CW00516638

# Oral History

# Studies in Narrative (SiN)

The subject of SiN is the study of narrative. Volumes published in the series draw upon a variety of approaches and methodologies in the study of narrative. Particular emphasis is placed on theoretical approaches to narrative and the analysis of narratives in human interaction.

## Editor

Michael Bamberg
Clark University

## Advisory Board

Susan E. Bell
Bowdoin College

Jerome S. Bruner
New York University

Jennifer Coates
Roehampton University

Michele L. Crossley
Edge-Hill University College

Carol Gilligan
New York University

Rom Harré
Linacre College, Oxford

David Herman
Nort Carolina State University

Janet Holmes
Victoria University of
Wellington

Charlotte Linde
Institute for Research
Learning

Dan P. McAdams
Northwestern University

Allyssa McCabe
University of Massachusetts,
Lowell

Eric E. Peterson
University of Maine

Catherine Kohler Riessman
Boston University

Theodore R. Sarbin
University of California,
Santa Cruz

Deborah Schiffrin
Georgetown University

Margaret Wetherell
Open University

Volume 10

Oral History. The challenges of dialogue
Edited by Marta Kurkowska-Budzan and Krzysztof Zamorski

# Oral History

The challenges of dialogue

*Edited by*

Marta Kurkowska-Budzan
Krzysztof Zamorski
Jagiellonian University, Kraków

John Benjamins Publishing Company
Amsterdam / Philadelphia

™ The paper used in this publication meets the minimum requirements of
American National Standard for Information Sciences – Permanence of
Paper for Printed Library Materials, ANSI z39.48-1984.

**Library of Congress Cataloging-in-Publication Data**

Oral history : the challenges of dialogue / edited by Marta Kurkowska-Budzan, Krzysztof
    Zamorski.
    p.  cm. (Studies in Narrative, ISSN 1568-2706 ; v. 10)
    Includes bibliographical references and index.
       1. Discourse analysis, Narrative. 2. Oral history. I. Kurkowska-Budzan, Marta. II.
    Zamorski, Krzysztof.
    P302.7.O73       2009
401'.41--dc22                               2008055548
ISBN 978 90 272 2650 1 (HB; alk. paper)
ISBN 978 90 272 8969 8 (EB)

© 2009 – John Benjamins B.V.
No part of this book may be reproduced in any form, by print, photoprint, microfilm, or any
other means, without written permission from the publisher.

John Benjamins Publishing Co. · P.O. Box 36224 · 1020 ME Amsterdam · The Netherlands
John Benjamins North America · P.O. Box 27519 · Philadelphia PA 19118-0519 · USA

# Table of contents

# List of editors and contributors

## Editors

Marta Kurkowska-Budzan
Jagiellonian University,
ul. Gołębia 13, 31-007
Kraków, Poland
e-mail: marta.kurkowska-budzan@uj.edu.pl

Krzyszof Zamorski
Jagiellonian University,
ul. Gołębia 13, 31-007
Kraków, Poland
e-mail: zamorski@jazon.hist.uj.edu.pl

## Contributors

Zibiah Alfred
University of Essex
United Kingdom, Flat F, Atlee,
Toynbee Hall, 28 Commercial Street
London E1 6LS
e-mail: zalfre@essex.ac.uk

Helga Amesberger
Institute of Conflict Research
Lisztstrasse 3, A-1030
Wien, Austria
e-mail: helga.amesberger@ikf.ac.at

Liisa Avelin
University of Turku,
Tervaskatu 3, FI-48770
Kotka, Finland
e-mail: liisa.avelin@utu.fi

James Chalmers Clapperton
University of Edinburgh,
Flat 8, 12 Yeaman Place
Edinburgh, Scotland, EH11 1BX
e-mail: jamesclapperton@hotmail.com

Mary Patrice Erdmans
Central Connecticut State University
New Britain,
CT 06050, USA
e-mail: ErdmansM@ccsu.edu

Kerstin Gunnemark
University of Gothenburg
PO Box 200 SE 405 30
Gothenburg, Sweden
e-mail: Kerstin.Gunnemark@ethnology.gu.se

Brigitte Halbmayr
Institute of Conflict Research
Lisztstraße 3, A-1030
Vienna, Austria
e-mail address: brigitte.halbmayr@ikf.ac.at

Charles Hardy III
West Chester University
500 Main Hall, West Chester
Pennsylvania 19383, USA
e-mail: chardy@wcupa.edu

Marta Kubiszyn
Maria Curie Skłodowska University
Niecała 6 m. 30, 20-080
Lublin, Poland
e-mail: martakubiszyn@gazeta.pl

Conor McGrath
Independent Scholar
10 Newbridge Avenue, Sandymount
Dublin 4, Ireland
e-mail:  conor.p.mcgrath@gmail.com

Anna Muller
Indiana University, USA
Ul. Dekerta 7/5, 80-262
Gdansk, Poland
e-mail: anmuller@indiana.edu

Sarah O'Brien
Mary Immaculate College
University of Limerick
South Circular Rd.
Limerick, Ireland
e-mail: Sarah.obrien@mic.ul.ie

Leena Rossi
University of Turku
20014, Finland
e-mail: leeros@utu.fi

Karin Stoegner
Institute of Conflict Research
Lisztstrasse 3 A-1030
Vienna, Austria
e-mail: karin.stoegner@ikf.ac.at

Sofie Strandén
Åbo Akademi University
Fabriksgatan 2, FIN-205 00
Turku, Finland
e-mail: sofie.stranden@abo.fi

Saara Tuomaala
Academy of Finland
P.O. BOX 59, 00014
University of Helsinki, Finland
e-mail: saara.tuomaala@helsinki.fi

# Foreword

Alessandro Portelli and Charles Hardy III
La Sapiensity University, Roma / West Chester University,
Dept. of History, USA

On November 8, 2007, scholars and oral history practitioners from more than fifteen countries gathered in Krakow for a conference on oral history, "Oral History: The Art of Dialogue," the first such meeting ever held in Poland. The meeting took place in the heart of Krakow, in the rooms of a 14th century college, now a conference center at Jagiellonian University, one of the oldest universities in Europe. What followed were two fascinating days of presentations and conversation that demonstrated the ongoing globalization of oral history and the breadth and quality of oral history practice in central and eastern Europe.

The meeting included presentations and discussions on the theoretical and ethical challenges of oral history interviewing; of, for example, the need to interview the perpetrators of atrocities, the collaborators and informers, as well as the victims, and the moral challenges of doing so. Conference presenters and attendees grappled with the importance and challenges of interviewing women, and with broader questions about the impact of gender in oral history interviewing. There were presentations on the lost history of Russians lives during the epic siege of Leningrad; public commemorations of the lost Jewish communities of Lublin and Berlin; photographs as densely coded cultural artifacts and scenes performance that take place in the memory long after a photo is taken and its subjects deceased; the use of non-directive questions to open up narrative space, and the meaning and use of false memories. The meeting included discussions of public memory and private biographies, borderline narratives, and how oral histories can "sensualize the past" by taking historians outside the text and into the lives of people. Presentations ranged from refugee communities in London to discothèques in Finland, from the state of oral history practice in Russia to oral history-based theatrical productions in the western United States. They documented and explored the succession of displacements – of Jews, Finns, Estonians, and other peoples – and the use of oral history to reclaim their identities. How extraordinary it was to observe a Finn discussing, in English, with a Latvian and Pole the ethnic inclusivity of their oral history projects.

Like the meeting in Krakow, the articles in this anthology provide a compelling demonstration of the ongoing globalization of oral history, and of the quality, richness, and variety of work taking place in central and eastern Europe. For scholars like us, coming from the United States and from Western Europe, this was a deep and exciting learning experience, concerning both the social and historical realities discussed, and the intellectual and methodological approaches our colleagues brought to them. While the dialogue and the presentations were firmly rooted in the specific and complex experiences of Eastern Europe, there was nothing "local" or parochial about the conference. Indeed, the meeting showed how Polish and other Eastern- and Northern-European scholars have been aware of, but not subaltern to, the contemporary international trends in oral history, and have been able to adapt them to their own situation and needs. We were especially impressed, as no doubt the readers of this anthology will also be, with the quality of oral history contributions to public history projects, at a time when memory becomes itself a significant political arena. Once more, then, oral history proved to be a fruitful terrain for international dialogue, for new ideas – there were many students in attendance – and for independent critical thought even in difficult contexts and times.

# From the editors

Marta Kurkowska-Budzan and Krzysztof Zamorski
Jagiellonian University, Institute of History, Poland

*dialoguing.*

There is no history without oral history. It is, after all, the oldest form or even "pre-form" of history's existence, and today with our contemporary possibilities of recording and transmitting the spoken word, oral history takes on greater meaning. Yet it never really ever disappeared.

In the shape of tales told, oral history was present not only in the courts of rulers described by Homer where, as is commonly known, those gifted with a talent for relaying the past – known as Aoides – were welcome guests. In fact, oral history existed in the courts of kings of various epochs and various cultures where oral tradition (among others) preserved knowledge of the past of a dynasty before it was set down in writing. Still longer it filled a part of the folk imagination regarding the world. Oral history took on the form of songs as well as the tradition verbally transmitted, dependent or independent of written history. The latter could become dominant in human culture only quite late – only after the onset of universal literacy which, for many European societies, did not arrive until the 19th century. Today where there are completely new possibilities of recounting human experience, the past takes on new meaning. How then is oral history resurrecting? What is it and what is it trying to be? No longer does it suffice to simply ask or ponder these questions, and hence this book which we invite readers to peruse.

Nonetheless, before we share the experiences of contemporary scholars of oral history, it would be worth pausing for a moment in the world of the mythical beginnings of history itself. Let us reach back to archetype. Greek tradition passes on to a us a certain metaphor regarding the functioning of history. In Homer's *Odyssey* a symbolic figure in the tale is the blind Aoide, Demodocus from the court of King Alkonoos in whom Homer purportedly saw himself. The elderly man spoke of Troy so fantastically that Odysseus, who was a guest of the court, could not maintain his anonymity. As Demodocus sang his tale of the conquering of Troy, he called forth an image of the past with such conviction that Odysseus could not hide his feelings. The tears flowing down his cheeks led Alkonoos to understand that this guest was special and exceptional.

It is difficult not to be caught under the spell of this situational coincidence and see it as the mythical genesis of oral history. Unfortunately, this concurrence could only be superficial and illusory. Demodocus was not, indeed, an eyewitness to the events he portrayed. The actual witness was, in reality, Odysseus. Homer in his chronicle captured the archetype of a cognitive experiencing of history itself perceived as an a-posterior reflection. Hence we are dealing here with history relayed by someone who did not participate in the events but is capable of seeing it and passing it on. Human culture is able to preserve well the memory of its famous heroes. As if to tell us "look Odysseus, what you and your compatriots have done has not vanished. These deeds still live on and we are able to remember them."

This is therefore not the classic, most often met cognitive schema of oral history. Here a blind old man transmits further a tale which he had once heard; he relayed what was known about the events in which not he, but another man, participated. Nevertheless, Demodocus was a link in an experience which – at the end of the 19th and first half of the 20th centuries – was labeled "tradition" in historical theory. To what did this correspond? Today we could say that, according to modernist concepts of history, he was conveying the state of the "collective consciousness" while, according to post- and post-postmodernist concepts, he was imparting "memory" of events.

In oral history the leading role is played by a person who remains in a clearly evident and rather intimate relationship with the incidents depicted in the story. In this case, the standard function of the narrator is performed by a "witness" – regardless of whether or not we would use this tag and regardless of the content we would assign to this storytelling.

In comparing this situation to the mythical metaphor illustrated above, we should then pose at least two specific questions. First of all, we should ask what part Odysseus plays – from the perspective of oral history – as the character who directly experienced the Trojan War. Secondly, we should – from this same point of view – ask about the role played by Demodocus. Herein we will be defending a thesis that oral history aims to lend a voice not only to Demodocus, but to Odysseus himself, releasing the latter to do more than weep at the sound of words recalling his personal trauma. Odysseus would then regain the possibility of telling his own tale – describing what he saw, describing what he experienced.

In this metaphorical example is expressed, among other things, the therapeutic function of oral history and more. Oral history stemmed from a feeling of coldness and emptiness: a lack of direct contact with the human experience of the past, precisely as it would exist in the consciousness of the participants of particular historical episodes. This void was created by the usurpation of history as an institutionalized academic discipline.

In contrast to this perspective, we aspire to populate our historicity with direct human experiences made available to all. We dream of the tale of Troy in words flowing from the mouth of Odysseus, Paris, or Helen. Hence we consciously move towards this goal: so that the narratives of our contemporaries will be available for the future, we care for, organize, and catalog them. One day in the distant future, in which the mythical Odysseus is wandering and lost, rather than the song of Demodocus in the court of Alkinoos he will hear his saga sounded out in his own voice.

Of course, at first glance, this looks to be a perspective hostile towards the honorable Demodocus. Yet, despite all our comments seeming to the contrary, his work also has its place within our discipline. In oral history we do not, after all, deny Demodocus the right to recite his moving narrative. Still we, the public audience, see that his point of view is not unambiguous.

Firstly, depending on our recognition of forms of the presence of history in the world, we perceive the storyteller as a mediator in the chain of history, or as a stimulator of historical consciousness, or as a reference point in the creation of collective memory. Secondly, the storyteller himself is testimony to a way of viewing specific events in future generations. The content of his tale, the way it is told, and the moment in which he tells it all constitute a source of knowledge about his own psyche and soul and that of his contemporaries. Here Demodocus becomes an oral historian of sorts – one who guarantees that memory of Troy will not vanish. And he does this in the best possible manner he can, applying all the talents with which he has been gifted by the Muses.

In fact, in the practice of oral history the position of the researcher – by preparing for and participating in the interview – is closer to that of Demodocus than Odysseus. After all, it is we who take on the responsibility of noting and recording the witness' story and then recounting it. And if this is the case, then we are as interested in the subject and content of the tale as in the form it is narrated. We, too, aim to achieve metaphorical perfection in relaying the voice and testimony of the observer. We set our sights (whether we want this or not) on the mythical situation in which Homer (if it is true that Demodocus was his counterpart) stands face to face with an eyewitness to the events and wins acceptance for the way in which that experience is presented.

This, in turn, leads us into the ethical side of oral history. How far can we go in utilizing the information gathered in conversations with narrators cajoled into telling their tales? Are there any limits and boundaries? Can we challenge the raconteur's statements?

The ideal principles regarding the status of the oral historian requires still further elucidation. In practice such a code of ethics is not and sometimes cannot be maintained. The more we want to treat the products of our interviews as research material, the more we will inject phenomena unknown to our heroes – those closer to our time-space continuum and comprehensible only within it. The world of potential reflection by Odysseus is one of initial, first reflection upon an experience of the recent past; the world of reflection by Demodocus is more derivative and regenerated. Inasmuch as Odysseus cannot escape the psychological burden of the events, the oral historian is responsible for critical consideration of that experience as well as its description. Furthermore, Demodocus will often want to take advantage of a tale in order to present his own imagination of the past.

These two types of reflection comprise the backdrop for the dialogue which, according to Alessandro Portelli, fundamentally defines the ethical and aesthetic framework of this methodology. Oral history puts the narrator in first place but allows the listener to participate in a sort of conversation with the storyteller. Humility and formality are dictated when facing the witness, yet the oral historian is not prohibited from endowing the dialogue with sense and meaning in current cognitive categories. Essentially we are seeking out the sense of history as Reinhardt Koselleck saw it when he spoke of the dialectics of the perspective of human experience and the horizon of the awaited future. In history, and especially in oral history, we want to deepen our experiences and share them with the reader, doing so in order to broaden our view of what is to come.

This above-described dialogue has its place in our human historicity which shifts and changes; each contact with a new experience influences our understanding of the past as a building block in human identity. Each oral history interview plays a role in an individually and socially specific way in which the past affects the partners in this conversation. There is no "present." After all, in our human life there is no clear border segregating living tradition from the dead. There is only a sense of history in which the past is nearer or farther away. Only past and future experiences exist which shape our personalities more or less.

Oral history is likely the most democratic discipline; it is neither contained solely within history, nor certainly even limited to academic history. To engage in this field one can be a professional historian, sociologist, anthropologist, teacher, or anyone with any educational background such as a journalist, clergyman, salesperson, or even a real estate agent. Neither class, nor ethnicity, nor age, nor gender limits the oral historian: pupils, university students, laborers, seniors, and gays can and do conduct such interviews. The minimal financial resources necessary to implement oral history are not great. And the wisdom which is the consequence of this work is created just as democratically. Herein lie the crucial ethical principles which oral history has developed over the years of its existence – the speakers or groups of speakers are subjects. They are not "objects" of analysis, but rather partners and participants in a dialogue about the past.

*it has been for some time now.*

All this means that oral history is gaining popularity in ever more countries and cultures; as a result it is becoming richer in shades and tones. In the Anglo-Saxon world it has been functioning for a long time and has a seemingly stable and anchored position in academia and society. Nonetheless, such status does not, fortunately, preclude continuing methodological and philosophical dilemmas and debates. In Europe – especially in Eastern Europe – oral history is in a phase of euphoric development. This blossoming is evident not only in increasing research but also in self-conscious reflection based on the body of experience and literature accumulated by countries in which oral history was born, enriched now by local historical-cultural contexts and the legacy of related fields of scholarly endeavor such as folklore studies, anthropology, and history.

The chapters comprising this book represent both the Anglo-Saxon tradition and concepts stemming from the relative newcomers to oral history – continental European countries. The reader will have an opportunity to familiarize himself with articles by authors from Austria, Finland, Poland, and Sweden as well as America, England, Scotland, and Ireland. Nonetheless, a segregation of the "old" and "new" traditions has been neither a constructive goal, nor the aim of this collection. The idea behind this publication was born during a conference organized in November 2007 in Kraków, Poland; the organizers were the scholarly periodical *Historyka: Studies in Methodology*, the Institute of History of the Jagiellonian University, and the "Artifacts" Association. Acting as symbolic patron for this international gathering was – and not without reason – thoughts drawn from Alessandro Portelli's *Oral History – The Art of Dialogue*.

What exactly is dialogue in oral history? Who takes part in it? Who bears the responsibility for the dialogue? In what physical, temporal, and/or cultural space can this dialogue take place, in what space can it not? What does it borrow from art? What are its principles, traps, and challenges? Contemporary oral history poses these questions before itself, just as anthropologists, theologians, and above all philosophers have done since time began. The dialogue, according to the words of a Polish philosopher and theologian, Józef Tischner, constitutes a chance to experience the existence of another human being, showing him his humanity and also acceptance for the otherness of another person. The dialogue is the heart of the concept of the "meeting," and poised at the opposite end of the axis from objectivization.

The texts found herein either undertake topics associated with the idea of oral history dialoguing, or they present concrete situations, research, persons, and their own stories built on the solid ground of discourse and within its context. The configuration of this book will perhaps recall that of the standard "Handbook of Oral History": the issues developed here correspond to the subsequent stages of research – preparing for and then conducting the interview itself, evaluation and analysis of the material, publication in the broad sense of the word, and, finally, the dilemmas or philosophical reflections with their accent on ethics. The reader will find immediate evaluation of the interviewer-narrator communication situation and the problems which appear before, during, and after this encounter.

Chapter 1 is entitled "Fieldwork challenges" because the texts it includes illustrate the technical aspects of "field research" – issues of making contact with the narrators, evoking recollections, and opening raconteurs up to the researcher. Sofie Strandén, a doctoral candidate at Åbo Akademi University in Finland, considers how the empathetic interview should be modeled so as to clarify the borders between empathy and sympathy. Leena Rossi from the University of Turku in Finland poses a very concrete and seemingly simply question: What is one to do if we hear our narrator admit to a crime for which he or she has not paid? Are we to break the rule of trust and inform the authorities? Kerstin Gunnemark of the Department of Ethnology at the University of Gothenburg shares her experiences with "The Memory Closet" experience in which things – personal mementos – act as an extraordinary catalyzer in intergenerational dialogue. Intriguingly enough, Liisa Avelin challenges the traditional understanding of the oral history interview when presenting her investigation conducted via an internet blog. Has dialogue made its way into this form of communication? Conor McGrath, an independent researcher from Scotland, describes the peculiarities of a historian's work among lobbyists.

Chapter 2 opens yet another set of doors in the subject matter: the gender issue in oral history. It opens with an article by Helga Amesberger, followed by analytical texts by Saara Tuomaala from Finland and Mary Patrice Erdmans from the USA. In the latter two cases we are provided with interesting material for comparison of the European and American methodological traditions in gender studies.

Chapter 3 continues the theme of narrative analysis. The pieces here present research conducted in various national and cultural milieus: James Clapperton among the eldest survivors of the siege of Leningrad (today's Sankt Petersburg), Anna Muller following a line of investigation in Poland, and Sarah O'Brien among Irish immigrants in England. The variations of these texts are expressed, too, in their methodological perspectives. This, in turn, convinces us that oral history provides great chances for fruitful studies by scholars of various visions. These articles lead the reader to ponder yet another issue: the cultural context of the dialogue between a researcher and a narrator.

Dialogue is not just an encounter between two people. The best proof of this is the functioning of oral history in the public sphere as public history. Sharing the results with a broad audience and repaying a debt to our narrators and the entire society through sociocultural work on their behalf is a practice sanctioned by the tradition and ethics of oral history. Adding to this is the digital revolution, rapidly introducing new chances as well as new challenges which we try to meet in various ways, in various countries and cultures. The internet space is very quickly being tamed by oral historians around the world, yet there is still a need for direct, interpersonal engagement among people and for people. Chapter 4 – "Public Spaces Challenges – commences with an article by Charles Hardy III who accurately defines the essence of oral history as public history:

> I am in the United States what is known as a 'public historian.' I have spent most of my career authoring histories for the listeners and viewers of public radio and television, for museum visitors, heritage tourists, K-12 teachers and students, and the general public. So one of my constant challenges has been to devise ways to bring the riches to be found in history, its lessons and morals, its conundrums and wonders – whatever select pieces of the great blooming mess that I am able to grab hold of – to folks who are free to walk past or turn the channel because something more interesting attracts, or promises to attract their attention.

By imparting his years of radio experience, Hardy encourages us to "think in sound" and to assume the challenge of contemporary technology, applying our imaginations and knowledge. Also included in this chapter is Marta Kubiszyn's contribution, presenting ideas of social education through the oral history program of the well-known and esteemed Brama Grodzka – Teatr NN (Grodzka Gate Center – NN Theatre) in Lublin, Poland. Next, Zibiah Alfred describes the functioning of a vast enterprise initiated by the Museum of London, the London Metropolitan University, and 15 refugee organizations: The Refugee Communities Oral History Project. These two texts, adjacent to one another, facilitate comparison of the state of public history in a Central European country vis-à-vis a Western one, and of the distinctiveness of each with regards to subject and form.

Dialogue occurs on a level of ethics (subject-subject); its guiding principle is the equality of the two sides – the fact that each is autonomous and has the right to its own view of the world. Therefore, the closing chapter touches upon philosophical and ethical dilemmas of oral history in general historiography perspective. Brigitte Halbmayr discusses the problem of conversing with former concentration camp prisoners while her friend, Karin Stögner of the Institute of Conflict Research in Vienna conducts a review of oral history in light of Walter Benjamin's philosophy, returning to the eternal pairing of truth and memory.

The volume at hand permits a view of the latest fieldwork carried out in Europe and the USA, in countries "old" and "new" to oral history. Here the reader will be able to compare the two traditions and deliberate upon the issues before which each of us – experienced or beginner, historian or anthropologist – stands face-to-face. This compilation of articles embodies the experiences of the authors, their efforts, successes, as well as failures in dialoging with narrators. Unveiled in these chapters is the extensive workshop of contemporary oral history stretching out towards its epistemological and methodological horizons.

SECTION 1

# Fieldwork challenges

# Trust in the empathic interview

Sofie Strandén
Åbo Akademi University, Turku, Finland

In this article, I discuss the concept of trust in the interview situation. I argue that my role, as an interviewer, is important in order to create trust for the interviewee. Along with the interviewee's expectations of what an interview is, I consider my own person, my professionalism, and my social background as the main factors when creating trust during my interviews. This article is based on the fieldwork for my folkloristic thesis to come regarding men's and women's narration about their experiences of war.

**Keywords:** emotions, empathy, fieldwork, interviews, reflexivity, trust

When conducting interviews about difficult subjects, one has to take into consideration that strong emotions will emerge sooner or later. It is difficult to anticipate whether your questions will trigger feelings of sorrow, unease, pain, shame, guilt, anger, relief, gratefulness, or something else. As an interviewer you also have to be prepared that you will react emotionally yourself during the interview. From my experience, interviews about war affect both the interviewer and the interviewee, and instead of regarding the emotions involved as an obstacle, I consider them an opportunity to delve deeper into the analysis of the interviews. The feeling of trust is thus important during an interview.

What I have chosen to call the empathic interview, is something that I see as a result of trying to understand the interviewees both emotionally and intellectually, both during the interview itself, and afterwards, during the analysis (Strandén 2005; Strandén 2007). In this article, I will discuss interpersonal dynamics in the interview situation. Above all, I discuss concepts that I feel create a trustful atmosphere during interviews. I use experiences from my own fieldwork in its specific context, and by my specific experiences I wish to show, on a more general level, how important and useful it is to distance yourself during and after fieldwork, and the need for thorough reflection.

The material for my forthcoming dissertation consists of twenty interviews with men and women who, in different ways, actively took part in the Winter War, the Continuation War, and the Lapland War from 1939–1945 in Finland.[1]

All of them were born and raised in the Swedish-speaking region Ostrobothnia, which is situated on the Finnish west coast. Eight of my female interviewees were members of the women's voluntary organization *Lotta Svärd*.[2]

In this article, I will refer to them in the singular as a *lotta* and in the plural as *lottas*, according to the way they are referred to in Swedish. The remaining two women interviewed were trained nurses, and worked in hospitals at the immediate front. The first seven interviews were conducted in a project called "*Ensign Stål* in our memories", where the main point was to let men talk about their relationship with the epic saga *The Tales of Ensign Stål* (1848 and 1860) by the Finnish national poet Johan Ludvig Runeberg, and a work of great importance for the Finnish nation state.[3]

Already during the first interview, and particularly during the second, I noticed that the interviewee gradually moved on to talking about his own experiences during the war, a tendency which grew stronger with the following interviewees. Therefore I decided to expand the project into a dissertation on narrating memories of the war on the basis of *The Tales of Ensign Stål* and the interviewees' own experiences. In addition to this amplification I also increased the number of interviews – three more interviews with men, and ten more with women (*lottas* and nurses).

In my opinion, you can concisely say that the folkloristic interview is characterized by open questions, where the interviewee can talk freely, and – supported by further questions that follow up what the interviewee has said – helped to develop his or her thoughts and reasoning. What is said during an interview is preserved as a recording and a transcript. However, an interview also consists – like all human encounters – of the emotions and thoughts of all participants (Banaka 1981:13). These interpersonal processes are impossible to record, and they are not evident in the transcript. Nevertheless, they are important to take into consideration when studying the communication between the interviewer and the interviewee. It has long been accepted that an interview is a two-way communication

1.   The interviews are filed at the Folklore archives at Åbo Akademi University.

2.   The name of the organization *Lotta Svärd* originates from *The Tales of Ensign Stål* by Johan Ludvig Runeberg. *Lotta Svärd* is the only woman in the epic saga, who has a poem named after her. The names "Stål" and "Svärd" are Swedish and mean "steel" and "sword".

3.   *The Tales of Ensign Stål* is based on the people and events of the Swedish-Finnish war against Russia in 180???–1809, when Russia conquered Finland.

in cultural sciences. Since the mid-1980s, discussions on reflexivity and representation have led to critical attention being directed to the encounter between the interviewer and the interviewee, as to what happens during the encounter and to how this is represented in the text (Fägerborg 1999: 56). The researcher's awareness of the significance of his or her presence, both when the material is created and when it is analyzed and interpreted, provides deeper insight into how knowledge is created (See for example Ehn & Klein 1994). According to Billy Ehn, the relationship between the interviewer and the interviewee plays an important role as to what the story looks like, as well as for social and cultural norms, values, and ideas (Ehn 1992: 200–210).

According to Lena Marander-Eklund, trust in the interview situation can be increased if you explain to the interviewee who you are, the reason why you want to interview him or her, and the purposes of the interview. You can accomplish a trusting atmosphere by showing that you have plenty of time, and by asking open questions (Marander-Eklund 2004: 98). I personally contacted all the interviewees by phone or, as in the case of some of the *lottas*, directly after a public talk given by them about their *lotta* activities. At the same time, when the first contact was made, I presented myself and explained what I do and why I wanted to talk to them. At the interviewees' homes, I told them again who I was, why I was there, and what I was doing.

It is not always easy for the people you study in your fieldwork to understand what you are actually doing. This is something that, for example, Susanne Wollinger also experienced when studying 20-year-old men in military service in Sweden. Despite having informed them both verbally and in writing as to why she was present in the company, it took several weeks before all of them had truly understood the reason why she was there (Wollinger 2002: 5). When I arrived at one house, that of a *lotta* called Lisa, I realised that she thought I was a medical doctor. She did not really understand why I wanted to talk to her about the war. I told her that I was about to write some kind of book, and she was happy with that explanation. As I entered her house, I noticed that she was nervous, though she simultaneously seemed happy and full of expectations. The interview was conducted in the winter, and as I knew that she lived in an old house, I had brought my woollen socks in order not to get cold feet. I told her that I had done so, and smilingly showed her how well darned they were. To my surprise, this was when the tension disappeared and she told me that she hardly needed to be nervous because I had brought with me my socks, which were full of holes and which I had darned. I took it to be the darned socks that had increased the interviewee's personal trust in me. This example shows that tiny details may make it possible to be successful in bringing about a trusting atmosphere between yourself and your interviewee.

## Gaining trust as an interviewer

In the Swedish dictionary the word *tillit*, trust, is defined as a "convincing of (someone's) trustworthiness or good intentions in relation to the person in question" (*Svensk ordbok* 1999). In addition to the possible incongruence in the interviewee's and the interviewer's understanding of what an interview is, I feel that there are three main factors characterising the interviewer which have an impact on the feeling of trust experienced by the interviewee in the actual interview situation: (1) the interviewer as a person, (2) the professionalism of the interviewer, and (3) the social context of the interviewer. In the following parts of this chapter I will look at the expectations of an interview, followed by the three factors mentioned above.

## Expectations of an interview

After a *lotta* lecture given by some of my future interviews, I presented myself to the six *lottas* present, and asked them whether I could interview them individually. Some of them were uncertain about what new knowledge they could possibly bring to my work. I believe that their insecurity concerning this was part of their idea of what an interview is, and their expectations of the knowledge generated in an interview. When I use the word "interview", I mean a situation where you, according to Eva Fägerborg, can "reach people's thoughts, their dreams, ideas, norms, fears and hopes" simply by letting the other person talk (Fägerborg 1999:61). It seemed to me as if they thought they were supposed to present me with correct facts. To the interviewees, the facts seemed to be the most important thing, while the narration of their experiences is much more important to me, as a folklorist. Something that most folklorists probably agree with Lena Marander-Eklund about, but nevertheless is important to point out, is that it is not the facts that are important, but the narrating itself (Marander-Eklund 2004:97).

The expectations of what an interview is supposed to contain varies drastically from interviewee to interviewer. It became my task as an interviewer to draw the interviewees' attention away from the facts, and make them tell me about what they had thought, done, and experienced, without paying attention to names, exact times etc. Several of my interviewees wondered if they really could contribute anything of importance to my work, and if they would be able to remember all the dates and names correctly and so forth. This became especially evident in the parts of the interviews dealing with *The Tales of Ensign Stål*. Quite a few of the interviewees thought it would be better if I contacted an "expert" if I wanted to know about Runeberg and his *Tales*. When I explained to them that I wanted to hear about how and where they had learnt the poems, what they thought of them etc, they were all willing to tell me. Many of them relaxed when they noticed that I was not about to discipline them for failing to know everything correctly, and several said to me with a smile as I was packing up my things and was about to leave: "I thought it was going to be much worse!"

## The interviewer as a person

According to Charlotte Hagström, variables such as sex, age, geographical home district, ethnical background, profession, education, hobbies, or sexual preferences can be significant to what is experienced as possible to talk about in an interview, and also to how well the interviewer and the interviewee understand each other. Hagström also stresses the importance of being aware that you are so much more than just an interviewer (Hagström 2002:50). According to Hagström, there are similarities and differences between you and the interviewee, which you can either emphasize or suppress according to what you want to talk about and study. Other qualities are constantly present and impossible to ignore (Hagström 2002:44). According to Hagström, the use of similarities and differences is a part of her way of working when she does interviews, but it happens more or less unconsciously in the interview situation. She stresses that everything that the interviewer and the interviewee are, do, and stand for – either consciously or unconsciously – have an impact on the other part of the interview. All of this is significant to what questions are asked and what answers are given (Hagström 2002:48).

Ethnicity, including language and varieties of language, sex, and age are the factors that I categorize as belonging to the interviewer as a person. The age difference between me and the interviewee was in some cases more than sixty years, and I am very much aware of the fact that this had an impact on what they told me. But I am not at all as sure that age had a very great importance for their feeling of trust.

All of my interviewees were, like me, born and raised in the Swedish-speaking region of Ostrobothnia on the Finnish west coast. Because of this we had a geographical background in common, even though we grew up at different times. Most of my interviewees had backgrounds as farmers, and even though my family were not farmers, I grew up in a small village in the countryside. My language background is, as that of my interviewees, Swedish. I consider both the local rural dialect and the, so to speak, normal Swedish variety spoken among the Finland Swedes to be my own languages. The interviews were conducted in the variety that I felt to be closest to the interviewee's. I am convinced that my Ostrobothnian rural background had a positive impact on the possibility of gaining the interviewees' trust.

After I had completed the first seven interviews with the men, I started to expand my material to comprise interviews with the women. I had a feeling that it would be different to interview women even if I did not know exactly what the differences would be (See for example Wollinger 2002). As a child I was much more familiar with elderly women than elderly men. My maternal grandfather died when I was a child, and my other grandfather and I were never really close. On the other hand, I grew up with my maternal grandmother, because she lived in the same house as my parents and I. My other grandmother and I became close when I was in my teens. Later, she said on several occasions that I am her only close female relative, and that she feels that I am the only one she has really been able to talk to, even about things she considers hard, such as her first years as a married woman. According to Birgitta Meurling, gender reflexivity has not had a prominent position in research. She feels that we have to become much more aware of the significance of gender when we create our sources. According to her, the interviewer's or researcher's sex has been noted to matter during fieldwork, but no profound conclusions have been drawn (Meurling 2002: 29–30). I dare say that my relationship to my two grandmothers, both as a child, and as a teenager, and an adult in the case of my paternal grandmother, has been valuable in my fieldwork with the women of my study.

Meurling writes that some researchers prefer and recommend homo-gendered and homo-social interview contexts, since they feel that these contexts favour the interaction and the production of knowledge (Meurling 2002: 31). According to her, they assume that women and men are different, that women understand other women better, and that women prefer to talk to women and men to other men. According to Meurling, there are examples when this has been the case, as well as it has been the other way round (Meurling 2002: 38).

At first, my interviewee Tilde had some doubts about letting me interview her. She had been misled in a previous interview for some other purpose, and she told me that she had promised herself never again to be interviewed about her time as a *lotta*. However, Tilde told me that she counted on me being different to the previous interviewer for two reasons. First, because I had been introduced to her by her good friend Ingegerd (another of my interviewees), and secondly because she thought that I would understand her better since I was a woman. Tilde seemed to be one of those who think that women understand other women better, and that a female interviewer is different in a positive way than a male interviewer. Tilde was very keen on making sure that I would not treat the things she told me in a bad way, as she had felt that the previous interviewer had done. I tried to explain to her how I intended to use the material. I also made a copy of the tapes from the interview and gave them to her. However, I will probably never get rid of the thought that Tilde might also be offended and feel misunderstood by me, even though I try to analyze and interpret what she and the other interviewees have told me as honestly as I possibly can, and also to present them in such a way that the interviewees will be able to accept them as just and fair.

I feel that I, in relation to the women, gained a lot of trust because I am a woman, something that was also commented on by some of the women themselves.

## The professionalism of the interviewer

Going into the field with questions and a voice recorder requires preparation. You have to know how the device works and feel at ease using it. I decided to consider the voice recorder as a kind of notebook, which was also what I called it when I talked about it with my interviewees. The way you conduct the interview is obviously also a factor that creates trust. Among other qualities in the interview, flexibility has an impact on how the interview transpires (see for example Marander-Eklund 2004). Qualities such as interest in and respect for people are, according to Bo Nilsson, necessary for the interviewer, as well as skills in showing understanding and a certain amount of smoothness in reactions. A certain amount of patience makes it possible to sit calmly and listen to what is being said (Nilsson 2002: 16).

Of course, preparations of other kinds are needed before you can enter the field. You study the theme you are going to ask about in order to ask well-thought-out questions. According to some researchers, it is very important to have thorough background knowledge. Sarah Forssell and Anita Marcus have done so-called Shoah interviews, which mean interviews that follow a certain pattern and which are done with survivors from the concentration camps during the Holocaust. The world wide goal is to collect stories of 50,000 survivors. Forssell and Marcus point out the importance of extremely thorough preparations, where the interviewers are expected to be familiar with the terminology used in the concentration camps and the war, they should know about the history, the politics, the society structure, and the language of the country from which the interviewee comes. According to Forssell and Marcus the interviews are supposed to be characterized by respect, trust, and knowledge (Forssell & Markus 2002: 68). In the beginning of my fieldwork I had in mind to ask questions primarily about *The Tales of Ensign Stål*. Consequently I had read a great deal about this subject. Already during the first interview I felt that I should have read much more about the 1939–1945 wars than about Runeberg and *The Tales*. According to Bo Nilsson,

ignorance and awkwardness can, however, be of assistance in an interview situation. The interviewee can instead show that he or she is an expert in a certain area
that the researcher knows much less about. Nevertheless, the interviewer may
never be so ignorant on a subject that he or she cannot ask essential questions
and inspire confidence (Nilsson 2002: 16). I believe that the trust I might have
lost due to my lack of knowledge about the war, I regained by honestly admitting
the shortcoming, and showing that I did not know much about it. If you look at
this from the perspective of power, my possible power position from being an
academic and an interviewer might have been softened because of this, and thus
brought me closer to my interviewees.

Furthermore, something that creates trust in an interview situation is self-po-
sitioning during the interview. It is important to show where you stand in relation
to the theme. In interviews about difficult subjects such as war, where there have
been strong opinions that, at times, have divided the nation, I found it necessary to, as neutrally as possible, show my own views on the matter. Anything
else would have probably been impossible. If I related that both my grandfathers
had been in the war, or that they had had nightmares for as long as they lived, I
would probably have received other kinds of answers than if I had not. On one
hand, I could show my gratitude and admiration towards the veterans and *lottas*,
while on the other I could feel sympathy for the young men that chose not to stay
in Finland and fight, but went to Sweden in order to escape the war. If I had not
shown my position, I would probably have been regarded with some scepticism,
and it seems likely that I would not have been given the amount of trust that I
actually received.

My role as an interviewer was also important when gaining the personal trust
of the interviewee. I tried to make it clear for the interviewees that it is the same "I"
who will conduct the interviews and who will continue to work with the material. I
regard this academic "I" as a combination of my personal and private "I", and of my
education. I wanted to appear as ordinary, but at the same time the unique person
that I am, who is interested in listening to what precisely they can tell, and, at the
same time, as an academic who wants to carry out research on that interest.

To me it has been very important to try to reach an emic understanding of
what I have been told. In the interview situation, I felt it was problematic to ask
questions about something of which I did not have an emic perspective. On the
other hand, the interviewees, in many cases, seemed eager to recount their experiences to a – from their point of view – young person. To them, my lack of emic
perspective did not seem to cause any problems. I also showed clearly that I really
wanted to find things out, things of which I did not know that much, and that I
did not just want to verify facts that were previously known to me. I asked several
of my interviewees to think of me as an interested grandchild when they talked

to me. For her master's thesis on roles, Anna Grönholm has interviewed elderly people. Grönholm talks about, among other subjects, lived roles, such as the one of the apprentice in the interview situation (Grönholm 2003: 30–31). I feel familiar with this role and see that it could be very much a variety of the grandchild listening to grandma or grandpa. My request that the interviewees tell me things as if I was a close relative might also have contributed to the reduction of the distance between them and myself in the interview situation.

## The social context of the interviewer

In the category of the social context of the interviewer, I include kinship between the interviewer and the interviewee, or knowledge of the interviewee's relatives. The fact that the interviewer and the interviewee are acquainted, or in one way or another have mutual acquaintances, I also put here. The persons' home district is also of significance in this case.

My interviewee Joel is a relative of my father and, consequently, also my relative. It was he himself who contacted my father and wanted to be interviewed by me. The fact that he let me know that he wanted to be interviewed, I took as a sign of trust on his behalf. Henrik's wife was also a distant relative of mine, and during the interview we discussed several times whose granddaughter I was. Margit, Åke, and Ingegerd knew my parents from their previous engagement in the local congregation. Brita had been asking friends about me, and she had found out who my parents and grandparents were. She told me that she was, so to speak, a bonus grandma to the children of a family who were acquainted with my parents. As a child, I had heard about her, but I had no recollection of having met her before. Despite this family research, I felt that Brita did not feel at ease with the interview situation. However, I am convinced that her research made her trust in me grow. I also regard her strivings as a sign of the importance of the person who conducts the interviews. The interviewee made, in this case, an effort to find out who I was before I arrived at her home and she was able to ask me more about myself and my relatives etc when I met her in person. To her it was important to be able to put me in a social context.

I also felt it important to be able to bring greetings from someone who I had already interviewed and who had recommended the person I visited. When I called Lisa, I told her that it was Margit who had thought that she could be a "good" interviewee. Axel had said the same thing about Vilhelm, as well as Janne about Henrik and so forth. This means, at the same time, that several of the interviewees knew each other and therefore might have had a certain idea of what they should talk about because the recommendation came from a specific person.

During a walk in my home village, I met Alice before I had even planned my dissertation project. By chance I found out that Alice hade been a *lotta,* and that she gladly wanted to tell me about her activities, if it turned out to be relevant later. I knew Alice because we used to live in the same village where I grew up, and because she was the grandmother of one of my classmates. I had also interviewed her previously about her handicraft skills for my master's thesis. Gunhild and I had known each other for one or two years because we had almost been neighbours and shared an interest in flowers and gardening. Axel and I had met earlier when I worked at a museum which was run by an association in which he was involved. Maria was shy in a way, and seemed afraid of putting herself forward. I did not know Maria, but it turned out that her son and I had attended the same handicraft course a few years earlier. I felt that this was important to her when it came to her trust in me.

Being part of the same community as the interviewees is, of course, not always a requirement for a successful interview. Sometimes it might be easier for someone to open up and recount his or her experiences to a total stranger, with whom he or she might not ever meet again. In those cases, a much larger emphasis is put on the professionalism of the interviewer. Nonetheless, in my work with the creation of the material, I made tremendous use of the fact that the interviews were conducted in a small community, of which I was considered a member by the interviewees. They placed and located me in their mental landscape, and thus I was attributed with certain qualities as a person who awoke trust within them.

## References

Banaka, W. H. 1981. *Djupintervju: Teknik och analys.* Stockholm: Natur och Kultur.

Ehn, B. 1992. Livet som intervjukonstruktion. In *Självbiografi, kultur, liv. Levnadshistoriska studier inom human- och samhällsvetenskap,* C. Tigerstedt, J. P. Roos & A. Vilkko (eds), 199–219. Stockholm: Symposion.

Ehn, B. & Klein, B. 1994. *Från erfarenhet till text: Om kulturvetenskaplig reflexivitet.* Stockholm: Carlsson.

Forssell, S. & Marcus, A. 2002. "Vem är du släkt med?": Etnicitetens betydelse i intervjuandet. In *Perspectiv på intervjuer: Genus, generation och kulturmöten,* K. Lövgren (ed.), 63–73. Stockholm: Nordiska museet. SAMDOK, <http://www.nordiskamuseet.se/Upload/Documents/18.pdf>, 30 October 2008.

Fägerborg, E. 1999. Intervjuer. *Etnologiskt fältarbete.* In Lars Kaijser & Magnus Öhlander (eds), 55–72. Studentlitteratur: Lund.

Grönholm, A. 2003. Ett rollspel i vardagen: Ett reflexivt studium av en intervjuares roll i ett levnadshistoriskt intervjuprojekt. *Budkavlen* (82): 22–35.

Hagström, C. 2002. En mamma möter pappor. In *Perspectiv på intervjuer: Genus, generation och kulturmöten*, K. Lövgren (ed.), 43–51. Stockholm: Nordiska museet. SAMDOK, <http://www.nordiskamuseet.se/Upload/Documents/18.pdf>, 30 October 2008.

Marander-Eklund, L. 2004. Att skapa och analysera ett muntligt forskningsmaterial. In *Metodkompassen: Kulturvetarens metodbok*, B. Henriksson, R. Illman & L. Marander-Eklund (eds), 93–115. Åbo: Åbo Akademi.

Meurling, B. 2002. Det mångtydiga könet: Om intervjuande, könskonstituering och reflexivitet. In *Perspektiv på intervjuer: Genus, generation och kulturmöten*, K. Lövgren (ed.), 29–41. Stockholm: Nordiska museet. SAMDOK:s e-publications 1651–1581, <http://www.nordiskamuseet.se/Upload/Documents/18.pdf>, 30 October 2008.

Nilsson, B. 2002. Kön som förutsättning och resultat: Om frågor och svar vid intervjuer. In *Perspektiv på intervjuer: Genus, generation och kulturmöten*, K. Lövgren (ed.), 15–27. Stockholm: Nordiska museet. SAMDOK:s e-publications 1651–1581, <http://www.nordiskamuseet.se/Upload/Documents/18.pdf>, 30 October 2008.

Strandén, S. 2005. Tillit, tankekontakt eller terapi: Att göra empatiska intervjuer. *Budkavlen* 84: 24–33.

Strandén, S. 2007. Släkt, bekanta och stoppade yllesockor: Tankar om tillit i den folkloristiska intervjun. In *Känslornas koreografi: Reflektioner kring känsla och förståelse i kulturforskning*, L. Marander-Eklund & R. Illman (eds), 92–103. Hedemora: Gidlunds.

*Svensk ordbok.* 1999. Stockholm: Norstedt.

Wollinger, S. 2002. Mellan seenden. In *Perspektiv på intervjuer: Genus, generation och kulturmöten*, K. Lövgren (ed.), 53–62. Stockholm: Nordiska museet. SAMDOK:s e-publications 1651–1581, <http://www.nordiskamuseet.se/Upload/Documents/18.pdf>, 30 October 2008.

# Oral historian – neither moralizer nor informer

Leena Rossi

Cultural History, University of Turku, Finland

In this paper, I discuss oral historian's roles in interviews in which crimes are revealed. First, I look at cases with the primary aim to collect information about statute-barred crimes. Second, I discuss cases in which the researcher does not study crimes, but the interviewee wants to disclose them. In the first case, the historian encourages the narrator to talk about crimes; in the second case she encourages her to keep silent. Oral historian should never accuse, reproach, or give therapy. She should not inform the authorities but encourage the narrator to do it herself. Finally, I suggest that the oral historian should be bound to professional secrecy.

Keywords: interview – oral historian's role, statute-barred crime, professional secrecy

## Background and purpose

I originally got the idea for this paper several years ago when I examined the smuggling of spirits in the Finnish coastal township, Koivisto (since 1944 known as Russian Primorsk) during the prohibition in the 1920s and 1930s. I also guided students who interviewed local people concerning smuggling in the Southwest Finnish archipelago. In addition, I studied sailors' lives and their involvement with smuggling and prostitutes in my hometown Turku. (Rossi 1999, 2003a, 2003b). While working on these projects I began to reflect on ethical problems, which arose during the interviews and in archives; and since then I have kept reflecting on them from time to time.[1]

---

1. I want to thank Professor Bruce Johnson, the University of Turku, for his inspiring comments on the topic as well as for editing my English. However, all the shortcomings remain mine.

In this paper, I will discuss the role of oral historians in particular cases in which crimes are revealed. Among others, David Henige (1982:114–115), Steinar Kvale (1996:115), Herbert J. Rubin and Irene S. Rubin (2005:99), as well as Linda Shopes (2006), have briefly raised this issue in connection with the confidentiality of interviews and the code of ethics. Mark Israel and Iain Hay have also dealt with the problem in a few pages of their book about research ethics in social sciences (Israel & Hay 2006:83, 86, 88, 92–94). In addition, John A. Neuenschwander has written the book *Oral History and the Law* in which he discusses criminal cases (Neuenschwander 2002:55–57). Yet, a more extensive discussion about the topic is welcome, to which here I will only make a small contribution.

First, I will look at cases in which the oral historian's primary purpose is to examine old criminal acts, which have already been protected or barred by the statute of limitations; in other words, cases in which the 'criminals' can no longer be punished. Second, I will talk about cases in which the scholar does not study crimes at all, but in which the narrator, either accidentally or intentionally, reveals certain illegal acts. What is the oral historian's role in these cases? What are her rights and duties? To whom is she ultimately responsible – to the narrator, the law enforcement officers, or to herself? What can or should she do? Who should she protect: herself, the narrator, or society?[2]

In her work, the oral historian meets with the same ethical problems as any other historian. Yet this is what makes oral history special: interviews in which the scholar, together with the interviewee, creates the most essential research material. It is the reciprocity of this face-to-face situation with the subjects that makes oral history emotionally, psychologically, and socially more challenging and demanding than ordinary archival research. No matter how hard their lives have been, people from the past in written documents are easier to deal with than living narrators. In an interview it is not enough for the researcher to simply listen attentively to the interviewee's account, but she must simultaneously encounter and manage not only her own emotions but also those of the narrator (Hochchild 1983).

Certain professionals – for instance, attorneys, clergy, psychiatrists, psychologists, and social workers – are frequently exposed to criminal and other more or less disturbing revelations by their clients. That is part and parcel of their daily work and they have special training for these encounters: encouraging the clients to disclose their secrets, hearing unpleasant news, or in dealing with their emotions. Very few oral historians have any professional training in human relations that would help them in interactive situations like interviews. Thus, they must work with the layman psychological and social skills and emotional intelligence

---

2.   Being a woman, I use the feminine pronoun "she" for both the researcher and the criminal.

that they happen to have. While some have naturally better abilities than others, they can be trained (Goleman 1998: 7).

It is not only crimes that cause ethical dilemmas in oral history but educational principles, child-rearing practices, and sexual matters as well as religion, politics, and practices of social policy that can cause similar problems; but these do not concern us here. Besides, I will only deal with 'milder' crimes and leave untouched the most serious ones, for instance, genocides and war crimes, which must be and have been discussed elsewhere (see, e.g. Evans 2002; Rousso 2002). Still, any crime, old or fresh, minor or major, might make the researcher feel anxious, angry, embarrassed, frightened, or perplexed.

## Crimes wanted

In terms of breaking the law, smuggling of various products might not be a legally demanding or difficult subject, particularly if the crime is already barred by the statute of limitations. However, it could interest social and cultural historians as a way of life or as a means of livelihood. Smuggling or any other comparable offence of the law, offers the oral historian real challenges, even in cases which have occurred a long time ago. Here, the researcher's major problem is how to make the prospective narrator accept the invitation to participate in the project and start recollecting her experiences and memories.

Indeed, all the interviewees are not necessarily willing to inform the researcher about past illegal acts that she or other members of the local community have committed. By refusing to co-operate they may be trying to protect their own identities and public images or those of their relatives, neighbours, and acquaintances. For these people, secrecy seems to be more a question of personal or public morals than a matter of legality. They often seem to be afraid of losing face, fouling their own nest, or the possible disapproval of other members of the community. In some cases, they might even be afraid of the researcher's disapproving reactions.

When studying the everyday life of the inhabitants of Koivisto, I wanted to know about the smuggling of spirits in the 1920s and 1930s, which was quite common on the coast. That is when I first noticed that people were somewhat reluctant to talk about the traffic. But when they realized that I would not condemn them or anyone else who was involved, they began to talk, interestingly, not about their relatives but about 'some villagers' or 'men in another village'. In the beginning, some people seemed to be slightly ashamed or embarrassed, though they had had nothing to do with the illegal actions, as they had been children at the time of prohibition. Realizing that I appreciated their experiences and even folk stories, they obviously felt relieved and began to narrate. The interviewees gave very lively descriptions about children's plays, which imitated the activities of adults, that is, those of the smugglers and law enforcement officers. A woman revealed, indirectly, that her family was involved, too: while thirsty, she drank water from a pitcher on the table, and when it tasted bad she realized that it was filled with diluted spirits (Rossi 2003a: 353–358).

In three communities in Southwest Finland, which had been very active centres of spirit smuggling during the prohibition, local people were very interested in the research project. They proudly brought various objects and photographs to exhibit, but most were reluctant to discuss the topic, despite the fact that the illegal activities had taken place more than sixty years ago. For several reasons, people wanted to keep silent. One reason might have been that the spirit traffic had not ended with the abolition of the prohibition law but had continued until the recent past. Another reason could be that several houses in the village had been built with smuggled money and every villager knew which houses these were. In addition, many inhabitants had profited in other ways. There were also those whose relatives had suffered badly for participating in the illegalities; for instance, they had been killed or confined to prison and lost their civil rights for a certain period.

An illustrative example of the reluctant villagers was an old sea captain who I wanted to interview because several neighbours had told me that he "knows a lot". When I asked him if he would like to be interviewed, he emphatically stated that he knows much more than others about smuggling, but nobody else would ever learn what he knows and he will ultimately take the information with him to his grave. While saying this to me he looked happy and proud of keeping his secrets. The skipper seemed to enjoy the power that he knew he had over me as a researcher and other contemporaries, as well as over the future generations (Rossi 2007; Rossi 2008). In addition, he obviously had a definite idea about what the right kind of history is and what is worth recollecting. He must have considered the smuggling of spirits to not be suitable material for public history. Of course, he might have wanted to protect certain people's reputations, including his own. He was so determined that it was impossible for me to convince him that his information would be worth recording and saving for future generations.

On the other hand, many of the retired sailors I interviewed in Turku quite willingly described how they or their colleagues had succeeded in smuggling brandy, chocolate, coffee, or nylon stockings after the Second World War, when all those luxuries were badly wanted at home. They did not seem to have any moral scruples about their deeds. Some also spoke openly (although not in first person) about the harbour prostitutes and their visits on board as well as the attitudes of captains and sailors towards the women. They did not find these matters disgraceful or embarrassing, but more or less amusing (Rossi 1999: 305–312).

When attempting to interview people of certain illegal activities for cultural history, the researcher might need all her skills to establish rapport with the interviewees-to-be and to convince the reluctant ones of the significance of the information they have in their memories and of the importance of their participation in the research project. She also has to convince them of the confidentiality of the interviews and guarantee their anonymity. The narrators must always feel safe and unthreatened both during the interviews and afterwards, no matter what they tell the interviewer (Kvale 1996:114–115; Rubin & Rubin 2005:98–99; Israel & Hay 2006:77–94).

Confidentiality in oral history means that the researcher does not pass any intimate or even neutral information about the narrator or about her recollections to anybody that she wants to keep secret – neither during the research process nor in the finished publications. She is also supposed to protect the anonymity of the narrator with a pseudonym or code if she wants to keep herself unidentified (Caunce 1994:197–198; Rubin & Rubin 2005:98). Of course, the identities of all parties to the crime discussed in the interviews should also be concealed. Confidentiality covers even the information that is irrelevant to the research topic or does not belong to the primary interests of the researcher.

In order to save valuable information for the future, the interviewer can suggest a compromise for the interviewee so that contemporary researchers would not have access to her recorded recollections but future scholars would. She might agree with the researcher to seal all the interview material or certain parts of it for a certain time, for instance, for the narrator's lifetime or until all the people have died who have been mentioned in the interview or who are otherwise concerned (Shopes 2006:146).

Thus far, I have spoken about old, statute-barred crimes that the researcher expressly wants to study and hear about, and for which the culprits can no longer be punished. Now, I will turn to cases in which interviewees reveal illegal acts, though the researcher does not particularly look for them and does not absolutely want to hear about them.


## Crimes not wanted

Regardless of her research topic, a historian might discover illegal acts while she is studying written documents in archives. She could learn of crimes that are not yet or never will fall under the statute of limitations: for instance, murder will never become statute barred. Although she does not have to face the lawbreaker face-to-face, it might not be easy for the researcher to decide what to do in such a situation – especially if she knows that the criminal is still alive. Should she simply forget what she has discovered in the documents or should she inform the law enforcement authorities? Does she have some moral obligations? For what or to whom is she responsible? For the order and justice in the society? To the victim(s)? Is she responsible for the integrity of the subject in the documents, or for her own sense of justice or peace of mind?

There are no simple or categorical answers to these questions. Usually the researcher has to decide alone if she will keep the crime a secret or if she will take certain judicial measures. In any case, the very same acts that create ethical problems could also generate powerful and even contradictory feelings in the mind of the researcher reading the documents (Bosworth 20020).

Oral historians can also encounter similar problems during interviews and will have to answer the same questions. Face-to-face interaction with another living person makes the situation emotionally, psychologically, and socially complicated. An interview in which the conversational partners produce research material together should always be an enterprise of mutual respect and confidentiality. As oral historians know, narrators tend to speak more during the interview when they are asked or encouraged to do so. Now that somebody is attentively and empathetically listening to them they could feel tempted to talk about their long buried secrets, which might burden their hearts. They simply cannot hold it back any longer, so they let the cat out of the bag, so to speak (Neuenschwander 2002: 55).

Is it still possible for the interviewer to keep up the respectful and confidential atmosphere if the impertinent information given by the interviewee concerns recent illegal activities? In this situation, the delicate balance of power could also be endangered and tipped even more to the side of the interviewer, who already has the upper hand since she is ultimately responsible for the conduct of the research. Nevertheless, a successful interview is not and should never be the scene of a power struggle between the researcher and narrator. The primary rule for the oral historian is: Do no harm to your conversation partner! (Rossi 2007: 92; Rossi 2008)

In oral history interviews the researcher hears many interesting things. Sometimes it can be difficult for her to keep silent about 'harmless' matters, for instance, love affairs of a well-known or even anonymous interviewee, which would be 'juicy' gossip. It could be even more difficult if the interviewee happens to disclose more morally questionable or downright unlawful activities she or someone else has been caught up in, for instance, drunken driving, drug trafficking, sexual abuse, shoplifting, or tax fraud, which could be taken to court if the authorities were informed.

I argue that from an ethical point of view, an oral historian is first and foremost a historian in the interview situation. She is definitely not a therapist or social worker and she should not try to be one by listening to criminal confessions and by trying to interpret the narrator's behaviour. Thus the questions are: What does it mean to be a historian in such a situation? What is her role? Does she have certain duties? What can or should she do?

## Researchers' choices

Anticipating ethically awkward situations that may occur during an interview, an oral historian might take certain measures in order to fulfil her primary obligation to be a historian. She could aim to completely avoid such problematic situations and consequential moral conflicts; or she could at least try to minimize the negative effects of the release of unwanted information. She can do that by acting either in advance, before any revelations have been made, or during the interview proper. If she suspects that the interviewee wants to unburden her heart too much, the interviewer might ask the interviewee not to give information that, if revealed, would put the narrator or other persons at risk of legal sanctions, public embarrassment, or other adverse consequences (Shopes 2006: 146; Israel & Hay 2006: 83). So far, this kind of warning is not standard procedure, but it could be made such in all oral history interviews.[3]

The interview situation is, however, psychologically and emotionally very delicate. The researcher can very seldom judge before the narrator begins her account if she has something unlawful on her conscience. Besides, the narrator might feel offended if she believes that the researcher even imagines that she could or might have done something illegal, and refuse to relate anything at all. But if the prohibitive suggestion against revelation of illegalities were a standard paragraph in the instructions at the beginning of every interview, there should be no reason for the interviewees to feel offended.

Even if she has not taken any precautions before the interview, the oral historian can take certain measures at the moment the narrator begins to uncover illegal undertakings that the historian is not looking for. Sometimes the narrator only mentions certain behaviour in passing, for instance, drunken driving. In such a scenario, it might be wisest to ignore the revelation and just continue with other questions. But if the interviewee intentionally begins speaking about illegalities, the researcher has two alternatives: either she finishes up the interview immediately or continues it on the condition that the interviewee refrains from telling about any illegalities. If the researcher finds the whole situation too ethically demanding, the ultimate alternative is to stop the interview, which may

---

3.  Zibiah Alfred brought this possibility to my attention in the Krakow congress.

sometimes be the best solution. Yet, if she chooses this course, she must clearly explain to the narrator why she has decided to drop the project. In addition, she might also recommend that the narrator seek a therapist, who could certainly help her work with the past, or that she should turn to the police if she absolutely wants to be punished for her crime.

If an oral historian expects to get essential information for her research topic from the interviewee and therefore absolutely wants to continue with the interview, but she does not want to learn more about any unlawful acts, she should ask the narrator to refrain from further disclosures. Then it is up to the interviewee to decide what to do: to continue on the researcher's conditions or miss the opportunity to participate in the project and contribute to research by recollecting her experiences. Of course, if the narrator decides to quit, the researcher might lose very valuable information. However, losing an interviewee and her account usually causes smaller damage for the researcher than losing her own peace of mind.

In his book about oral history and law, Neuenschwander writes that there is certainly no privileged relationship like that of doctor-patient or lawyer-client that would prevent the interviewer from informing law enforcement officials of serious crimes that a narrator has admitted. However, I argue that in any interview situation in which the researcher has learned about crimes, albeit not yet protected by the statute of limitations, it is not the researcher's duty to let the police, or any other authority, know about the narrator's revelations. And she has to make it absolutely clear that she will *not* report her. Moreover, as Neuenschwander says, there is no legally enforceable duty for an oral historian or any other citizen to report a past crime unless a special statute imposes such a requirement (Neuenschwander 2002: 56).

The researcher's promise of confidentiality for the interview requires that she assure the interviewee that nothing about the conversation will leak out, and then keep her promise. In my mind, the researcher must not report crimes, even if the narrator asks her to do so. It is the interviewee's duty to confess her illegal acts herself. A historian is not a law enforcement authority whose duty it is to protect the law and order in society. If the researcher regards her primary obligation to get criminals arrested and punished, I suggest that she changes her profession. Neuenschwander also urges caution in reporting a crime that the interviewee has knowledge of or actually has admitted to. In addition to statutes of limitation, the interviewer should carefully consider other important legal issues, for instance, potential defamation or claims of defamation, and legal sanctions for breach of confidentiality (Neuenschwander 2002: 57).

## No moral lectures

Regardless of what the narrator says, in my opinion it is imperative that during the whole research process the oral historian refrains from any kind of reproach and reprobation. Moral condemnation and lecturing is not a part of her role. Naturally, as a private person she might have many opinions or attitudes, but as a professional historian she should be committed to good manners and empathy in and out of the interview situation.

However, the researcher has the right and – I would say – duty to question the justification of the interviewee's illegal deeds and to express her own attitude or those of other laypeople and authorities in a 'civilized' manner and in general terms. She would hardly offend or hurt the narrator with the following statements: "I understand your behaviour in that particular situation very well but I cannot accept it, and I am afraid, neither would the authorities or other citizens", "Have you thought that people might morally condemn your behaviour or consider it unlawful?" or "You probably know that the police would immediately arrest you if they learned about the activities you spoke about".

Moral reproach in an oral history interview situation would certainly destroy whatever remains of the rapport between the historian and the narrator, if there ever were any. Probably the researcher would also destroy all her and her colleagues' chances in the future to enter the field to interview the same person or other members of her community.

Hearing about past criminal acts not only causes moral dilemmas but also instigates various and often very strong emotions in the researcher's mind towards the narrator, victim(s), or authorities; for instance, anger, anxiety, disgust, fear, hatred, malicious pleasure, pity, rage, sadness, or shame. (Wincup 2001: 24–27; see also Rossi & Aarnio 2008) Such feelings could be seen as normal, adequate, and appropriate provided they are expressed in an acceptable way. However, as Rubin and Rubin say: "If you find yourself sympathizing with interviewees who are killers, racists or religiously intolerant, or who are abusing public trust, you might begin to question yourself" (Rubin & Rubin 2005: 33).

In an oral history interview, it is not enough that the researcher encounters and manages her own feelings, but she also has to encounter and control those of the narrator, who might experience and express very strong emotions while recollecting past events. In socially interactive situations both parties tend to follow the rules for managing and expressing emotions they have learned earlier in their lives. In scholarly communities one of the elementary 'feeling rules' (Hochschild 1983) is that nobody should direct any physical aggression towards others. Even shouting and loud speaking are considered neither appropriate nor desirable. The same rules are also valid in the research interview. Most historians are probably rather good in controlling their emotions, since the academic community favours restrained behaviour and veiling one's feelings, but they are often helpless in encountering interviewee's emotions. Here it might be natural to follow Juliene G. Lipson's advice: "trust in your own gut feelings about what is right in the immediate situation" (Lipson 1994).

In the last section I will only briefly stress the main points of the oral historian's roles and suggest that they should be bound to professional secrecy in their work, as professionals are in many other fields. I will also connect these issues with the current discussion in oral history.

## Professional secrecy

If an oral historian wants to study old or statute-barred crimes that are interesting in social, societal, or cultural respects, her major problem is more often than not in convincing the interviewees-to-be of the importance of their recollections and in persuading them to participate in the research project. On the other hand, the interviewer's role is to keep the narrator silent if she begins disclosing unlawful deeds that she or someone else has committed in the past, regardless of the research topic and the historian's interests. This she can do either in the beginning or during the interview.

An oral historian should always remember that she is primarily a historian: she is not supposed to be a moralizer, informer, or therapist, even if an interview can have a therapeutic impact on the conversational partner. She should never accuse, lecture, or reproach. If she feels that encountering recollections of criminalities disturbs her too much, she might perhaps choose another less upsetting research project or field of history.

"What duty if any is there to report past criminal behaviour that the narrator either has knowledge of or actually admits to during the course of an interview?" asks Neuenschwander, adding that the question has surfaced repeatedly among oral historians at gatherings and on electronic discussion lists (Neuenschwander 2002: 55). It is difficult or impossible to find a conclusive answer to the question since different countries and states have different legislation and historians, and, thus far, lack a common code of ethics. Thus I suggest that oral historians apply and adapt the code of ethics in the neighbouring disciplines of anthropology or sociology.

According to the American Anthropological Association's *Code of Ethics* (Approved 1998), researchers have primary ethical obligations to the people, species, and materials they study and to the people with whom they work. In cases of conflicts of interest, these individuals must come first. The researchers must do everything in their power to ensure that their research does not harm the safety, dignity, and privacy of the people with whom they work, conduct research, or perform other professional activities (Shopes 2006: 146). The anthropologists make it clear that their primary responsibility is to the narrators, who are usually their subjects, too.

Since I firmly agree with the anthropologists, I suggest that we oral historians commit ourselves to professional secrecy, like professionals in the fields of law, therapy, and social work, although we are not required to give any vow or promise of silence. If we cannot, in general, keep secrets we should perhaps pursue another profession. Having promised confidentiality to the interviewees we should not break it and inform the law enforcement authorities of illegalities learned during interviews. We should only encourage the narrator to do it herself. In health sciences, Lipson also recommends the promise of secrecy to researchers dealing with persons with criminal background or who are otherwise stigmatized (Lipson 1994: 348).

It is true that "professional ethics may conflict with the researcher's perceived civic duty or moral sensibility" as Shopes says. In other words, as a private person the professional might want to report a client or an interviewee, but her professional secrecy binds her to silence. She continues: "researchers must live with themselves and thus decide for themselves how to handle such conflicts" (Shopes 2006: 146). Here, I definitely agree with Shopes.

I make my suggestion despite Rubin and Rubin emphasizing that if they keep silent, oral historians, at least in the U.S., are not immune to court sentences, as certain other professionals are. They also say:

> Because of this threat that hangs over research, researchers need to be very clear about what they will do if they somehow become embroiled in such legal proceedings. If you cannot imagine yourself going to jail for contempt of court for refusing to turn over interview notes, then you should not promise confidentiality to an interviewee who might be engaged in some unlawful activity.
>
> (Rubin & Rubin 2005: 99)

Interestingly, there are a few cases in which researchers have gone to jail rather than reveal information disclosed by their subjects (Kvale 1996: 115; Israel & Hay 2006: 88). Indeed, I would call this civil courage.

As long as the information given by the narrator is kept secret and in a safe place, confidentiality does not cause problems. But if, for one reason or another, unconcerned people come across information rendering someone guilty of certain crimes, they can take legal action against her. We should try to prevent this by protecting our oral history material as well as possible.

## References

Bosworth, M. 2002. The past as a foreign country? Some methodological implications of doing historical criminology. *British Journal of Criminology* 41: 431–442.

Caunce, S. 1994. *Oral History and the Local Historian*. London: Longman.

*Code of Ethics of the American Anthropological Association*. Approved 1998. <http://www.aaanet.org/committees/ethics/ethcode.htm> 5 December 2007.

Evans, R. J. 2002. History, memory, and the law: The historian as expert witness. *History and Theory* 41: 326–345.

Goleman, D. 1998. *Working with Emotional Intelligence*. New York NY: Bantam Books.

Henige, D. 1982. *Oral Historiography*. London: Longman.

Hochschild, A. R. 1983. *The Managed Heart: The Commercialization of Human Feelings*. Berkeley CA: University of California Press.

Israel, M. & Hay, I. 2006. *Research Ethics for Social Scientists: Between Ethical Conduct and Regulatory Compliance*. Thousand Oaks CA: Sage.

Kvale, S. 1996. *InterViews: An Introduction to Qualitative Research Interviewing*. Thousand Oaks CA: Sage.

Lipson, J. G. 1994. Ethical issues in ethnography. In *Critical Issues in Qualitative Research Methods*, J. M. Morse (ed.), 333–355. Thousand Oaks CA: Sage.

Neuenschwander, J. A. 2002. *Oral History and the Law*, 3rd edn, revised and enlarged, 55–57. Waco TX: Oral History Association.

Rossi, L. 1999. Merimies on erimies. In *Turun sataman historia*, J. T. Lappalainen (ed.), 293–318, 423–426. Turku: Turku Turun satama.

Rossi, L. 2003a. *Koiviston arkielämää 1880-luvulta 1930-luvulle*. Porvoo: Koivisto-Säätiö.

Rossi, L. 2003b. Kulttuurihistoriantutkija ei ole tuomari eikä poliisi. In *Kekui ja trokarei: Kertomuksia salakuljetuksesta saaristossa*, U. Clerc (ed.), 17–22. Nuotta.

Rossi, L. 2007. Valta muistitietotutkimuksessa. *Sananjalka, Suomen kielen seuran vuosikirja* 49: 79–94.

Rossi, L. 2008. Who has power in oral history? Forthcoming.

Rossi, L. & Aarnio, T. 2008. Feelings matter – historian's emotions. *Historyka. Studia Metodologiczne* XXXVII–XXXVIII.7

Rousso, H. 2002. *The Haunting Past: History, Memory, and Justice in Contemporary France*. Translated by R. Schoolcraft. Philadelphia PA: University of Pennsylvania Press.

Rubin, H. J. & Rubin, I. S. 2005, *Qualitative Interviewing: The Art of Hearing Data*. 2nd edn. Thousand Oaks CA: Sage.

Shopes, L. 2006, Legal and ethical issues in oral history. In *Handbook of Oral History*, T. L. Charlton, L. E. Myers & R. Sharpless (eds), 135–169. Lanham MD: Altamira Press.

Wincup, E. 2001, Feminist research with women waiting trial: The effects on participants in the qualitative research process. In *The Emotional Nature of Qualitative Research*. K. R. Gilbert (ed.), 17–35. Roca Baton FL: CRC Press.

# Memorable belongings

Kerstin Gunnemark
Department of Culture Sciences, University of Gothenburg, Sweden

The aim of this article is to present a methodology which highlights the necessity of integration between oral history and artefact collection. Memory Closets are evaluated to give opportunities for dialogues in geriatric care and schools. In the creation process of the closets employees and volunteers were invited to workshops with emphasis on autobiographies, elderly people were interviewed, and pupils wrote essays. Even if many people are not used to talking about materiality, everyone finds it enjoyable when they understand how selected things can awaken memories of their own, their cultural heritage. The dialogues around the Memory Closets, when the past can be used in the present, support their quality of life for the elderly as well as younger persons.

**Keywords:** Memory Closets project, dialogues, workshops, cultural heritage, quality of life

People are usually able to draw attention to objects and places that they associate with special occasions, events and feelings they can easily remember. When the intention is to search for further memories more things begin to stand out. Different kinds of belongings connected with everyday life are generally good tools when the issue is to try to remember earlier decades and describe experiences in an autobiographical manner. Many listeners and readers find individual narratives very interesting. Their ability to imagine previous times increases when the narrator makes references to subjective opinions within the narration of the past. It is also advantageous when artefacts in museum collections are associated with narratives of this kind. Lack of contextual references with regard to personal preferences is often problematic (Silvén & Björklund 2006). The methodological approach should be further evaluated for this purpose. The aim of this paper is to present the possibilities for maintaining a methodology which highlights the necessity of integration between oral history and artefact collection. The method of narration and collection is also favoured within geriatric care and schools.

**Memory Closets**

In homes for the elderly, the residents in their eighties and nineties do not usually converse with each other about all kinds of memories. The expectations of appropriate subjects can be rather limited. Of course there are some canons on what older men and women are interested in. For instance everybody has especially good memories from their childhood and youth, and love to retell episodes from those days. Men speak about their jobs and sports interests, while women tell about their family and home. These are common assumptions amongst the elderly as well as the staff at many homes. The employees sometimes find it difficult to communicate with the elder people and stimulate them to talk more with each other. There is also an issue of time. Practical duties generally get priority at homes for the elderly in Sweden. Time for conversations is not usually prioritised in the weekly routines or evident in the employers' time schedules. Dialogues sometimes take place without any preparation, trusting to spontaneity. Often this has a satisfactory outcome. However, most elderly people want more opportunities for dialogues and the staff are often frustrated that they do not have enough time (Anebäcken 2002).

My project is regarded as a national initiative by the Swedish Government to stimulate enterprising innovations within the sector of geriatric care. As an ethnologist I have cooperated with the head of a library and a culture and leisure coordinator in an old district of Gothenburg. We have evaluated a series of Memory Closets, and I have written a book about the methodology to create and use them, entitled 'Gallery of Memories' (*Minnenas Galleri*, Gunnemark 2004). The aim is to give opportunities for dialogues within and across generations, and to arrange meetings around Memory Closets with employees or volunteers of different ages. With cooperation from geriatric care and schools, it is also possible to invite elderly people and children into dialogues.

**Creation and narration**

In the series 'Gallery of Memories', five Memory Closets were created on different themes. Common to all items in the closets is their relation to narratives. The purpose in interviewing elderly people, staff, and residents of different ages about memorable belongings was also to inform them about the project and stimulate an interest in using the Memory Closets when they were completed. Two themes, 'Birthdays' and 'Holidays', had a time spectrum from the beginning of the last century to the present. The contributions to these themes from children and teenage pupils were drawings and school essays. The other themes were limited to particular decades, for example, old districts of 'Gothenburg' with special attention to the time before the extensive demolition and modernisation of old blocks in the 1960s and 1970s.

In the workshops the participants got the opportunity to decide on a theme for 'their' Memory Closet. One group of female employees chose 'Teenage Time'. They were teenage girls in the 1950s and 1960s and very interested in clothes and fashion. The aim was also to create a closet with reference to a subject, to which young employees could associate their own experiences. The members of the second workshop were volunteers between 50 and 75 years of age who wanted to recall their memories from their homes in the 1950s. At each meeting the participants read or retold their individual narratives and discussed why they had remembered theses belongings. Sometimes they brought photos or objects with them, which they had found in attics or cellars. At the end of the workshops we went to flea markets together, to search for things they had mentioned in their narratives. There was no obligation to give any personal belongings to the closets, although some of the participants in the workshops enjoyed doing so.

The Memory Closets were decorated by the employees in different colours and patterns associated with the themes. They also made protective covers for the closets and for some of the chinaware. I have selected narratives, school essays, drawings, and interview quotes in files for each closet. The files are together with some novels and magazines in pockets inside pockets in the doors. There, one can also find instructions for the conversation leader. The sizes of shelves and drawers vary inside the closets, depending on the space each object needs.

## Reminiscence of everyone

The process of narrative documentation as well as using the completed Memory Closets has obviously been to encourage subjectivity. No one is participating as a representative for an entire group with reference to class, gender, or ethnicity. Here individuality is emphasized and desirable. It also means that the members of a conversation group must respect the differing opinions and experiences of the others. The main aim of Memory Closets is not to teach cultural history, but to stimulate memories. And everyone is an expert on his or her own life.

The conversation leader makes a reservation for a Memory Closet and arranges meetings once a week. The purpose is not to show every single item at the first meeting. Some artefacts are hidden in drawers or behind small doors in the closet and can be revealed later. At the beginning, the leader can encourage someone to pick up an object and talk about it or introduce the meeting with a personal narrative. During each session it is also important that everyone in the group gets time to express some reminiscences of their own. After four or five meetings the group can choose another closet or a new group may be established. However, it is important to have some kind of stability within a group if the engagement of the members is to increase. It is not desirable to have to take time introducing new members at every meeting.

The ability to remember varies between elderly people. The most important issue when a group is constructed is to invite people with comparable abilities to ensure the quality of the dialogues. The Memory Closets are not created for individuals who suffer advanced senile dementia, even if the concept also gives opportunities for their comprehension. The series 'Gallery of Memories' is not 'owned' by any special group. Different groups with varying abilities to remember can use them in a variety of ways. Too often elderly people with good memories are regarded as expressing independence. But they also need stimulation on *their* own terms.

## Dialogue

If a dialogue is to be successful it is important to exchange roles during the conversation, giving the narrator the opportunity to also be a listener. Many times when children are visiting homes for the elderly or the seniors are in schools the dialogue is unbalanced. The adults are narrators and children just listeners. The most common subjects are memories from the time when the elderly were children. From this point of view the children would not have any interest in the history of everyday life without these narrations of childhood. The duty of the elderly is to teach cultural history through their memories. It used to be that the adults showed no interest in listening to children's descriptions of what it is to be a child nowadays. And the hierarchical structure of generations was evident (Johansson 2005: 23).    _across generations_

In the Memory Closet project the approach is different, with special attention to the opportunities for dialogues. If the purpose is to create meetings for school pupils and the elderly, it is important to shape the closets with belongings from both generations. When the children are narrating their memories with regard to things they find in the closet they also become aware of what the listeners do not know. It is encouraging for 7–10 year old girls and boys to have something to give the adults. These conversations are on more equal terms and are usually interesting for the elderly when they realize how joyful it is for the children to explain their games and their attitudes to the belongings. As adult listeners it becomes easier to make comparisons over time and discuss likenesses and differences. In these dialogues the adults are not supervisors in all aspects and the children get the role of experts in their own lives.

This example shows the curiosity of the elderly for the present and other generations when they are listening to narrations of everyday life from subjective points of view. Within the Memory Closets project it is evident that the elderly are not just interested in the past when they were young. They have lots of memories from different eras of their lifetime and can make many comparisons with the present day. During the 1950s this generation was middle aged. They had already settled down and were generally not moving to newly built areas at that time, but they bought new things. Many senior citizens are very fond of talking about the 1950s. When they touch objects from this decade they remember individual events and the national spirit of the time. By focusing on the 1950s they can stimulate each other to compare the times before as well as those after (Gunnemark 2006).

## Deposits of everyday life

Generally when people talk about memorable belongings, they have heirlooms in mind. Anecdotes about these things are sometimes related at Christmas or other occasions when relatives of different generations are together. But the interpretation of what constitutes an heirloom is rather limited. Many families only count their old things which also are attractive at the antiques' market. However, there are other objects in a home which have symbolic value. They have been kept for years in closets, drawers, and wardrobes for different reasons. The owners have preserved these belongings because they are memorable. But even if they are reminders from different phases of a lifetime, the owners have seldom told anyone why they have been collected or any episode in connection to them. From the perspective of the owners it is obvious that collections of belongings have been made on a scale from very conscious to entirely unreflective. Some things bring special memories alive directly. When the owners look at them, emotions of joy or sorrow are evident. Other belongings have been kept in attics and cellars more like deposits of everyday life. They are more or less hidden in boxes waiting to be sorted out some day. The owners' hesitation to throw them away is obvious. These things generally have very little or no financial value but they correspond to experiences, lifestyle, and identity. And on reflection it is also possible to recall the historical context with subjective references to these belongings (Löfgren 1998).

## The art of dialogue

Meetings around Memory Closets are activities in the present where the cultural heritage of everyday life is in focus. This means, for instance, that the historical perspective to living memory is regarded differently by different generations. Comparisons between past and present are also considered. There are no specific chronological demands. A meeting can start with a dialogue about a thing which is fairly new. The same principle is also used for the narration of life stories. The varied themes of the Memory Closets provide opportunities for autobiographical presentations without the predictability of beginning in childhood and ending in old age. With regard to belongings, the memories usually bring narratives with different contents to the surface. There is no requirement to construct links between various memorable belongings or the contexts which surround them. Like photos in an album, the narratives describe situations from different places and times. Using Bruno Labour's actor-network theory it is possible to analyse how belongings are reminders and interact with the narrator in the recall process (Latour 1999). When separate situations were in focus, many aspects of life were mentioned in rather unexpected and contrasting ways when comparison with the canons of elder's interests (Bergvall 2007: 45).

The employees in geriatric care have been given new opportunities for dialogues with elderly men and women. When they arrange meetings around Memory Closets, nothing else should be done. The conversation activity is registered in their time schedules. With the obligation of conversation leaders to relate memories of their own, their contact with the elderly people often deepens. With the exchange of life stories, unknown aspects come to the surface. When all participants are confident in the group, recalled emotions of grief and pain are as welcome as joy and pleasure, and then the quality of the dialogues develops (Armitage 2002). In addition to the staff, volunteers have also found that talking about collected belongings is very useful when new people are introduced at a home for the elderly. The activity makes it easier for them to get to know other residents. With the creation of Memory Closets and the dialogues around memorable belongings, the pleasure of work has increased.

During a lifetime there will be several requirements for socialisation in each new phase (Liljequist 1993). For instance, when a person leaves the working life or later moves to a home for the elderly. It is not surprising that these adaptation processes sometimes take time. The elderly must be comfortable in their new living situation. The quality of life will be strengthened when elders feel that their experiences can be useful. Few activities stimulate narration of everyday life with historical perspective. Culture programs are generally directed at the elderly as passive consumers rather than active participants. There are also expectations as to which events are worth relating with reference to established historical genres (Portelli 1998). With the obligation to speak about trivial things in the Memory Closets, the traditional concepts of historical genres are challenged. Even if many people are not used to talking about materiality, everyone finds it enjoyable when they understand how these selected things can awaken memories of *their own*. The dialogues around the Memory Closets, when the past can be used in the present, support their quality of life.

A genuine apprehension towards using reminiscence perspective is common within geriatric care in Sweden. But as far as I can understand, the extent to which this approach was realized in practice, varied a great deal. It is a question of the interests of the managers of homes for the elderly, and also which models assistant nurses have. In England, as described by Joanna Bornat, the practice of reminiscence methods has been widespread. There were also workshops for working class history established in the 1970s and the Centerprise Publishing Project was successful in editing narratives of everyday life (Bornat 1998). In Sweden this kind of workshop was rather common 1975–1985 concerning industrial work with references to Industrial Archaeology in Great Britain (Alzén 2005). I have also been inspired by this field of oral history. In various projects I invited inhabitants of Gothenburg to write autobiographies which focus on everyday life in their neighbourhoods. As a workshop leader for groups of one or three generations, with only females or both men and women, I share experiences with other oral history researchers. The participants do not merely deliver everyday life stories; they are also to a large extent self-reflecting on their lives (Armitage 2002; Bornat 1998). When their narratives were published, and they got response from the readers, they also became conscious of the values of cultural heritage within living memory (Gunnemark 1991, 2000). It is seldom possible to arrange a workshop of this kind within a home for the elderly. The task of writing autobiographical narratives is, for most elderly people, too ambitious. The meetings around Memory Closets, however, have methodological links to workshops with writing obligation and especially to those which emphasize materiality as reminders. Memory Closets can be created on various themes and the art of dialogue about memorable belongings is also useful in museums for contextual documentation of oral history.

## References

Alzén, A. 2005. Kulturarv i rörelse – en jämförande studie. In *Kulturarvens gränser. Komparativa perspektiv,* P. Arnosson, B. Hodne, B. Skarin Frykman & J. Ödemark (eds). Göteborg: Arkipelag.

Anebäcken, E.-M. (ed.). 2002. *Kultur och meningsfull vardag inom äldreomsorgen.* FoU-centrum för vård och omsorg [FoU-rapport 1:2002]. Linköping: Linköpings universitet.

Armitage, S. H. 2002. Next step. In *Women's Oral History. The Frontiers Reader,* S. H. Armitage, P. Hart & K. Weathermon (eds). Lincoln NB: University of Nebraska Press.

Bergvall, C. 2007. *Liv, lust och mening – om krukväxters kulturella betydelser.* Stockholm: Carlsson bokförlag.

Bornat, J. 1998. Oral history as a social movement: Reminiscence and older people. In *The Oral History Reader,* R. Perks & A. Thomson (eds). London: Routledge.

Gunnemark, K. 1991. *Våra liv i Kortedala. Kvinnor i två generationer skriver och berättar.* Göteborg: Etnologiska föreningen i Västsverige.

Gunnemark, K. (ed.). 2000. *Återblickar och framtidstro i Majorna.* Göteborg: Etnologiska föreningen i Västsverige.

Gunnemark, K. 2004. *Minnenas Galleri, om minnesskåp och kulturarv.* Stockholm: Carlsson bokförlag.

Gunnemark, K. 2006. *Ung på 50-talet. Om förälskelser, mode och boende i en brytningstid.* Stockholm: Bilda förlag.

Johansson, B. 2005. *Barn i konsumtionssamhället.* Stockholm: Norstedts Akademiska förlag.

Latour, B. 1999. *Pandora's Hope. Essays on the Reality of Science Studies.* Cambridge MA: Harvard University Press.

Liljequist, M. 1993. Socialisation från vaggan till graven. In *Kultur och erfarenhet. Aktuella teman i svensk etnologi,* B. Ehn, (ed). Stockholm: Carlsson bokförlag.

Löfgren, O. 1998. My life as consumer. Narratives from the world of goods. In *Narrative and Genre,* M. Chamberlain & P. Thompson (eds). London: Routledge.

Portelli, A. 1998. Oral history as a genre. In *Narrative and Genre,* M. Chamberlain & P. Thompson (eds), London: Routledge.

Silvén, E. & Björklund, A. 2006. *Svåra saker. Ting och berättelser som upprör och berör.* Stockholm: Nordiska museets förlag.

# Oral history & e-research

## Collecting memories of the 1960s and 1970s youth culture

Liisa Avelin
University of Turku, Finland

Whether we like it or not, computer-mediated methods are no doubt becoming more and more a part of an oral historian's toolbox. I describe here one online data collection method – the blog – which is part of the ever-increasing e-research family. I highlight the process, benefits, and challenges of this form of data collection and analysis with one case study, which was undertaken to collect memories and data for my cultural history study: 1960s and '70s disco culture in Finland.

**Keywords:** computer-mediated research, online data collection, blog, pop-culture in Finland

When a researcher's purpose is to find out people's thoughts and the meanings they give to things, interviewing has traditionally been his/her main method. The interviewer usually records the interviews in one way or another and also very often transliterates them. If not always using the practical paper-and-pencil (P&P) method, he/she will exploit some computer-aided system and text processing software for turning the oral data to textual format. I view oral history as a method of historical documentation, which uses interviews and other methods with living "survivors" of the time under investigation. Let us not forget all the benefits that the use of ICT tools (for example, computer-assisted interviews, digital voice recorders, and software for managing data) provide for the researcher. Can ICT tools provide additional help to a researcher? Is it worth to use the Internet, instead of interviews, when collecting oral history data? Does the data obtained from such methods differ from traditional methods – and if so, how?

## What is e-research?

"Is the computer [ – ] a genie in the bottle which, once released, will transform the activity of field research in unnoticed and unwelcome ways?" Nigel G. Fielding and Raymond M. Lee ask this question while discussing the possibilities and challenges ICT offers in qualitative research (1991:6). Their article was published in 1991, and until now we have been wise enough to know that the computer does nothing by itself, and we hopefully do not conduct research led by computers.

The use of the Internet and other new technologies such as voice recognition systems, e-mail systems, Internet telephones, virtual interviews, and the blog are all considered to be electronic data collection methods, known as "e-research" (Singh & Burgess 2007:29). Innovative tools and technologies can be applied to case study research, focus groups, surveys, as well as the analysis of data, which makes doing research a more interesting experience.

Web sites and web pages are potential sources of data that support both quantitative and qualitative research. The most simple e-research method is virtual interviewing, or interviewing by Internet. This means an interview where the researcher is communicating virtually with people by computer who can be physically far away. Virtual interviews are done by e-mail or via the Internet among groups or individuals, in public or private, synchronously or asynchronously. E-mail can be used to do structured or unstructured interviews (Tiittula et al. 2005:264–266; Mann & Stewart 2002). Oral history research is well suited for virtual interviews, which I will point out while considering the requirements of this method (Mann & Stewart 2002:603–628).

Computer-mediated communication (CMC) creates a base, which CSSN (computer-supported social networks) gives life to. Internet blogs – defined here as frequently modified web pages in which dated entries are listed in reverse chronological sequence – are an increasingly popular form of communication in the World Wide Web. The first present-day format appeared in 1996, and the term "blog" was first applied in 1997 (Herring et al. 2007). In a blog the author (blogger) writes something and publishes it for others to read. The more public a blog, the more important is the rhythm of the news the blogger posts. A conversation becomes possible when readers are allowed to comment on the written entries.

## How to use blogs for research purposes

Using a blog is quite a new method for collecting oral history research materials. The literature of the subject is wide, but it seems to concentrate on giving advice to bloggers on technical and content matters, not for research purposes. As far as

**Table 1.** Top five themes in the blog

| A week's headline | Comments per week |
| --- | --- |
| Pop generation is speaking | 263 |
| Nothing is useless, if it give you memories | 226 |
| Let's recall past, as long as we still remember | 209 |
| Messages, hints questions and links | 208 |
| Twelve point for Finland in the Eurovision Song Contest | 205 |

I have been able to ascertain, Torill Mortensen and Jill Walker – who are research-ers of online games, texts, and culture – are two of the few academics using a blog for research (Mortensen & Walker 2004). Cameron Barrett, who runs the popular "CamWorld" blog, encourages people to build a blog for one's special industry, speciality, or occupation. According to him the world is in need of more spe-cialised blogs (Barett 2002: 33). David Kline and Dan Burstein describe how the blog is "the Internet's fastest growing communications phenomenon", and how it is changing politics, business, and culture. Even they do not pay any attention to its effect on science (2005: passim).

Blogs are a form of CMC, which means that communication through blogs comes with certain changes compared to face-to-face (FTF) communication. In some ways communication will be poorer and in others it will be enhanced. Through a textual conversation people will have a different experience than when the same people have a face-to-face conversation. On the other hand, when using the Internet it is possible to communicate in a simple and inexpensive way with people on the other side of the world (Wijnia 2004). In my research I found the blog to be the best way to get in contact with my target group, now middle-aged and spread out, working and living all over the world.

My blog <http://disco.kymp.net> was built as a forum to discuss and share memories in public. I launched it in 2006 and ran it for 45 weeks. In addition to the fact that the people were able to share memories (by reading and writing about them), they could participate in the research and also follow the progress of the research. Everyone had equal access to the blog community, because there were no passwords. I introduced a new subject every week, so there were 45 themes to discuss.[1]

The blog was read on all continents and in more than 80 countries. It had over 50,000 visitors altogether, 74–636 per day. It is very important to have a real conversation in a blog, especially when you try to collect data with it. The writers really built up a living on-line community. In almost all occasions they knew each

---

1.  Music was absolutely the most popular theme from the beginning to the very end.

other from the '60s–'70s and continued the conversation which was interrupted nearly 40 years ago. The blog made it possible for people to join the community once again.

For me as a researcher the blog was a very interesting and stimulating way to collect oral history data from certain themes. As a matter of fact, we can consider the process as one kind of interview, in which the writers answered my questions consequentially and where the questions were absolutely the same for everyone. On the other hand, to be honest, the blog proved to be very demanding as a research tool. Running it took much more time and effort than I could have ever imagined. While it took almost all my leisure time for one year, I started to feel sympathy for the bloggers, who were also suffering from burnout. Nevertheless, the highlight for a blogger is when you find out that you are not writing a monologue in a dark space.

What was my blog's meaning? From a research point of view, the results are very remarkable, but from a subjective point of view they are very embarrassing. At first it was a way to collect memories for research purposes, but it soon became something else, too. It offered the people a forum to share memories, make contact with old and new friends, get rid of depression, and develop love affairs. The data is still plentiful: the blog covers 4,698 comments, more than 100 photographs, and plenty of other contemporary material and documents from the '60s and '70s. There were many regular writers who wrote almost every day. 12.5% of the visitors produced all the research data.

It is important to remember ethical principles, especially in the world of ICT, where knowledge can be reached freely by anyone. Several difficulties may occur; for example, it is not simple for the blog writer to direct his/her text. I mean, it is impossible to know all the readers on the Internet. What should one say about his/her youth experiences to the whole world? The need for the conversation is private and human; but, on the other hand, when you satisfy it openly, it is full of risks. As a form of media, blogs can be too public.


## How to use e-research in interviews

Couper and Hansen see computer-assisted interviewing (CAI) simply as a method where the interviewer reads the questions from the screen and types the answers during the interview (2002: 557–560). Obviously, this annoying method is different from the traditional method, both from the interviewee's and the interviewer's point of view. It has a huge effect on their communication and interaction. We must say, that it is strongly recommended to print the questions on paper. The interaction between the interviewer and interviewee remains alive, and the interviewer can concentrate better on the situation itself and observe, for example, the respondent's speechless communication.

What benefits are found when one records an interview using a computer? I approach the problem from the point of view of my research question. What kind of data is relevant to my research? How do we infer meaning when my respondents describe their youth experiences? I recorded my interviews using open-source software and a digital voice recorder.[2] I wanted some interviews to be transliterated, and for that purpose I used different open-source software designed to manage qualitative data.[3]

An interesting feature of the software is that it creates graphics from the speech which can in some cases be used when analysing the meanings. Sometimes, when the interviewer is telling a very remarkable story for him/her, the volume goes up and the speed increases. On other hand, speeches slow down, pauses between words become longer, the voice lowers and it can sometimes even fade away as you see here:

**Figure 1**

A researcher needs to be very careful with this. As oral historian Alessandro Portelli points out, the matter is not a simple one. The speed and changes of a respondent's speech vary during the interview, but there are no fixed interpretative rules. When the speech is slowing down, it may mean greater emphasis but also greater difficulty. Also, acceleration may show a wish to glide over certain points (Portelli 1998: 34). Still, one benefit using this method is that graphics can in some cases give extra information when analysing.

Interviews recorded on a computer can be transformed by certain software which offers tools for transcribing, identifying analytically interesting clips, assigning keywords to clips, arranging and rearranging clips, creating complex

---

2.  The software is called Audacity 1.2.6. See <http://audacity.sourceforge.net>. 15 February 2007.

3.  Transana was originally created by Chris Fassnacht. It is now developed and maintained by David K. Woods at the Wisconsin Center for Education Research, University of Wisconsin-Madison. The newest versions 2.20 and 2.21 are not open source anymore. Transana Website <http://www.transana.org/about/news.htm#NotFree>. 3 January 2008.

collections of interrelated clips, exploring relationships between applied keywords, and sharing the analyses with colleagues. The researcher can simultaneously listen to the interviewee's speech while transliterating and categorising it. All can be done with the same equipment. However, in oral history research it is always important to ask if it is really dependable, from a validity and reliability point of view (not to mention economical) to transliterate the interviews.

For example, Portelli raises the question of the value of authentic spoken words. According to him transcription is not necessary in oral history research at all; on the contrary, in a careless transcription you may even spoil the data. Language is composed of traits which are bearers of meaning – for example, tone, volume range, and the rhythm of popular speech. Portelli points out that while the transcription turns aural objects into text, it will inevitably make changes and leave room for interpretation. That is why he also believes that it is unnecessary to give excessive attention to the quest for new and closer methods of transcription (Portelli 1998: 33). Historian Raphael Samuel also warned to the perils of the transcript already in 1971. Some distortion is bound to arise, whatever the intention of the writer, simply by cutting out pauses and repetitions. In the process, the weight and balance of the spoken word can easily be upset (Samuel 1998: 389–392).

In any case, if you still want to transcribe your data, e-research can be a lot of help. Qualitative research software can help you manage, shape, and make sense of unstructured information. But one must remember: it does not do the thinking for you.

> As the use of computers in qualitative research develops, do qualitative researchers need to be reminded, as quantitative researchers have long been, of the "gigo" principle – "garbage in, garbage out"?                              (Fielding & Lee 1991: 15)

The anxiety comes from the fear that the machine will "take over" the analysis. There is the possibility that the use of computers may tempt qualitative researchers into "quick and dirty" research, with its attendant danger of premature theoretical closure. Qualitative research software can be used in analysing your data.[4] For example the Ethnograph allows one to import text-based qualitative data, typed in any word processor, straight into the program.

The main point in using this kind of software is that you must carefully study the possibilities it offers. That is the only way to find out how to correctly and effectively use it in your research. The larger your data, the more important it is to keep your own thoughts clear. The program does not do anything by itself; it is your problem to decide, for example, the indexing categories, segments, and code words. It takes time and is not easier than when using traditional methods. The

---

4.  For example, NVivo, XSight and Ethnograph.

point is that once you have created the categories, you can easily do searches and selectively or globally modify existing coding schemes, or construct a possibly large and highly structured hierarchical indexing database into the documents to be analysed. I am sure this method suits some of us extremely well. For example, on Transana's website, one user's comment was: "Oh my god!!!! This is $&#%ing brilliant!!!!"

## How to do e-research?

> Does my interviewee really exist?
> Where did he disappear during the interview?
> How could I politely end this two year long "interview"?

When you are not familiar with e-research, it is easy to encounter problems such as those described above (Tiittula et al. 2005: 264–265). That is why it is important to discuss some basic things in using e-research methods, virtual interviews, and blogs. They have many similar problems, which I will now introduce.

Virtual interviews are, according to Christine B. Smith, an economic alternative to labour intensive and expensive face-to-face and/or telephone interviews. She emphasises that e-mails are rapidly becoming an indispensable tool for gathering detailed information on selected populations (Smith 1997). Persuasive arguments for using e-mail surveys are: extreme cost reduction, quick turnaround, ability to facilitate interaction between the researcher and respondent, collapsed geographic boundaries for research, user (respondent) convenience, and candid and extensive response quality (Mann & Stewart 2002; Smith 1997; Singh & Burgess 2007; Tiittula et al. 2005).

Arja Kuula reminds us that a researcher always has to respect the respondents' self-determination and give them a chance to decide whether to take part in the research or not (Kuula 2006: 59). Chris Mann and Fiona Stewart add that one way for researchers to dispel respondents' feelings of caution and to increase trust is to be as open as possible about the purposes and processes of the research. They want to know if the faceless researcher is trustworthy. It is also important to note that the more individuals know each other in a virtual community, the more likely it is that trust, satisfaction, and a sense of being in a safe communication environment will ensue (2002: 616–617). In a blog, this requirement is extremely important to understand, to make and keep it a living forum. In virtual reality all those requirements mentioned are highlighted because of the lack of physical contact.

A researcher needs ICT skills, but also interactive skills when launching a blog or doing virtual interviews. Good relationships are important. Otherwise the researcher suddenly discovers that he/she is the only writer in the blog, the interviewees disappear, or they do not bother to answer your questions at all. A blog conversation requires that a blogger continually keeps his/her eye on the page and tirelessly follows the discussion. Mann and Stewart put it this way: human relationships have the same kind of variability and rules on-line as they do in real life. Rapport on-line is possible – it comes from being very up front with what you are doing and responding as you would with anyone (2002: 613, 617).

A virtual environment is text-based, which is also a challenge. The primary ways for the writer to express him/herself are the choice of the words, verbal descriptions of feelings, and the structure of the text. The interviewer or blogger cannot be seen face-to-face, but the respondent can use emoticons, big letters and punctuation to show his/her feelings (Tiittula et al. 2005: 264, 271) (see, for example, the above-mentioned Transana user's enthusiastic comment). Nevertheless, misunderstandings on the Internet are embarrassing but possible, when the expression given is different from the expression received (Goffman 1971: 39–40).

The researcher's feedback is emphasised in a virtual world. Participants may need regular confirmation to make sure that they are communicating in an appropriate way and that their contributions are valued. Participants may experience an interviewer's or blogger's pause to "listen" as absence. Cues that an interviewer is listening reassure participants of continuing interest. Mann and Stewart give an e-researcher some advice on how to show listening in a virtual world. A researcher may express listening with interest by responding promptly to questions, overtly expressing interest in a particular point made, asking follow-up questions, or perhaps enthusiastically sharing similar experiences as those described by the respondent. Because of the possibility of misunderstandings, it is also worth informing the interviewees when you are absent due to travelling, illness etc. (Mann & Stewart 2002: 617–618).

If I promise to participate in e-research as an interviewee, can a researcher be certain that my identity is real and that it is really me answering? Although this was not problem in my blog, the fact is that the interviewer can never absolutely know for sure who is behind the answers. It is possible for the participants to create whole new identities for themselves in a virtual world.[5]

---

5. It happened in my blog that when there was a new writer, one of the regular writers usually asked: "Excuse me, could you tell us who you are?" People wanted to find out each others identities. It is interesting that the demand for revealing each others identities came from the writers' community, not by me. I tried to encourage everyone to join the blog and write using their name, pseudonym, or remain anonymous. Common history and the spirit of a virtual community seemed to be more important for the writers than the research, and so demanded that writer's real identity should be revealed.

If a researcher receives an answer written at 3:10 a.m. on Saturday, what does it tell about the person answering? Interviewees and blog writers can choose the right time and place for them to write. The e-researcher must pay attention to this point. We must also remember that only those with enough technical abilities can answer virtual interviews and write in the blogs. Due to this, e-research only works with certain types of respondents and the voice is muted of those whose voice is normally low. A writer states in my blog: "I think that people who write here have things in order. Those people who have a pc at home, laptop in their summer cottage or a screen open on the desk. What would those people write who don't have that equipment?".[6] If the target group of the research is not just *the Bold and the Beautiful*, it is the researcher's task to take care of the research data triangulation.

When a researcher is using a blog method for data collection, he/she has to step into the public with unfinished research, which is usually unpleasant and even frightening. According to Erving Goffman, we preferably like to show just the result when presenting our products to the public. So we make sure that we are being evaluated only on the finished, refined, and packed performance (Goffman 1971:56). It is typical for the blog that the research goes forward in cooperation with the public. That can also be one of the method's benefits.

Lastly I want to discuss the quality of the oral history data produced by e-research. Is the result different that of traditional methods? Is there a difference between the data produced by speaking or by writing? Tiittula, Rastas, and Ruusuvuori have, for example, paid attention to this. They point out that the language has a tendency to adapt to the tool. Often – but not always – the writers' language is more explicit, considered, straight, and systematic. E-mail allows more time for writers to choose their words (Tiittula et al. 2005:268–269; Pöysä 2006:230). For example, one writer in my blog sketched out his texts for days, checked the facts and dates before posting. On the other hand, there can also be certain streams of consciousness without checking spelling. As we know, language is developing and also reveals something about its time.

As I have pointed out, in addition to its many benefits, the new technology has also some potential risks. Those risks should be taken into consideration in advance. From an oral history point of view, I see many possibilities in e-research. For example, it is hard to imagine another method which has been so comprehensively reached among people as the blog.

The researcher has to decide how to ensure the storage of the blog and other e-research data. The material should be filed in its original context. When e-research

---

6.  Jusu M., comment in the blog http://disco.kymp.net. 18 August 2006.

methods develop and the usage of the method increases, this will be a big challenge for archives in the future.[7]

Whatever the method, the most important thing is to make sure that it does not weaken the quality of the data. My methodological objectives were to create and develop new ways in using ICT tools for oral history research. Transana software made the transcribing process easier and more interesting and also produced visual information of the interviews. The blog made it possible for my target group to join the online community whenever they wanted. For me it offered an information channel to make my study transparent and public in collecting oral history material.

Above all the people found that the public discussion in the blog made them remember old things better and clearer. Photos, links, and drawings published in the blog helped stimulate memories. The possibility to read one's own thoughts on a screen encourages reflecting on them and also activates long term memory processing. The memories become shared, diversified, multiplied, and accumulated. I find the e-research method very encouraging from an oral history and cultural history point of view. As a researcher you need just three things: time, time, and time.

## References

Barrett, C. 2002. More about blogs. In *We've Got Blog. How Blogs are Changing Our Culture*, R. Blood (ed.), 28–33. Cambridge: Perseus.

Couper, M. P. & Hansen, S. E. 2002. Computer-assisted interviewing. In *Handbook of Interview Research. Context & Method*, J. F. Gabrium & J. A. Holstein (eds), 557–560. Thousand Oaks CA: Sage.

Fielding, N. G. & Lee, R. M. 1991. *Using Computers in Qualitative Research*. Newbury Park CA: Sage.

Goffman, E. 1971. *Arkielämän roolit*. Translated by Erkki Puranen. Porvoo: WSOY.

Herring, S. C., Scheidt, L. A., Bonus, S. & Wright, E. *Bridging the Gap: A Genre Analysis of Blogs*. School of Library and Information Science, Indiana University Website: <http://www.ics.uci.edu/~jpd/classes/ics234cw04/herring.pdf>. 12 June 2007.

Kline, D. & Burstein, D. 2005. *Blog!* New York NY: CDS Books.

Kuula, A. 2006. *Tutkimusetiikka. Aineistojen hankinta, käyttö ja säilytys*. Tampere: Vastapaino.

Mann, C. & Stewart, F. 2002. Internet interviewing. In *Handbook of Interview Research. Context & Method*, J. F. Gabrium & J. A. Holstein (eds.), 603–628. Thousand Oaks CA: Sage.

---

7. My blog data is stored in The Finnish Social Science Data Archive (FSD). See: http://www.fsd.uta.fi.

Mortensen, T. & Walker, W. 2004. *Blogging Thoughts: Personal Publication as an Online Research Tool.* <http://imweb.uio.no/konferanser/skikt-2/docs/Researching_ICTs_in_context-Ch11-Mortensen-Walker.pdf>. 10 February 2008.

Portelli, A. 1998. What makes oral history different. In *The Oral History Reader,* R. Perks & A. Thomson (eds), 63–74. London: Routledge.

Pöysä, J. 2006. Kilpakirjoitukset muistitietotutkimuksessa.In *Muistitietotutkimus. Metodologisia kysymyksiä,* O. Fingerroos, R. Haanpää, A. Heimo & U.-M. Peltonen (eds), Helsinki: Suomalaisen Kirjallisuuden Seura.

Samuel, R. 1998. Perils of the Transcript. In *The Oral History Reader,* R. Perks & A. Thomson (eds), 389–392. London: Routledge.

Singh, M. & Burgess, S. 2007. Electronic data collection methods. In *Handbook of Research on Electronic Surveys and Measurements,* R. A. Reynolds, R. Woods & J. D. Baker (eds), 28–43. Hershey PA: Idea Group Reference.

Smith, C. B. 1997. Casting the net: Surveying an internet population. *Journal of Computer- mediated Communication* 3(1), <http://jcmc.indiana.edu/vol3/issue1/smith.html>. 8 February 2008.

Tiittula, L., Rastas, A. & Ruusuvuori, J. 2005. Kasvokkaisesta vuorovaikutuksesta tietokonevälitteiseen viestintään. In *Haastattelu. Tutkimus, tilanteet ja vuorovaikutus,* J. Ruusuvuori & L. Tiittula (eds.), 264–272. Tampere: Vastapaino.

Wijnia E. 2004. Understanding blogs: A communicative perspective <http://elmine.wijnia.com/blog/archives/wijnia_understandingblogs.pdf> accessed 30 August 2007.

## Websites

Ethnograph Website <http://www.qualisresearch.com/>. 10 February 2008.

Transana Website <http://www.transana.org/>. 10 February 2008.

University of Carolina website. Herring, S. C, Scheidt L. A., Bonus, S. & Wright, E. 2004. Bridging the Gap: A Genre Analysis of Blogs. School of Library and Information Science, <http://www.ics.uci.edu/~jpd/classes/ics234cw04/herring.pdf> 12 June 2007.

# Oral history and political elites

## Interviewing (and transcribing) lobbyists

Conor McGrath

Independent Scholar, Dublin, Republic of Ireland

This chapter discusses some of the methodological issues which arose in my interviews with lobbyists in Washington, London and Brussels. While all research projects are different, this chapter attempts to highlight some key issues around interviewing which researchers need to consider – such as interview structure, the ethics of transcribing, and editing transcriptions for publication – and to provide an account of how they were addressed in the course of this particular project. It ends by urging that such transcripts become generally available to other researchers, as they constitute a potentially fruitful data resource of no less importance than the quantitative datasets which tend to be more commonly available.

Keywords: political elites, oral history interview, ethics of transcribing, editing transcriptions

## Introduction

The motivation behind this chapter is centered in my own experience of interviewing a number of lobbyists for a book (McGrath 2005).[1] As a former lobbyist myself, the thing I have most often found lacking in scholarly monographs about lobbying is the lobbyist himself or herself. It is by no means uncommon to read a work which seeks to explain what lobbying behavior is likely to be undertaken or

---

1.   I am deeply indebted to the lobbyists who have been generous enough to speak to me during my research. Andrew Roman has suggested that, "Writing authoritatively about lobbying is as difficult as writing authoritatively about the practice of espionage. Anyone who has any relevant current information is likely not to be writing about it but practising it, yet will not tell you how, or with what success" (qtd. in Stanbury 1988: 305). I have been fortunate in having spoken about lobbying with so many experienced professionals who have been so willing to share their views.

effective in a particular situation, but for that author not to have actually spoken to a single lobbyist in the course of the research. Highly mathematical models of lobbying are produced, which are undoubtedly extremely internally rigorous but which nevertheless are based entirely on previous mathematical models of lobbying rather than on any insights which could be offered by lobbyists themselves (for one example, see Grossman and Helpman 2001). One of the aims of my own book was therefore to provide a space in which lobbyists could discuss their experiences and expertise at some length, in their own words. What this meant in practice was that the final third of the text (approximately 30,000 words) consisted of edited transcripts of my interviews with 16 named lobbyists. While others were quoted more briefly (and generally anonymously through the text), these detailed transcripts constitute the backbone of the work as a whole.

The closing statement of Sammy Finer's influential work on British lobbying pleaded for "Light! More Light!" (1966: 145). Academic scholars can help to interpret and explain what is found when light is shone on lobbying practices, but that light itself comes from lobbyists being prepared to speak to us about their activities. It is my hope that the contributions recorded in my book may go a little way towards encouraging other lobbyists to speak to other researchers openly, in detail, and in their own words, about their work.

This chapter, then, discusses some of the methodological issues which arise in the interviewing of members of the political elite in Washington, London and Brussels, and then moves on to consider how such interviews can best be transcribed and edited. It ends by urging that such transcripts become generally available to other researchers, as they constitute a potentially fruitful data resource of no less importance than the quantitative datasets which tend to be more commonly available.

What I hope this chapter contributes, particularly to early-career researchers, is a sense of some of the issues which do need to be considered and resolved before interviewing people professionally involved in politics, the questions associated with producing an interview transcript, and the importance of finding some means by which to create an accessible record of those transcripts in order that they can be followed up by future researchers. While this chapter is centered around my own particular project, the questions which that work raised with me have a more general applicability for all scholars undertaking interview-based research. Interviewing is clearly more of an art than a science. Thus, while the literature abounds with advice on what to do and not do, a 'right' answer can never be arrived at, and so each discussion of how that advice was used in the course of a specific project is a valuable addition to our stock of knowledge about interviewing.

## Interviewing political elites

It is common to find expressed in the literature the idea that interviewing elites is different from interviewing 'ordinary' people. So, what constitutes an 'elite' interviewee? According to Seldon, elite interviews are "those conducted with individuals selected because of who they are or what they did" (1996: 353). Political elites are therefore "loosely defined as those with close proximity to power or policymaking" (Lilleker 2003: 207). My group of interviewees – lobbyists – certainly fit Lilleker's definition as their professional lives are spent intervening in and attempting to influence the public policymaking process.

One of the most prolific interviewers of political elites took a somewhat different approach to what constituted an 'elite interview'. Dexter regarded *any* interview as elite if the interviewee was accorded what he termed "special, non-standardized treatment" (1970: 5). By this, he meant that the interview was largely steered by the respondent rather than the investigator – instead of simply asking everyone a set of common questions and providing them with a range of possible answers (as might occur in a questionnaire, for instance), an elite interview is characterized by an emphasis on the interviewee's perception of what is relevant and important and a consequent willingness by the interviewer to allow the respondent to set the frame of the discussion. (And, as an aside, my experience has very much been that the most productive interviews were those which proceeded like discussions rather than 'question-answer-question-answer' sessions: those elite figures whom I interviewed appeared to strongly prefer this mode, albeit that these were discussions between an interviewee with substantial lobbying experience and an informed interviewer with less personal lobbying experience. Perhaps political elites positively enjoy 'teaching' someone who is keen to learn from them?) This sense of "the virtue of allowing the subjects to tell the interviewer what's relevant and what's important rather than being restricted by the researcher's preconceived notions about what is important" (Berry 2002: 681) has, in my experience, been at the core of an interview in which both participants feel they have enjoyed the encounter and said/heard something useful and interesting.

This was the approach I decided to take with my own interviews: having selected the interviewees largely on the basis that I had, through desk research, established that they had a particular set of experiences or expertise which was relevant to the overall project, I tended to allow them to discuss that in a form and sequence largely of their choosing, while of course always being able to introduce specific follow-up questions intended to encourage them to address a particular situation I knew they had dealt with in the course of their work. As Dexter put it "the interviewer confronted with genuinely prominent people or the prestigious well-informed is unlikely to feel that he can insist on their hewing to a standardized line of discussion" (1970:6). Indeed, my own reflection in hindsight tends to reinforce this approach, as it seems to me that many of the most interesting nuggets of information which lobbyists offered would have been unlikely to have resulted from the confines of a more structured interview technique – "If the interviews are individual-specific a list of headings or objectives are often more appropriate; this will allow the interview to be fluid and organic and the interviewer can alter the line of questioning pragmatically" (Lilleker 2003:210). It is frequently the case that an interviewee will introduce a new thought or interpretation which can then be followed up in that and subsequent interviews.

Other researchers may well prefer to conduct more structured interviews in order to obtain quantitative data which can be analyzed in the light of a specific hypothesis. In this project, though, I was primarily interested in 'soaking and poking', in gaining each respondent's individual opinions and experiences. As Beth Leech has commented, relatively unstructured interviews "are most appropriate when the interviewer ... wants an insider perspective.... [They] are best used as a source of insight, not for hypothesis testing" (2002:665). Even so, my interviews were not entirely unstructured, in the sense that my background research had identified topics I then raised with each interviewee on the basis that I believed they would have something valuable to say on those topics. The precise order in which the topics were covered, and the precise way in which I framed questions and subsequent probes, were however generally more or less spontaneous or unscripted. As Williams wrote of the interviews he conducted while researching a political biography:

> my object was always to get the informant to talk naturally and spontaneously and to limit the use of questions.... The strategy by no means implied an absence of questions on my part; just the contrary, it was all the more important to know exactly which points one wanted answered, in order to seize any opportunity to divert the conversation into fruitful channels.                    (1980:305)

Discussing her experience of interviewing senior politicians, McEvoy concurs that such a semi-structured approach both allowed her "to investigate their opinions" and gave her interviewees "the freedom to expand on areas, thus providing 'rich' information" (2006:185). Similarly, in my own research, I found that a semi-structured approach – a synthesis between the use of a highly rigid interview schedule and an entirely unplanned interview – was most likely to produce an effective and efficient exchange. Some degree of forethought by the researcher helps to ensure that interviews can be systematic in terms of covering a range of subjects (both internally and between interviews, so that it is possible to compare the answers of several respondents). At the same time, some degree of flexibility permits respondents to both reply to questions in their own personal and individual manner and to suggest pathways not previously considered by the interviewer. Putnam's study of politicians in Britain and Italy, for instance, relied upon a semi-structured interview approach which he intended would "suggest certain topics for discussion, striving for a formulation as constant as possible across interviews, but striving also to maintain the tone of a genuine conversation" (1973: 19).

Whatever degree of structuring is involved, researchers do need to have thought prior to the interview about the manner in which questions ought to be formulated, even if (as in my case) the exact wording of the questions was not determined beforehand. In keeping with the elite or non-standardized approach I was using, my questions tended to be rather exploratory or open-ended – "Elites … do not like being put in the straightjacket of close-ended questions. They prefer to articulate their views, explaining why they think what they think" (Aberbach and Rockman 2002: 674). Obviously, follow-up questions asking for clarification of a particular point or concrete examples to illustrate a point may be less open-ended.

It is also worth considering in advance *why* one wants to undertake elite interviews as part of a research project: they are, after all, only one of a range of possible methodologies, and can be very time-consuming and potentially expensive. So it is essential to ask oneself what sort of project one wishes to undertake, what sort of information needs to be obtained for that project, and how that information can best be obtained. Interviews will not always be the most effective or appropriate methodology to adopt. That said, though, I very consciously wanted to draw in my book on the thoughts of lobbyists themselves, and felt that it was important to allow them to express those thoughts in their own ways. One writer suggests that "interviews yield rich insights into people's biographies, experiences, opinions, values, aspirations, attitudes and feelings" (May 2001: 120); another argues that "interviews are only necessitated when a researcher wishes to produce a work with textural depth as well as empirical strength" (Lilleker 2003: 208).

Another consideration which affects the decision as to whether or not interviews will be employed relates to the extent to which it is thought necessary for the research to be statistically representative of the whole population of (in this instance) lobbyists. In the case of my project, I was not attempting to 'prove' anything about lobbyists as a collective, but rather was seeking to focus in depth on some lobbyists selected by virtue of their perceived ability and expertise and not because they were deemed to be typical of all lobbyists. In practical terms, if one wanted to achieve a representative sample of lobbyists, a questionnaire would make much more sense than conducting hundreds or thousands of interviews. Conversely, interviews are much more revealing than standardized surveys if the aim is to encourage fewer lobbyists to be more open and discursive. My aim was not to achieve some kind of balance, but nor was it entirely random or *ad hoc*;

I purposely wanted to interview a selection of lobbyists whom I had reason to believe would have useful experiences to relate. Again, this comes back to the nature of elite interviews – Seldon and Pappworth argue that an elite interviewee "is taken to be someone of interest because of the position he or she holds, rather than because he or she is representative or typical of a group" (1983: 6). Interviews are thus particularly useful as a means of obtaining a depth of material from a relatively small sample of elite figures, while surveys would be more appropriate for gathering wider but shallower information from a larger population.

While the implication that elite interviewees are somehow more interesting or worthy than anyone else is unfortunate, it is – however clumsily expressed – an important and necessary distinction which does need to be made because it has implications both for how an interview is conducted and for how it is later transcribed.

## Transcribing political interviews

Early-career researchers will find much advice in the literature on how best to write up an interview. Opinions vary of course, with some arguing in favor of note taking – for instance, it is suggested that some people will become unnaturally "verbose in front of a tape recorder" and that being seen by an interviewee to be taking notes "can be used to guide the conversation" in that an interviewee may gauge how valuable his or her remarks are according to how frantically notes are being taken (Seldon and Pappworth 1983: 71). The obvious difficulty with note taking is that of taking sufficient notes to be able to accurately and comprehensively reconstruct the responses. While a personal form of shorthand can be used while the interview is taking place, it is crucial to make a more detailed note very soon afterwards. It is also possible to spend so much energy and concentration on taking notes while the interview proceeds that inadequate attention is paid to the content of what is being said, and thus fail to probe particular comments or ask for clarification of a point. There will be some interviewees who find having the discussion recorded permanently on tape to be somewhat inhibiting and thus reveal less than may otherwise have been the case (but in my experience these tend to be civil service officials rather than elected politicians or lobbyists).

My own practice was to ask when arranging an interview if the person would object to me making a tape recording of the interview (none did – it may be that political elites are well accustomed to being recorded at meetings and by journalists), and to focus during the interview on listening to what was being said rather than on writing it all down. That sort of approach, I believe, encourages a greater rapport between interviewee and interviewer, and eliminates the undoubted distraction and lack of eye contact which note taking necessitates; it is, nonetheless, important to make a few notes as the interview progresses, even if only as reminders of specific observations one wants to return to and probe a little more.

Tape recording an interview should not, though, be regarded as simply an easy option. For that recording to be of most utility, it then has to be transcribed, and this can be a very difficult and time consuming process. To begin with a practicality, I initially had some tapes typed up by an experienced secretary, but quickly found that reviewing the transcripts thus produced and going back to the tapes to fill in blanks was both time consuming and frustrating. The frustration was eased when I began to type up the tapes myself, although it certainly took me longer to type them personally. Moreover, as I had also conducted the interviews (or more precisely, had also participated in the conversation which had been taped), I was already familiar to some extent with the speech patterns of the individual lobbyists, which allowed me to produce a transcript which reflected those as far as possible.

Once I had typed up a verbatim transcript of each interview, I would then begin to edit it: firstly for punctuation, spelling, grammar and so on, to produce a 'clean' copy; and then for content. Opinions differ in the literature as to the appropriateness of this sort of editorial work, but in both cases it was necessary for this particular project. While one of my aims as interviewer was to provide lobbyists with an opportunity to speak at length in their own words about lobbying, as high-profile figures within the political elite, one of the aims of the interviewees was to ensure that the final text reflected them to their best advantage. Clearly, there is always a balance to be struck here; for this project, having considered the range of options, I concluded that it was preferable to have each lobbyist speaking on their own behalf, even at the expense of making them appear somewhat more coherent than may have been the case. It is certainly true that simply adding punctuation marks into a transcript does alter the text, and this must be done with some consistency and an awareness that it has implications. Equally, though, as Powers has observed: "I apply punctuation for ease of reading and comprehension. I take it for granted that I influence the transcript in many ways, and I feel punctuation is the least intrusion I make" (2005: 45). Given that the subject matter was of a professional rather than a personal or emotional nature, that seems to me to be a reasonable *modus operandi*.

In terms of the actual content of the interviews, I consciously edited the transcripts with as light a touch as possible. Sections were deleted if they were overly repetitive or digressive, and some sentences were re-ordered for the sake of coherency, but the final product remained firmly in the speaker's own words. Idiosyncratic use of language or sentence construction, the ways in which each interviewee defined particular terms, the phraseology employed to discuss an event or professional technique – all these were the real meat of the interviews, and accordingly were not edited out or standardized across transcripts. There is of course another balance to be struck here, between the demands of "precise accuracy of detail" and readability, and here I lent towards the view that "corrected transcripts are more straightforward" (Humphries 1984:44) – in other words, what I tried consciously to achieve in the work was to produce detailed and interesting and true transcripts which could easily be read and analyzed and used by future researchers. It seems to me that both academic utility and readability can be achieved, provided that the author is always conscious of the balance which is being struck: Yow cautions the author to "stay as close to the narrator's words as you can while still having a readable text. The least possible tampering with the primary source – *according the most respect for the narrator's unique way of speaking* – is the best way" (2005:327) (emphasis in the original).

There are without question potential hazards involved in any transcription, and these multiply the more the transcript is edited. People do not tend to speak in perfectly grammatical prose as it might appear on paper. Every transcript distorts to some extent – "The oral interview is a multilayered communicative event, which a transcript only palely reflects" (Dunaway 1984:116) – but that ought not be an argument for not producing transcripts. Transcripts can remain useful academic tools – if they are produced with care. Samuel notes that the degree of distortion is dependent "upon how far the writer is aware of the temptations to which he is prone" (1998:389).

In accordance with the commitment I had given each lobbyist at the time of the interview, I then sent each a copy of the edited transcript of their interview, asking that they review it. My covering letter advised each lobbyist:

> I am very keen that [the book] should not only allow students and professionals to learn from the expertise of those whose transcripts are included, but also that it should reflect as best as possible the words of those professionals…. I have therefore tried in producing the attached transcript to be as faithful as possible to the actual recording I made, to your authentic speaking voice perhaps. I hope that each transcript allows something of the character and personality of the professional to come across; therefore, I would be very grateful if you would review the transcript essentially for details of accuracy and confidentiality rather than for precise language or grammar.

This seemed to me to be a necessary part of this particular project, certainly in terms of gaining the trust of the interviewees when I first met them, as they could be reassured that they would have an opportunity to see in black and white what they had actually said to me. In the event, only one person refused to allow their transcript to be used, claiming that they did not recognize as their true belief a particular view expressed in the transcript (and on the tape recording of our meeting). All the other lobbyists read their transcript, returned it promptly, and generally made quite minimal suggestions or requirements for change.

Researchers differ on whether allowing interviewees to see transcripts before publication is appropriate. On one hand, some argue that to do so runs the risk "that the informant might become alarmed at what he has said and want to make major changes" (Seldon and Pappworth 1983:86); another scholar notes that this practice is considered by many "to be indulgence to the interviewee" (Morrissey 1998:112). Conversely, others believe that it is proper "to try to ensure that the representation of the respondents' information was as accurate as possible" (Davies 2001:76). In terms of my book, I felt that since it was important to base the work around transcripts of lobbyists, it was reasonable to give them the chance to see their transcript before it was published and (hopefully) read by their peers: "Review [by the respondent] is especially necessary when all or part of a transcript is to be published" (Powers 2005:89). Other than this practical or pragmatic rationale, there is too a more ethical principle at play here – as Yow notes "there is something about print that gives it a formality that taped sound does not have. Therefore, there has been a change and the narrator has a right to see what you have done" (2005:322). Acknowledging that a change has been made, it still seems to me to be desirable and useful to produce and publish relatively lengthy edited transcripts of interviews; after all, without such publication how do we learn of others' experiences and attitudes and perspectives?

## Interview transcripts as a data resource

While many books, journal articles and conference papers on lobbying are based in part on interviews with lobbyists, almost always they include only brief extracts from each interview. It is therefore difficult, if not impossible, for other researchers to use those interviews in their own work: a short quote may be all that the original interviewer gets from an interview that is relevant to their particular project, but there may have been a great deal of other information that would be useful to someone else working on a different project. The problem lies in the accessibility of the interview transcript. We tend to think of interview transcripts as 'ours', and rarely publish them in full or place them in an archive where they can be read and used by others. As Bale puts it, "The practice of poring over another political scientist's interview transcripts is less common than playing with the numbers those transcripts may even have helped to generate. It is also less common than it should be" (1996:63). There are reasons why this situation has evolved (for instance, some interviewees may have requested anonymity and simply leaving their name off the top of a transcript may do nothing to erase the internal clues to their identity contained in what they said; and some academics undoubtedly regard transcripts as something valuable not to be shared with colleagues), but my own starting point is that it is very much in the interests of the original researcher to make his or her detailed transcripts easily accessible in some form.

As scholars, we all want other academics to find our writings useful and important, and often how this is expressed in practical terms is through others citing our work in their own publications. But if I want to quote from an interview conducted by another political scientist, the only such quote available to me is that which he or she has included in some previous work; it is at the very least problematic for me to gain access to the full transcript of that interview, in order that I may use a different (and previously unpublished) quote from it. In order to do so, I would have to contact the original interviewer, even assuming that that was possible and that he or she could be tracked down, and then I am entirely at his or her mercy in terms of obtaining copies of the transcripts. Referencing and citing very brief and previously published extracts from someone else's interviews is not always particularly valuable – as an eminent British historian has observed: "where [a] source is an oral interrogation of which only the author has the text, anything more than a general reference seems pointless: what is the point of recommending a reader to check a source which is out of his reach?" (Hugh Trevor-Roper, qtd. in Seldon and Pappworth 1983: 131–32). There is, in addition, a more internalized notion among academics that they should do their own interviews rather than re-analyze those conducted by others – we all want to produce original work, but the possibility of producing original work which is partly based on interview sources obtained by someone else seems to strike us collectively as somehow undesirable.

Why this should be so, is unclear to me. No scholar could write anything without referring to material previously published by others – indeed, we consciously want to build on work which has gone before us. Few academics are at all reluctant to re-assess statistical data on which previous work has been based. Indeed, the funders of academic research generally insist that quantitative datasets are made available in some archival form precisely so that they can be examined and further tested by other researchers. But, curiously, grant-awarding bodies rarely make the same stipulation with regard to qualitative data (for instance, writing in 1996, Bale noted that while the Data Archive at Essex University in the UK held 1,322 studies derived from interviews, all of which were easily accessible to other researchers, some 1,319 of these made available the statistics which arose from the coding of the interviews but only three provided access to the interview transcripts themselves).

While transcripts can never precisely reproduce every detail of an interview, as Powers states "they can be well-crafted forms of the original that allow for further appreciation, insights, or analysis" (2005: 3). Unless the transcripts are commonly available, though, they can only be appreciated and analyzed by the original researcher. From the perspective of interviewees, presumably one motivation which lies behind them agreeing to be interviewed is that they wish to make a contribution to academic debate and to impress their beliefs and opinions on it. They, too, will prefer (as a general rule of thumb) that their comments can inform more than one researcher's work. Certainly, my experience has been that a lobbyist open enough to talk to me frankly, positively wants his or her words to be heard by an audience of more than simply me. The fact that I approached them asking for an interview which would eventually result in a detailed transcript of their words being published in a book, I believe encouraged some of them to make the time available to meet with me: they thought that this was presenting them with an opportunity to influence the thinking of the wider academic community as well as that of their professional peers.

So, what can be done? If it is accepted that interview transcripts constitute potentially significant and useful sources of secondary research, and if it is inherently desirable that they should be able to inform general academic debate, it is essential that such transcripts can be easily obtained by researchers. If the interviews which I have conducted provide useful material, why do I include only a small fraction of that data in my next book or article, and thereafter hoard the full transcripts in a cardboard box in my office for the rest of my career, only for it to be thrown out by my children after my death? If the material is actually useful, it deserves to be actually used – and not just by me, but by any researcher who can put it to use. As Wallot and Fortier assert: "research findings can only be critiqued fully when the sources used in the research are available to other researchers. Transparency is needed for any public debate or scientific undertaking" (1998: 370). In other words, if we want our work to be examined by others properly, we need to enable them to see detailed interview transcripts rather than merely the one or two brief quotes we have extracted from them.

Ideally, bodies which provide research funding will begin to make a pre-condition of such support that interview transcripts are made available to the academic community generally. But even as individual researchers, we can find ways of ensuring that transcripts are accessible. It is possible (though neither easy nor fast) to find, as I did, a publisher which was open to the idea of publishing detailed transcripts as part of a larger book (for instance, see Reeher's 2006 book based on interviews with state legislators). We can put transcripts on websites so that they can be located easily by others – as Thompson notes in a different context, "Oral historians can think now as if they themselves were publishers: imagine what evidence is needed, seek it out and capture it" ( 1998: 24). If fellow academics take the interest to contact us and ask to see transcripts, we can respond helpfully and positively. We can encourage others to make transcripts available simply by asking to see 'their' transcripts. The pay-off for us is that our work is disseminated more widely than would otherwise be the case, and (hopefully) is cited more frequently by a greater range of colleagues than would otherwise be the case.

## Conclusion

In any field, interviews can be an enormously rewarding and stimulating activity: it is impossible to undertake a number of interviews with a range of people in any sphere of life and not come away from them collectively with a sense of knowing more about the subject and of better understanding its nuances and interpretations. They certainly enliven a text, providing textual depth and color to an analysis; as Peabody et al. assert, "One of the most potent, high-yield ways of studying political elites is to interview them" (1990: 454). Indeed, the increasing use of oral history methodologies in recent decades has vastly improved and expanded our understanding of both history as a discipline ('what constitutes history?') and the practice of historical investigation ('how to do history?'). Interviewing has been key to this, for interviews explicitly presume that history encompasses contemporary events as much as it does those of centuries past; and interviews require the historian to consider anew how best to access source material.

In particular, interviewing has been instrumental in simultaneously both expanding the conceptualization of history such that it includes the history of 'ordinary' people and communities, and also – the particular focus of this chapter – enhancing the practice of history by allowing us to probe in detail the experiences of elite figures. However, interviews are not always the most appropriate research methodology – for instance, questionnaires will be more efficient if a large and statistically representative sample is to be questioned, and interviews are less useful in testing hypotheses than they are in providing 'rich' insight – and even when they are, they still raise substantial issues which the researcher must be aware of. When conducting elite interviews, a semi-structured approach allows the interviewer to raise pre-selected topics while permitting the interviewee to bring up areas he or she believes to be important. Each interviewer, each interviewee, and each research project will bring different requests or demands regarding the best way of recording interviews or taking notes during them. If interviews are recorded, transcribe them with care and deliberation, and ensure that both participants have a shared understanding of what use is to made of the recordings and transcripts.

And certainly interview transcripts constitute a very valuable resource for the wider academic community. They should be shared with all who can derive insight and illumination from them. Raphael Samuel has made this argument most persuasively:

> The collector of the spoken word – of oral history and tradition – is in a privileged position. He is the creator, in some sort, of his own archives, and he ought to interpret his duties accordingly. His role, properly conceived, is that of archivist, as well as historian, retrieving and storing priceless information which would otherwise be lost …. His greatest contribution may well be in the collecting and safe preservation of his material rather than in the use he can immediately find for it, or the way he writes it up.                                              (1998: 391–92)

While we all hope and believe that our published work is of some interest or significance, the interviews on which they are based are equally of inherent importance – "in the long run the interviews themselves will prove much more useful to scholars than the texts grafted upon them" (Grele 1998: 43). The most practical manifestation of this utility is for more and more academics to make freely available the transcripts of their interviews.

# References

Aberbach, J. D. & Rockman, B. 2002. Conducting and coding elite interviews. *PS: Political Science and Politics* 35(4): 673–676.

Bale, T. 1996. Other people's words: Creating a market for interview material in political science. *Politics* 16(1): 63–67.

Berry, J. M. 2002. Validity and reliability issues in elite interviewing. *PS: Political Science and Politics* 35(4): 679–682.

Davies, P. H. J. 2001. Spies as informants: Triangulation and the interpretation of elite interview data in the study of the intelligence and security services. *Politics* 21(1): 73–80.

Dexter, L. A. 1970. *Elite and Specialized Interviewing*. Evanston IL: Northwestern University Press.

Dunaway, D. K. 1984. Transcriptions: Shadow or reality. *Oral History Review* 12: 113–117.

Finer, S. E. 1966. *Anonymous Empire: A study of the Lobby in Great Britain*, 2nd edn. London: Pall Mall Press.

Grele, R. J. 1998. Movement Without Aim: Methodological and theoretical problems in oral history. In *The Oral History Reader*, R. Perks & A. Thomson (eds), 38–52. London: Routledge.

Grossman, G. M. & Helpman, E. 2001. *Special Interest Politics*. Cambridge MA: The MIT Press.

Humphries, S. 1984. *The Handbook of Oral History: Recording Life Stories*. London: Inter-Action Imprint.

Leech, B. L. 2002. Asking questions: Techniques for semistructured interviews. *PS: Political Science and Politics* 35(4): 665–668.

Lilleker, D. G. 2003. Interviewing the political elite: Navigating a potential minefield. *Politics* 23(3): 207–214.

May, T. 2001. *Social Research: Issues, Methods and Process*. Buckingham: Open University Press.

McEvoy, J. 2006. Elite interviewing in a divided society: Lessons from Northern Ireland. *Politics* 26(3): 184–191.

McGrath, C. 2005. *Lobbying in Washington, London, and Brussels: The Persuasive Communication of Political Issues*. Lewiston NY: Edwin Mellen Press.

Morrissey, C. T. 1998. On oral history interviewing. In *The Oral History Reader*, R. Perks & A. Thomson (eds), 107–113. London: Routledge.

Peabody, R. L., Hammond, S. W., Torcom, J., Brown, L. P., Thompson, C. & Kolodny, R. 1990. Interviewing political elites. *PS: Political Science and Politics* 23(3): 451–455.

Powers, W. R. 2005. *Transcription Techniques for the Spoken Word*. Lanham MD: AltaMira Press.

Putnam, R. D. 1973. *The Beliefs of Politicians: Ideology, Conflict, and Democracy in Britain and Italy*. New Haven CT: Yale University Press.

Reeher, G. 2006. *First Person Political: Legislative Life and the Meaning of Public Service*. New York NY: New York University Press.

Samuel, R. 1998. Perils of the Transcript. In *The Oral History Reader*, R. Perks & A. Thomson (eds), 365–378. London: Routledge.

Seldon, A. 1996. Elite interviews. In *The Contemporary History Handbook*, B. Brivati, J. Buxton & A. Seldon (eds), 353–365. Manchester: Manchester University Press.

Seldon, A. & Pappworth, J. 1983. *By Word of Mouth: Elite oral history*. London: Methuen.

Stanbury, W. T. 1988. *Business-Government Relations in Canada*. Scarborough, Ontario: Nelson Canada.

Thompson, P. 1998. The voice of the past: Oral history. In *The Oral History Reader*, R. Perks & A. Thomson (eds), 21–28. London: Routledge.

Wallot, J. P. & Fortier, N. 1998. Archival science and oral sources. In *The Oral History Reader*, R. Perks & A. Thomson (eds), 365–378. London: Routledge.

Williams, P. M. 1980. Interviewing politicians: The life of Hugh Gaitskell. *Political Quarterly* 51(3): 303–316.

Yow, V. R. 2005. *Recording Oral History: A Guide for the Humanities and Social Sciences*. Walnut Creek CA: AltaMira Press.

# Doing gender

# Doing gender within oral history

Helga Amesberger

Institute of Conflict Research, Vienna, Austria

At the focus of the article is how the process of generating oral history contributes to the creation of gendered history. I follow two paths to proof my hypothesis that researchers participate in the creation and reinforcement of gender stereotypes and engendering the subject. First, I analyse life story interviews with female and male survivors of the Mauthausen concentration camp, concerning how the interviewees draw genders, and about which gendered topics do wo/men speak (or do not speak). Second, I look at the role of the interviewer: what kind of questions does s/he ask women respectively men, and do gender-specific questions produce otherwise non-mentioned topics or reduce interviewees to their assumed gender roles. The analysis shows that doing gender is a common pattern in oral history interviews and therefore needed to be reflected on.

**Keywords:** gendered oral history, concentration camp survivors, role of the interviewer

_such as._

Debates within the (feminist) historiography about gender specificity of the Holocaust and the National Socialist persecution have been going on for more than two decades. These discussions roughly oscillate between two positions: one that traces disparity to the different socialization of women and men, and another that places women's "openness to violation" ('_Verletzungsoffenheit_') at the centre of analysis (Bock 2005: 7–21). At the same time, historiography still suffers from oblivion regarding the gendered aspects where general history is concerned. This is not due – as one might assume – to a lack of oral or written testimonies by women. As Maria Ecker (2004) discovered in her research about Holocaust testimonies in the USA, more female than male survivors wrote about their experiences in the period from 1945 to 1960. Even after this period the number of publications written by women or men was rather equal, whereas we have much less oral accounts of women survivors from 1945 up to the late 1970s.[1] Ecker, therefore, rightly concludes: "It's not that women wrote or talked less than male survivors, but that they received less attention" (Ecker 2004: 5). Most of the time, women are only focused on in the specific context of the history of women. General history is seemingly genderless, meaning that the history of men is the standard, from which the history of women deviates.

In my article I want to address the conflict between the use of the gender category to render women's history visible and the danger of enhancing gendered stereotypes through the research process. Therefore, the focal point of this paper will be the way the research process – or more precisely, the process of generating Oral History – contributes to the creation of (non)gendered history.

I will follow two paths to prove my hypothesis that researchers participate in the creation and reinforcement of traditional genders and of (non)engendering the subject. First, I analyze life story interviews with female and male survivors of National Socialist concentration camps: In which way do interviewees produce gender and what gendered topics do women/men speak (or not speak) about? Second, I will look at the role of the interviewer: What kinds of questions does she/he ask women or men, and do gender-specific questions produce otherwise unmentioned topics or reduce interviewees to their assumed gender roles?

Before elaborating on my findings, I would like to clarify my premises concerning the production of oral history/narration and my definitions of "gender" and "doing gender".

### Premises

Concerning the production of life stories, in my view two premises are important for the understanding or classification of the data obtained:

1.  Life stories are never (exclusively) purely subjective constructions, nor are they entirely "true" events. Rather, they reflect social conventions, norms, values, and rules of discourse (Scholz 2003: 141–144; comp. Scheffer 2003: 99) and, thus, gender relations.

---

1.  Constanze Jaiser, who did a similar research about published testimonies in Germany reported at the workshop "Experiences of Sexualised Violence during National Socialism", organized by the Institute of Conflict Research in Vienna in November 2007, that in the immediate aftermath of the Holocaust (1945–1949) half of the memoirs were written by female survivors, until the 1960ies the percentage of women's memoirs decreased, and in the 1970s and 1980s the number of publications by women and men are equal again. Later on published memoirs by women outnumbered testimonies by men.

2.  Every interview – and also, therefore, the narrative-biographical interview – must be read as an interaction between at least two individuals. Even if the interview is directed as little as possible by interview guidelines, as is the case in the narrative interview, it must be assumed that the interviewer is "co-producer" (Scholz 2003:143; comp. also Ecker 2004:5) of the biographical construction. Socio-demographic characteristics (of interviewees as well as interviewers) such as age/generation, gender, educational background, etc. influence the content and course of the interview as does the concrete social, political, and economic situation. Similarly, expectations placed on the person opposite (and in the interview) affect the biographical (re)construction.

From (1) and (2) follows that, essentially, narratives are related to the present, the situation, and the addressee. Biographical accounts are, therefore, rather "stories about what her life is and more importantly, what a life should be like" (Welzer 2003:186). This means that the (re)construction of a biography cannot occur completely arbitrarily. Through our specific social situation, we perceive things in a specific manner, interpret them in our own individual manner, and incorporate them – matching with our recollections – into our memory. This means that these biographical identities change and vary in their emphasis. In this context, Welzer (2003:199) mentions that autobiographical memory is always also a social memory.

3.  A basic constant of modern societies is the engendering of individuals, whereby the engendered identity is constructed as strictly two-gendered and essentially hierarchical. In everyday life when assigning gender to individuals, we almost exclusively fall back on appearance, such as hairstyle, clothing, or figure since biological criteria such as chromosomes or genitalia cannot (usually) be seen. Besides, these features are not always as unambiguous as it might seem. (comp. Gildemeister & Wetterer 1992:209; West & Zimmerman 1998:169–170) Simultaneously with the assignment to a gender category, a connection is made to seemingly intrinsic, behavioural, and psychological traits, which are based on the different reproductive functions of the genders. Although the two-gender construction is a result of history, it is viewed as a "natural" consequence and as an unquestioned fact. (West & Zimmerman 1998:169–170)

Consequently, if engendering is a basic constant of our society and if the narratives are essentially related to the present, the situation, and the addressee, then the production of gender is part of everyday communication/interaction and, thus, of every interview situation. Gender assignments and productions of gender images are seldom deliberate, but rather an unconscious act.

Therefore, we need to ask how gender is produced during (biographical-narrative) interviews by both the interviewee and the interviewer alike and how processes of doing gender co-design the construction of life stories.

## What is "doing gender"?

I am unable to refer here to the extensive debate about or justified criticism of the differentiation between sex as a biological and gender as a social sexual category.[2] The term "doing gender" emphasizes that gender is not determined by biological traits, which in turn produce gender roles, habits, attitudes, behaviour, and so on, but by the meaning attached to such physical traits – especially the difference in reproductive functions – that produces gender. "Doing" refers to the production process of gender; a production done not only by men but also by women. We can define "gender" as the accomplishment of normative concepts of "(true) femininity" or "(true) masculinity". Cancade West and Don Zimmerman conclude: "Doing gender means creating differences between girls and boys and women and men, differences that are not natural, essential, or biological. Once the differences have been constructed, they are used to reinforce the 'essentialness' of gender" (West & Zimmerman 1998: 178).

## Database and approach

Although doing gender is not confined to the phase of data gathering, but is part of the entire research process, I will focus on the interview situation as far as it is reflected in the following interview transcripts. The basis for analysis are life story interviews with female and male survivors of the Mauthausen concentration camp, conducted in 2002/2003 by various researchers in various European countries, Israel, and the USA. This documentation about survivors of the Mauthausen concentration camp was conceptually developed and organized by the Institute of Conflict Research, in co-operation with the Ludwig Boltzmann-Institute of Social Science History, and the Documentation Centre of Austrian Resistance. The interviews were conducted by regional teams. Most of the interviews I used are translations from various languages into German. This fact implies several

---

2.    For a thorough discussion comp. Gildemeister & Wetterer (1992). The theoretical differentiation of sex and gender produces according to the authors two main aporias: first, a "shifted biologism" since sex is still biologically determined; and second, a "latent biologism" because of the tacit parallelizing of sex and gender.

problems such as the difficulty to transfer the specifics of one's mode of narration, of sentence construction/syntax, and so on into another language. Still, this database has the advantage that all interviews are conducted according to one single guideline. That is, (theoretically) the differences regarding our topic cannot be a result of different research interests and/or research methods.

In the following article I elaborate on the process of doing gender in interviews regarding:

a.   content level, that is, what is talked about; and
b.   interactional level; that is, how does the interaction/communication between interviewee and interviewer produce gender? (Scholz 2003)

Within these levels we can distinguish direct and indirect references to gender.

## Doing gender at the content level

At the content level, the evidence of doing gender is ample. It would require too much time to present a thorough analysis of the content of the various life story interviews. Therefore, I shall concentrate on topics that are mentioned in Holocaust literature as major differences between women and men, such as the preoccupation with "social bonding" in women's memoirs (Goldenberg 1998: 335). I will also select a few themes that have indirect references to gender, such as solidarity versus aggression/violence, family and children, and themes that address gender directly, such as depictions of female perpetrators and the representations of mothers and fathers.

### Indirect references to gender

Whereas Myrna Goldenberg found a greater preoccupation in women's memoirs with "social bonding" than men, Constanze Jaiser, who compared memoirs written shortly after liberation and more recent memoirs, concluded that in early reports the "picture of greater solidarity and of non-violence among women" (Jaiser 2005: 130) appeared less frequently than in later reports. That is, female survivors seem to smooth their narration about women (over time) to fit common representations of femininity.

My comparison between the interviews with female and male Mauthausen survivors does not confirm Goldenberg's findings either. Women and men alike speak about friends/relatives with whom they were together and shared food and clothing, and/or who supported them in various ways. There is no evidence that men construct themselves more than women do as lone fighters, but, in sum, they mentioned a smaller number of individuals than women. How about references to aggressive acts committed by fellow prisoners and prisoner-functionaries? With respect to this, women spoke less frequently about physical violence among prisoners than men. Furthermore, aggression and revenge – if reported at all – were always less severe than those reported by men. How can we explain this difference? Does this mean that women acted less aggressively than men? Not necessarily, as all women also mentioned violent female prisoner functionaries, the so-called Kapos. There is also the possibility that such deeds are not mentioned because they seem to be unwomanly and do not conform to the ideal of the peace-loving woman. Additionally, all male interviewees also reported that acts of revenge took place, they just denied participating in such acts against Kapos, fellow prisoners, or SS perpetrators. Apparently, men merely wish to distance themselves individually from violence, but not the group of men as a whole. From this it follows that male interviewees do not draw a picture of men/masculinity that opposes traditional features of masculinity, but refer – at least indirectly – to the "idea of combat/struggle" (Enloe 1983:12, quoted according to Lentin 1999:75). Thus, both women and men adhere, to traditional role models, at least to a certain degree.

Ronit Lentin states in her article about the (en)gendering of genocides through mass media that women and children have turned into symbols of barbarity of genocidal wars. Women are only seen as victims (not as bystanders and perpetrators), whereas the trope of 'motherhood' and 'cracked female beauty' is the embodiment of suffering (Lentin 1999:72). Do we find such tropes in the interviews, too? Are there any differences between memoirs of female and male survivors concerning this theme? To answer these questions, I want to draw your attention on the representations of children, mothers, and female perpetrators in the interviews. Analyses revealed that almost only women narrate about the fate of children in concentration camps. Despite the fact that men were also deported together with children and that children were also imprisoned in predominately male concentration camps, hardly any man mentioned children. Our female interviewees – irrespective of their age and/or to which group of victims they belonged – addressed children's suffering from hunger and thirst, forced separation from their mothers, abuse of children for medical experiments, killings of newborns, and so on.

> They brought them here together with the children! [moanful] They have taken away [entire – Transl.] families, children were among them. Well, the husband was with the partisans, they found out about it. /Well, they killed some of them

and some/.[3] And toward the end, they took most of them to Auschwitz together with the children. They took the children from them. Oh, this is a nightmare what has happened here! How is it possible? A small child, and they are taking her away from her mother! (Stanewa 2002: 26)

These female narratives about children (and mothers) point to three aspects. First, there are victims who suffered more than women (from the women's perspective). According to these narratives, the "true" victims are the innocent children. It then follows that women do not want to position themselves in the hierarchy of victims as the most pitiable (that is, the most powerless and helpless). In fact, female resistance fighters especially represented themselves as women who did not quit the struggle even in the concentration camps. Second, along with children, mothers were the most afflicted ones. In these narratives, therefore, children and mothers symbolize the regime's barbarity. Third, interviewees of both genders reproduce the stereotypical representations of women and men with this (non-) reference to children. Women, and only women, are assigned to the reproductive sphere and their responsibilities for caring, whereas men are assigned to politics and the public sphere, as the quote expresses so clearly.

Nevertheless we find some contradicting evidence when we turn our attention to the topic of separation from ones own children in the course of persecution, marriage, and starting a family. Many female interviewees did not speak about the separation from their own children while in detention; they hardly mentioned the existence of children or being married at all.[4] Although we asked about the interviewee's life story, we usually received information about these aspects of life only when asking specifically.[5] How can we interpret this contradiction? Is it a contradiction at all? First of all we must view this in the context of the complete interview. In general, the interviewees neither spoke at length about their life after liberation nor about their life before the war. Asked for an interview because they are survivors of the Mauthausen concentration camp, they focused their narration on the period of persecution. This could be one reason for not speaking about starting a family and about children. Another reason could be that in retrospect, this part of life was not as important to them. In this case, the rare mentions of family,

---

3.  A slash indicates that the sentence was not completed by the interviewee.

4.  These findings correspond to another study by Amesberger et al. (2004: 275–287). Ecker's (2004: 7–8) findings are slightly different in this respect. The interviews with interviewers suggest that female interviewees tend to speak more about founding a family, children and so on than male interviewees.

5.  None of our male interviewees had children at the time of persecution, but they, too, rarely spoke about founding a family after liberation.

etc. by female interviewees would be evidence of the ambivalent embodiment of gendered norms, values, and concepts of femininity/womanhood, whereas in the case of men, it would be congruent with traditional representations of masculinity/manhood. Furthermore, there is the possibility that women themselves share and/or reproduce the societal devaluation of the reproductive work of women, so that it is not worth mentioning this part of one's life. Many men, who did not have a career, did not speak a whole lot about their later professional life either.

## Direct references to gender

So far we have seen that we can partly trace the process of doing gender through indirect references to gender via solidarity, children, and family. Now I want to turn to the direct references, that is, when in narratives, women and men are directly addressed as such. I will illustrate this with the representations of female perpetrators, mothers, and fathers. As an example, I quote a paragraph from an interview with a female Belgian resistance fighter:

> Then I saw a girl; she worked in the cesspit. I also worked in the cesspit. I say, 'be careful, she is watching us'. And suddenly the girl fainted, and we brought her back to consciousness. But the SS woman did not lose sight of her. These were female SS soldiers. [peremptory] And [pauses for four seconds] shortly thereafter, she faints again/. 'Oh,' the woman says, 'if she is unable to work, she might as well perish,' and she pushes the girl into the cesspit and presses her down with her foot until the child has drowned [stamps her foot agitatedly]. These are the Nazis. [solemnly] That is Fascism. That is Fascism. And then you see that same woman a quarter of an hour later as she hangs a bird cage for a little bird into a tree. That makes you want to kill her. [solemnly] Afterward she was killed, indeed. And then one returned and had to tell the mother, because this we had promised to one another, that her child [slowly] had died. This is impossible to tell a mother. But I lied. I said that she had fallen asleep. That she had died as everybody else – from exhaustion. One cannot tell such a thing to a mother. (Ulrix 2003: 11)

The SS-woman here stands for the cruelty of the regime and of Fascism. This is emphasized through the repeated expression "That is Fascism" and the accompanying bodily expression – she stamps her foot. The expression "That is Fascism" further implies that only Fascism "produces" such cruel women; women in a democratic society are not cruel, violent, etc. The barbarity of the woman and the regime is boosted by the dramatic device to tell how nicely and caring the SS-woman acted with the bird, an animal.

The depiction of the so-called Kapos by the interviewees are another example where one can trace the process of doing gender. Here quite often the link is made between the beauty of the female Kapo (and also of the female SS) and her barbarity. Again, beauty, standing for femininity, boosts cruelty. Sometimes the description of violent females is concluded with statements like: "they were more barbarous than men" (Vrachoritou 2003:13). Such comparisons of women and men reveal that while the female SS wardens, female Kapos, etc. do not meet the expectations concerning women's appropriate social behaviour, it is well in the range of "normal" male behaviour to be violent (comp. also Amesberger et al. 2004:78–79).

The process of doing gender is not limited to representations of women. In interviews with female survivors we also find depictions of men – prisoners and perpetrators. Ms Ulrix remembers the following situation when arriving at the Mauthausen concentration camp.

> When the prisoners, the men of Mauthausen – the prisoners who saw us when we arrived – the men had, of course, pity with us women. But their pity was suppressed by another feeling. And one could read this in their eyes: the feeling of their inability to save us. [with emphasis] I don't know whether I express myself correctly [to tell] you. One could read [with emphasis] this in the men's eyes. The powerlessness these people experienced as they were unable to do anything for us. And these unfortunates were themselves mere living corpses. (Ulrix 2003:18)

Besides noticing sympathy for the female prisoners, the interviewee refers to what under civil circumstances is the appropriate role model, behaviour, and duty of men – to protect and save women. Their inability to do so causes these men emotional distress, emotions that are deeper even than their sympathy for the women. At the same time, their inability rendered them not only unmanly, but unsexed and non-human, too, which is emphasized in the concluding sentence: "And these unfortunates were themselves mere living corpses".

Now I want to turn to the representations of mothers in the interviews. The interview passage quoted above about the cruel SS female who drowned a girl in the cesspit was followed by the interviewee's account of her difficult duty to tell the mother about the girl's death. According to the interviewee, a mother – that is, a "real" mother – cannot bear to hear of her child's death. Even if we can imagine that this was as hard for the interviewee as for the mother, we also have to notice the production of mothers and gender in this narration. The interviewee assumes that every mother must love her child and, indirectly, that fathers do not suffer as much from the loss of a child. She did not say: "One cannot tell parents of such cruelties." She repeatedly refers solely to the mother. We find a similar construction of motherhood in interviews with male survivors. In their narratives about returning home after liberation and their reunion with their families, mothers and other female relatives "fainted" or "nearly went mad" because their beloved sons had returned. In interview passages about family reunions, fathers are mostly absent, but when present, they do not react as hysterically as mothers.

In the narratives of men, women are significantly less represented than in the narratives of women. This hardly surprising fact can be explained, on one hand, by the segregated "world" of civil society of the 1930s and 1940s and especially of the concentration camps. On the other hand, it reveals that women are not perceived – besides their reproductive functions – as fellow resistance fighters, fellow inmates in ghettos, prisons, concentration camps, etc. Who were the women mainly mentioned by men or by women? In the stories of men, female relatives prevailed compared to other groups of females (such as individual female prisoners and/or resistance fighters), whereas relatives are only one group among others in the memoirs of women. Usually, male interviewees spoke about having seen female prisoners in the concentration camp only after specifically being asked by the interviewer. This question almost always produced a narrative about camp brothels and the women who had to work there. The existence of a women's camp in Mauthausen starting in September 1944 was rarely mentioned either.

If one examines the list of other people mentioned in the interviews, it is striking that many male interviewees, apart from mentioning other people to a significantly lesser extent, mention, above all, "famous" well-respected men. This behaviour is hardly found among women. This cannot be read merely as a (subconscious) strategy of self-aggrandizement. Rather, the "world of men" altogether is endowed with more weight and significance.

## Doing gender at the interactional level

For an analysis of the interactional level, I investigated who was asked which questions. Even though all interviewers underwent the same training program for interviewing Mauthausen survivors and were equipped with the same interview guidelines, the outcome varied greatly. One notices that not all interviewers agreed to ask questions about life after liberation, especially about the so-called private life – family and children. And there is a tendency that male survivors were not asked about starting a family, whereas female survivors were not asked about their later professional life. A rather common pattern is that interviewers ask about the political attitude of the interviewee's father, but not that of the mother. Not only do we learn nothing about the mother's political affiliation, women seem to be apolitical and their lives are reduced to the so-called private sphere, or womanly areas like religion, as can be seen from the following section from the quote of an interview:

"Interviewer: But your father was a Communist?
Interviewee: Yes, yes, yes.
Interviewer: Yes. And how was your mother's relation to religion? How was your [family's] attitude to religion?
Interviewee: At the time, my mother used to be a singer in our church choir. (...)." (Kononenko 2003: 16)

Although the interviewer extended his question concerning religion to the whole family, the interviewee only heard the question about his mother's affiliation. This question is followed by a lengthy narration of his mother's beautiful voice; but we do not learn anything about her attitude to politics in the course of the entire interview, nor were we informed about the religious life of the other family members.

However, doing gender is not only a matter of examining what is and is not asked to various people; it is also a matter of the questions' implicit codes. For example, the simple question, "How were the female SS wardens dressed?" (Primozic 2002: 45) does not seem to be gendered. Theoretically, the question could have also been asked about the male wardens. But I am sure that the outfit of the male SS staff would be of interest only in the rarest cases (and, in fact, in none of the analyzed interviews was the question asked at all). Indeed, it is the proper and stylish outfit of female SS wardens that became a code for their viciousness. Maybe the interviewer wanted to evoke a story of violence, which the interviewee had experienced or witnessed; if so, she succeeded in that, but it also resulted in the boosting of the violent act by means of reference to the woman's beauty. Violence seems to be more repugnant because of the female's beauty.

If the various identities of both the interviewees and the interviewers had an influence on the interview itself, then one may ask whether same-sex interview settings differ from mixed-sex interview settings with regard to topics addressed, style and length of narration, and so on. I heard more than once from female survivors that they prefer to be interviewed by a woman because of bad experiences with male interviewers. I am unable to expand here on the ways in which the interview setting influences content and style of narration. Here, I have to limit myself to the length of the interviews. Sylka Scholz came to the realization that same-sex interviews are much longer than interviews where the partners are of different sex (Scholz 2003: 149–153). My analysis cannot support these findings. The length of an interview seems to depend much more on the interviewer's interviewing skills, empathy, and historical knowledge, as well as the interviewee's experience with narration and level of traumatisation, and finally, the rapport that developed between interviewer and interviewee.

## Concluding remarks

In this contribution, my focus was on the analysis of the interview situation. The analysis proved the hypothesis that interviewees as well as interviewers produce and reinforce representations of gender in various and multifaceted ways. However, gender – and this I wish to emphasize – has already been produced in advance when determining the questions, developing research tools and methods, as well as afterward during the evaluation process. Yet, this question also brings about the danger of reproducing and reinforcing the seemingly strict duality of the gender categories. When we ask, for example, how women and men experienced the National Socialist persecution, our starting point is, on one hand, the dual categorization of the sexes, and, on the other hand, an implicit assumption that an undisputed assignment to one sex/gender is possible (comp. West & Zimmerman 1998: 173–174). Thus, we (researchers and interviewers) contribute to the process of doing gender. We cannot avoid it. Not including gender as a societal relevant category would mean to neglect existing power relations and inequalities as well as a loss of information with the consequence of inaccurate analysis. Therefore, as researchers we have to live with this ambivalence. Yet, we are able – and even have an obligation – to reflect on how we do gender in the research process and how we encourage our interviewees to do gender, the same way as we have to consider how other identities of both the interviewee and the interviewer alike might interfere. Avoiding gender-sensitive questions will not solve the problem.

## References

Amesberger, H., Auer, K. & Halbmayr, B. 2004. *Sexualisierte Gewalt. Weibliche Erfahrungen in NS-Konzentrationslagern*. Wien: Mandelbaum Verlag.

Bock, G. 2005. Einführung. In *Genozid und Geschlecht. Jüdische Frauen im nationalsozialistischen Lagersystem*, G. Bock (ed.), 7–21, Frankfurt: Campus-Verlag.

Ecker, M. 2004. The impact of gender on oral testimonies of holocaust survivors. Ms, lecture at the Annual Meeting of the Oral History Association, Portland OR.

Enloe, C. 1983. *Does Khaki Become You? The Militarization of Women's Lives*, London: Pluto Press.

Gildemeister, R. & Wetterer, A. 1992. Wie Geschlechter gemacht werden. Die soziale Konstruktion der Zweigeschlechtlichkeit und ihre Reifizierung in der Frauenforschung. In *Traditionen Brüche. Entwicklungen feministischer Theorie*, G. Knapp & A. Wetterer (eds), 201–254. Freiburg im Breisgau: Kore.

Goldenberg, M. 1998. Memoirs of Auschwitz survivors: The burden of gender. In *Women in the Holocaust*, D. Ofer & L. J. Weitzman (eds), 327–339. New Haven CT: Yale University Press.

Jaiser, C. 2005. Repräsentationen von Sexualität und Gewalt in Zeugnissen jüdischer und nicht-jüdischer Überlebender. In *Genozid und Geschlecht. Jüdische Frauen im nationalsozialistischen Lagersystem*, G. Bock (ed.), 123–148, Frankfurt: Campus-Verlag.

Lentin, R. 1999. (En)gendering Genocide. Die Feminisierung der Katastrophe. *Zeitschrift für Genozidforschung* 1(1): 70–89.

Scheffer, B. 2003. Verschweigen eher Ja, Kontrolle eher nein. Zu den biographisch-emotionalen Driften bei Wissenschaftlerinnen und Wissenschaftlern. In *Die biographische Wahrheit ist nicht zu haben*, K. Bruder (ed.), 89–113. Gießen: Psychosozial-Verlag.

Scholz, S. 2003. Das narrative Interview als Ort eines "männlichen Spiels"? Prozesse des Doing Gender in der Interviewinteraktion. In *Die biographische Wahrheit ist nicht zu haben*, K. Bruder (ed.), 139–161. Gießen: Psychosozial-Verlag.

Welzer, H. 2003. Was ist autobiographische Wahrheit? Anmerkungen aus Sicht der Erinnerungsforschung. In *Die biographische Wahrheit ist nicht zu haben*, K. Bruder (ed.), 183–202. Gießen: Psychosozial-Verlag.

West, C. & Zimmerman, D. H. 1998. Doing Gender. In *Feminist Foundations: Toward Transforming Sociology*, K. A. Myers, B. J. Risman & C. D. Anderson (eds), 167–190. Thousand Oaks CA: Sage.

## Interviews

Kononenko, V., interview by A. Koslowa, 16 January 2003. Archive of Mauthausen Memorial (AMM), Vienna, AMM OH/ZP1/654.

Primozic, S., interview by V. Frenkel, 12 November 2002. Archive of Mauthausen Memorial (AMM), Vienna, AMM OH/ZP1/517.

Stanewa, L., interview by A. Koslowa, 25 September 2002. Archive of Mauthausen Memorial (AMM), Vienna, AMM OH/ZP1/491.

Ulrix, C., interview by F. Aarts, 02 February 2003. Archive of Mauthausen Memorial (AMM), Vienna, AMM OH/ZP1/544.

Vrachoritou, S., interview by A. Menexiadis, 22 February 2002. Archive of Mauthausen Memorial (AMM), Vienna, AMM OH/ZP1/ 624.

# The dialogues in-between

## Phenomenological perspective
## on women's oral history interviews

Saara Tuomaala
Academy of Finland, Department of History

In this article, I consider aspects of the process of recalling one's subjectivity and body in different experiential levels in oral history interviews of elderly women in Finland. I discuss this dialogical process, including the dimension of gender, from the phenomenological point of view, especially philosophy and feminist Maurice Merleau-Ponty's phenomenological interpretations combined with experiential and narrative analysis.

**Keywords:** gender studies, the sites of memory. oral narration, body phenomenology, experiential analysis

In this article, I approach aspects of the process of narrating one's subjectivity and body in two experiential levels: as a woman in oral history interviews and in her past as a girl. I discuss this narrated and embodied gender from the phenomenological point of view, especially by reading Maurice Merleau-Ponty's phenomenological philosophy and feminist interpretations of experiential and narrative analysis.

My interview material is based on the study of rural childhood and youth in Northern and Central Finland, where I interviewed 67 narrators during the years 1990–96. Narrators were born in the 1910s, 1920s, and 1930s; of these, 32 women recalled their lives as girls and their transitions into womanhood. Empirically and as case studies, the oral history data of this paper have been previously discussed in several papers and presentations, both in conferences and in published articles, including my Ph.D. thesis. I have primarily studied narrating the local: how interviewees recall their rural childhood, adolescence, and early adulthood; how these personal and intimate recollections are continuously interpreted in various ways within cultural and social structures, and therefore, politically. In my research I use life-historical analyses and a combination of narrative and phenomenological methods in order to interpret institutional interaction between the peer groups of the children and young people, home, school, and civic organizations in their localities. I started my oral history interviews as thematically structured, but the later interviews transformed into life history interviews.[1]

In these oral history interviews, the narrator remembers her life course as a relationship in which the girl of the past and the elderly woman of the mobile present are experientially juxtaposed. In this narrative process, the remembered body of the young person overlaps the actual body of the elderly person. During an interview this kind of pondering occurs simultaneously, both in alienation and recognition of the past self and life. In my research, Maurice Merleau-Ponty's phenomenological body philosophy offers a starting point to characterize these narrated and embodied transitions in the interview dialogue. On the other hand, according to feminist interpretations of phenomenology, the lived and living body brings its experiential and layered past into each new situation unavoidably as gendered and gendering (Young 1995; Butler 1993; Davis 1997).

## Experiential narration and the question of "reaching the body"

Oral historian Selma Leydersdorff, among others, has stressed the experiential layering reflected in reminiscence narration, within which lived and narrative dimensions of recalling become intertwined. In other words, in life-historical narration individual experience is connected to a broader set of cultural meanings. At the same time, conventionally central frames of reference, for example of the nation state, are made problematic or left aside. In experiential narration there exists the simultaneous existence of many contextualisations and layerings, for example, in the meanings of gender and gendering one's life history. The special nature of studying oral history is in listening to and bringing to the surface the

---

1.  This text is part of the post-doc project: "Rural Youth, Citizenship and Gender in Finland, 1917–1940" at the Academy of Finland. My Ph.D. thesis was published as a monograph: Tuomaala, S. 2004a. *Työtätekevistä käsistä puhtaiksi ja kirjoittaviksi. Suomalaisen oppivelvollisuuskoulun ja maalaislasten kohtaaminen 1921–1939* (*From Working Hands to Clean and Writing Ones. The Encounter Between Finnish Compulsory Education and Rural Children 1921–1939*), Helsinki: Suomalaisen Kirjallisuuden Seura; in English, see, Tuomaala S. 2004b. How Did Shepherd's Life Story Become a Patriotic Song? Narrating past rural childhood of the 1920s and 1930s in Finland. In: *History and Change*, A. Lahtinen & K. Vainio-Korhonen (eds.), 57–77. Helsinki: Finnish Literary Society. This paper is based in some parts on the article Tuomaala, S. 2005. ¿Por qué reía Anna? Fenomenología y género en la historia oral (Why Did Anna laugh? Phenomenological and Gender Perspective to Oral History). *Historia, Antropologia y Fuentes Orales* 3(1):37–47,

variety of individual experiences. According to Leydersdorff, the study of oral biographies offers an alternative to research, which has a tendency to define overly-unifying generalizations of individual and social experiential dimensions. They are "powerless to deal with the great variability and cacophonic voices of the experiences" (Leydersdorff 1999: 604).

In my point of view, elderly Finnish women's memories narrated in interview encounters reflect the dialog and tension between lived experiences and their crystallized representations. In other words, memory and information about oneself as a girl and a woman, "history of one's own" (Ukkonen 2000) is created primarily through the practices and encounters of everyday life and its altering repetitiveness. Furthermore, to get them recalled, these practices and encounters are interpreted symbolically through linguistic devices of metaphors and metonymies. In interviews these symbolic levels of expressing and interpretation are mingling intensively with the embodied level.

More specifically the remembered body of the narrator overlaps with her present body, and the juxtaposition is presented to the listener as an embodied biography, which applies to a variety of verbal, paralinguistic, and physical techniques. This embodied – and constantly changing – "whole" takes shape as experience narratives, including laughter, sounds, voice stresses, gestures, postures, and even as scars on the narrator's limbs (Barcelona 2003; Thomas & Ahmed 2004; Tuomaala 2004b).

What data and knowledge do body language or nonverbal communication, as a part of reminiscence narration, offer to the researcher? Considering the dialogue between the human body and surrounding social world I refer to Jamilah Ahmed's conclusions pointed out in her article *Reaching the Body: Future Directions* (Ahmed 2004) about the increasing research on the body and bodily identities across the humanities and social sciences. Therefore, in her point of view the focus is shifting from the theoretic direction toward the historically materialised and experiential body:

> A concern with the role of the body in the social framework can ignore the more immediate issue of what it means to have and be a body (Turner 1984). While 'the body' has gained a certain currency in sociology, it can also be used as an object or symbol for sociocultural constructs without concern for the material realities of bodies. (…) This would mean that the representation of the body – as a symbolic construct – might no longer be prioritized over the concept of the body as a lived reality.(…) The system of dualisms lingers in contemporary sociology that divides private from public, nature from culture, woman from man, and the body from the mind.                                      (Ahmed 2004: 285)

Maurice Merleau-Ponty's phenomenological body philosophy offers one starting point for characterizing and interpreting dialogues between narrator and
researcher in an interview situation.[2] According to Merleau-Ponty, the body of
a person is always part of her/his consciousness and the experienced bodily situation forms the origin of consciousness. It is the first space and place in the world
and it cannot be studied objectively from the outside. Subjective consciousness
and corporeality overlap as inseparable given definitions. As Finnish philosopher
Martina Reuter has stated, the layering of this phenomenological being is made
up of "the creation of the construction of meaning through the actions of an embodied subject living in the world" (Reuter et al. 1997:159). The duality of body
and subject, as well as their ambiguity and multi-mindedness, permit their layering. They also offer tools for a historical and reflected body-subject for character-
ization. In other words, the body brings its layered past into each new situation
(Rautaparta 1997:132). A person's models for action, as both a narrator and a
researcher, are linked to her layered past, which is created in relation to cultural
expectations, necessities, and possibilities, as well as personal feelings and goals.

Oral and life historical approaches, combined with, for example, a body phenomenological approach, offer an alternative to crossover and tie-together dual-
isms of the body and the mind within human sciences. Andrew J. Strathern has
stated that according to Merleau-Ponty, the characteristics of our bodies limit
all our mental functions (Strathern 1996:132). Merleau-Ponty's objective was to
show the subjectivity of bodiedness, *carnality*, and dismiss the Cartesian juxtaposition of mind and body. Active subjects show their intentions in their movements
and gestures with their bodies, while simultaneously expressing their relationship
to the past. As a radical example, Merleau-Ponty uses a lost or paralyzed arm,
which subjectively feels present or even usable to its owner. According to him,
this phantom limb is not caused by cognitive error or an emotional protection
mechanism, but instead there is a question of a bodily layered past. Objectively,
a lost limb does not exist, but it still exists in the armless person's experience of
himself. It still affects his feelings, decisions, and actions. The issue here is of a
lost body part's "ambiguous presence", not of a conscious or unconscious decision
(Merleau-Ponty 1962:76–81, 103–141).

---

2.  Among Finnish researchers, the philosopher Sara Heinämaa has particularly studied the
body phenomenology of Merleau-Ponty in connection with gender and sexuality. Heinämaa
defines the phenomena of concepts in philosophy as relative to research, according to which
generalizations related to reasons and consequences are only abstractions of "what is really apparent" (Heinämaa 1996:42). Merleau-Ponty describes the relationship between the phenomena and science by comparing it to "the relationship of landscape and map": scientific information is like a map drawn for certain movements in relationship to "the landscape, in which we
have learned what is 'a forest, meadow, or lake'" (Merleau-Ponty 1962:iii).

## The presence of the embodied past as a subjective sediment

The past is part of a narrator's bodily and subjective layering, which also affects the present and actual experiences in the interview situation. In other words, a personally experienced and interpreted past supports historical probabilities, which contain different phenomena, such as narratives dealing with the narrator's early age experiences. According to Merleau-Ponty, this past – although it might not be determinative – at least has a special emphasis: it is not the remote sum of the events one has left behind, but it shapes one's atmosphere in the present (Merleau-Ponty 1962: 442).

Maurice Merleau-Ponty calls the presence of the past a sediment (*la sédimentation*), which, as a habitual body, shapes a subject's repetition and reinforced postures in special historical and social situations (Merleau-Ponty 1962: 441). In the historical study of women (and therefore, of girls), there is reason to stress that even the life history of a single individual is made up of different subjects and body politics shaped at different times. The body-subject of a child, its freedom, limits, and circumstances are different from those of a young person, an adult, or an elderly person. However, a personally experienced childhood, for example, is a layer which the narrator brings to the interview situation. It is positioned and directed both inward (as the presence of the narrator's past and her lost subject) and outward (as dimensions of present and future, including the interview encounter with the historian). Therefore, the narrator is composed of two interwoven dimensions: her present body and her habitual body, which are shaped over the course of her life and adapted in certain positions from interacting with the world.

Merleau-Ponty has received criticism because he concentrates on an intentional, moving, and acting subject. Visibility and direction outwards are stressed in this body-subject, which is not gendered and left sexually undefined. Luce Irigaray has stated that Merleau-Ponty "takes reversibility too far because he does not acknowledge that certain tactile experiences cannot be rendered visible" (Parkins 2000: 62). Nevertheless, Monika M. Langer and Andrew J. Sthrathern, among others, have stressed that Merleau-Ponty's goal was, in any case, to characterize the body from the perspective of the world lived in instead of the objectivistic and mechanistic concept of body politics. The body contains the memory of the subjective "project" and "bodied intentionality". In this manner, observations are formed as conditions of memories of bodily personalities. A person is the comprehensive center of her/his memories, which builds the past and its meanings in present and in everyday life situations. As Langer states, the Merleau-Pontian phenomenological concept of the body is essentially "an expressive space", a term of the significant world, through which other expressive spaces are formed (Weiss 1999: 122; Strathern 1996: 37; Langer 1989: 25–34, 40, 47).

## Layering of oral narration: A bodily site of memory

According to Merleau-Ponty, the existence of an individual unfolds in a social and temporal context, relative to other people around her/him. Memory, which is a condition and prerequisite of reminiscences, is created essentially in a dialogue between people and their encounters. The horizon of the shared past – which means simultaneously personal and common interpretations of human observations, directions, and actions – is formed in memories.

The body is a structure that expresses and in which shared meanings change and become layered. The continuous overlapping of language and body is essential to the process through which personal and shared meanings are formed. The spoken word creates new meanings in which culture becomes carnal and personal, and is transmitted forward. At the same time, this carnal historicity is crystallized when spoken (Merleau-Ponty 1964: 18; Langer 1989: 18; Strathern 1996: 38–39). Thus, historicity means the realization of a person in certain spaces and events, in which s/he is oriented towards situations of human contact, such as in an interview of one's life history. Therefore, lived situations are a central part of actions creating cultural meanings, which begin when people meet and interact both as narrative and embodied beings.

In experiential narratives of one's past, the most important is the question of once lived, material, and continually bodily experiences from which linguistic and symbolic marks have formed. Therefore, the narrativity and narrative nature of these life-historical marks permit their construction as material and bodily memories, able to be interpreted with the assistance of concepts like the site of memory and history (Nora & Goldhammer 1997; Peltonen 2003). A bodily site of memory is a trace or mark associated with an experiential narrative, which shapes the actual metaphorical space of speech, performance, writing, or illustration that is orientated towards the past. As such, the environment, buildings, objects, texts, pictures, as well as oral narratives associated with one's lived past are also able to form the specific sites of memory (Peltonen 2003; Korkiakangas 2001).

The oral memories that deal with one's own bodily expressions are included in the life-historical category of reminiscence as sites of memory, as well as the marks of the recalled life (such as scars or paralinguistic marks like laughter or tears) that are associated with the history of body. They shape, for example, the sites of memory of a personal girlhood and womanhood. This circumstantial nature directs and takes an attitude towards the past as a primarily subjective and bodily process, still revived in different phases of one's life cycle. Also, these expressions invoke different cultural meanings in narrators' and researchers' interpretations. The personal nature of these meanings strengthens the connection to the past as "history of one's own", in other words as experiences, feelings, and interpretations as both personal and shared that are present in the here and now, in actual and performed interview speech.

### Conclusion: The formation of historical narratives in oral and embodied contexts

Life-historical experiences are created, for example, as physical marks, movements, symptoms, and feelings. As such, bodiliness is simultaneously a physical and social process, which is localized historically and produces different kinds of identities. Examined from a phenomenological perspective, this multilayered body is a historical process, which is expressed as subjective attitudes, movements, and actions in a cultural and material space. From the perspective of body phenomenology, in Merleau-Pontian's sense, the bodiliness of narratives is expressed as a layering of personal experiences. It is also expressed in the specific situation and social setting. In the interview dialogue and situation, I interpret these subjective dimensions of bodiliness as historical traces, which are produced in different interdependencies that are layered in terms of time, space, and community.

When the embodied expressions included into the narration of women's pasts are interpreted as expressions regarding the life those people have lived, they become socio-cultural recorders and, as such, (auto/biographical) historical sources. Therefore, the interpretations regarding historical sources and experiential narratives form different kinds of historical narratives (Feixa & Nilan 2006). Historian Hayden White, who has remarkably analysed the formation of historical narratives from different traces concerning the past, concentrates on the textual world (White 1978, 1987). The view ignores the idea that history – and hence historicity – is continually bodiliness and subjectivity, which is expressed and takes shape in the realization of the past in voice and silence, as skin and on skin, in gestures and in other bodily expressions. In other words, according to my interpretation, history is not "just a narrative"; instead, it is the continuation of materiality, as loaded linguistic-social forms of being and action, which are expressed in the body and as bodiliness.

Therefore, bodily and non-verbal traces can be interpreted as historical sources and at the same time life-historical narrative constructs, which bring up the special learning experiences of one's life span. As Finnish cultural researcher Ilona Reiners concludes in her study of the bodiliness of subjective memories in the context of the Holocaust, the presence of the past is expressed as a potential world of meanings in the here and now, in the actual world of remembering and interpreting (Reiners 2001). Thus, in an interview situation, the elderly narrator's body and its expressions are, through meanings embedded therein, partly combined with the body of the child and young person s/he used to be. The expression of this kind, as a reflective site of one's own experiences, also acts as a bodily-given meaning through which the narrator historicizes her/his past. Therefore, the meanings of subjective embodied expressions are created in a particular historical and cultural context.

The construction of gender produces vitally important means for the narration, recollection, and interpretation of one's life and identity within cultural and political discourses, which girls and boys, women and men encounter in their social environment. Their gendered experiences are implemented in the private and public institutions of production and reproduction, and they are reflected in the autobiographical and literal data (Yuval-Davis 1997; Skeggs 1997). However, questions still remain for further study of gender and femininity in oral history narration: How do these two levels, discursive and embodied, differ from each other, and how do they converge? And, in methodological terms, how should one interpret both, paradoxically, differentiating and homogenizing embodied and narrative processes for recalling girlhood and womanhood in a specific culture, society, and era?

One possible way to start approaching this question, which I mention briefly here in my article, would be through analyzing the intermingling metaphors and metonymies. They are constantly polarizing and connecting experiential narration and embodied narratives. The metaphorical and metonymic level with simultaneously embodied and discursive practices, structures the processes of recalling subjective girlhood and womanhood. In other words, this symbolically and bodily-laden level spins together meaningful relationships, places, and material objects. As diversified combinations, they construct the cultural, unavoidably gendered, and material space of subjective experiences (Tuomaala 2004a; Tuomaala 2004b).

As Finnish social scientist Anni Vilkko has observed, the use of familiar metaphors in life stories, through feminine and masculine images and figures, offers us a glimpse of how one's lifetime can be conceptualized in our culture (Vilkko 2003: 49–51, 61). Intensively charged metaphors and metonymies not only disclose the way in which the narrator articulates her life experiences to her listener, but they also communicate them to other people. Therefore, symbolic and embodied narratives represent life by shaping and ordering it. On the other hand, the oral story may be incoherent and fragmentary, but it is created anew in the interpretative acts of listening and telling, and later on, in reading. From this perspective, the woman actively constructing her embodied subjectivity in oral reminiscence practice is emphasized.

The gendered voices of women and girls are construed as both verbally and non-verbally embodied sites of memory, where their personal experiences are framed by differentiating cultural models and social processes. By combining oral history interpretation with a phenomenological gender perspective, elderly women's oral narration and reminiscence of their early age become embodied as a function of recalled subjective actions of their girlhood. Therefore, narrators create bodiliness and subjectivity of their own, by constantly negotiating with representational resources and gendered images of both the ideal and averted girls and women in their specific culture. In an interview narrative, a recollected age-bound life history is reflected as the presence of different "times". More definitely, the experiential dimension of life sequels is historicized. It is the subjectively placed and socially located positioning of the past, in which different historical meanings are constantly created and interpreted.

## References

Ahmed, J. 2004. Reaching the body: Future directions. In *Cultural Bodies. Ethnography and Theory*, H. Thomas & J. Ahmed (eds), 2–24. Oxford: Blackwell.

Barcelona, A. (ed.). 2003. *Metaphor and Metonymy at the Crossroads*. Berlin: Mouton de Gruyter.

Butler, J. 1993. *Bodies that Matter: On the Discursive Limits of Sex*. London: Routledge.

Davis, K. (ed.). 1997. *Embodied Practices. Feminist Perspectives on the Body*. Thousand Oaks CA: Sage.

Feixa, C. & Nilan, P. 2006. *Global Youth?: Hybrid Identities, Plural Worlds*. London: Routledge.

Heinämaa, S. 1996. *Ele, tyyli ja sukupuoli, Merleau-Pontyn ja Beauvoirin ruumiinfenomenologia ja sen merkitys sukupuolikysymykselle*. Helsinki: Gaudeamus.

Korkiakangas, P. 2001. Esineiden nostalgisoituminen: ylevöityneen, arkisen ja kansanomaisen nostalgia. In *Pandoran lipas. Virvatulia esineiden maailmasta*, I. Vesterinen & B. Lönnqvist (eds.), 75–101. Helsinki: Suomalaisen Kirjallisuuden Seura.

Langer, M. 1989. *Merleau-Ponty's Phenomenology of Perception: A Guide and a Commentary*. London: Macmillan.

Leydersdorff, S. 1999. Gender and the categories of experienced history. *Gender and History* 11(3): 604.

Merleau-Ponty, M. 1962. *Phenomenology of Perception*. London: Routledge.

Merleau-Ponty, M. 1964. *Visible et l'invisible: suivi de notes de travail*. Paris: Gallimard.

Nora, P. & Goldhammer, A. (eds). 1997. *Realms of Memory. Rethinking the French Past*, Vol. 3, *Symbols*. New York NY: Columbia University Press

Parkins, W. 2000. Protesting like a girl. Dissent and feminist strategy. *Feminist Theory* (1)1: 59–78.

Peltonen, U.-M. 2003. *Muistin paika: Vuoden 1918 sisällissodan muistamisesta ja unohtamisesta*. Helsinki: Suomalaisen Kirjallisuuden Seura.

Rautaparta, M. 1997. Ruumis subjektina Merleau-Pontyn filosofiassa. In *Ruumiin kuvia. Subjektin ja sukupuolen muunnelmia*, S. Heinämaa, M. Reuter & K. Saarikangas (eds), 129–135. Helsinki: Gaudeamus.

Reiners, I. 2001. *Taiteen muisti. Tutkielma Adornosta ja Shoahista*. Helsinki: Tutkijaliitto.

Reuter, M. 1997. Anorektisen ruumiin fenomenologia. In *Ruumiin kuvia. Subjektin ja sukupuolen muunnelmia*, S. Heinämaa, M. Reuter & K. Saarikangas (eds), 136–167. Helsinki: Gaudeamus.

Skeggs, B. 1997. *Formations of Class and Gender.* London: Sage.

Strathern, A. J. 1996. *Body Thoughts.* Ann Arbor MI: The University of Michigan Press.

Thomas, H. & Ahmed, J. 2004. *Cultural bodies. Ethnography and Theory.* Oxford: Blackwell.

Tuomaala, S. 2004a. *Työtätekevistä käsistä puhtaiksi ja kirjoittaviksi. Suomalaisen oppivelvollisuuskoulun ja maalaislasten kohtaaminen 1921–1939.* Helsinki: Suomalaisen Kirjallisuuden Seura.

Tuomaala, S. 2004b. How did shepherd's life story become a patriotic song? Narrating past rural childhood of the 1920s and 1930s in Finland. In *History and Change*, A. Lahtinen & K. Vainio-Korhonen (eds), 57–77. Helsinki: Finnish Literary Society.

Tuomaala, S. 2005. ¿Por qué reía Anna? Fenomenología y género en la historia oral. *Historia, Antropologia y Fuentes Orales* 3(1): 37–47.

Ukkonen, T. 2000. *Menneisyyden tulkinta kertomalla. Muistelupuhe oman historian ja kokemuskertomusten tuottamispuheena.* Helsinki: Suomalaisen Kirjallisuuden Seura.

Weiss, W. 1999. *Body Images. Embodiment as Intercorporeality.* London: Routledge.

White, H. 1978. *Tropics of Discourse.* Baltimore MD: Johns Hopkins University Press.

White, H. 1987. *The Content of the Form: Narrative Discourse and Historical Representation.* Baltimore MD: Johns Hopkins University Press.

Vilkko, A. 2003. Gender and life stories. In *Gender and Qualitative Methods*, H. Järviluoma, P. Moisala & A.Vilkko (eds.), 46–68. London: Sage.

Young, I. M. 1995. *Throwing Like a Girl and Other Essays in Feminist Philosophy and Social Theory.* Oxford: Oxford University Press.

Yuval-Davis, N. 1997. Gender and Nation. London: Sage.

# The problems of articulating beingness in women's oral histories

Mary Patrice Erdmans

Department of Sociology, Central Connecticut State University, USA

Based on an analysis of women's oral histories, this article examines the problem of articulating motherhood. Despite the fact that motherhood is a primary identity, self-reflections on being mothers are circumscribed for several reasons. First, the omnipresent and ethereal nature of the mother identity makes it difficult to capture in words. Moreover, everyday routines are taken for granted and less visible unless they become problematic. Finally, activities in the public sphere are perceived as more significant and worth discussing than those performed in the private sphere. In sum, when using oral histories to document the lives of marginalized populations, it is important to consider how the subordinate position influences the content and form of the narrative.

**Keywords:** marginalized people, content and form of oral narratives, motherhood

The oral history program at Columbia University was established in the late 1940s for the purpose of documenting and preserving a record of "significant lives." Beginning in the 1960s, however, social historians interested in writing history "from the bottom-up" began collecting oral histories of *ordinary* people. The oral histories of significant people and ordinary folk differ in both content and narrative style. Significant lives are usually public lives, and public figures are used to speaking on record, putting their thoughts into words, and having others value their opinion. They generally believe that what they think and what they do is important. In contrast, ordinary folk are not public figures: they are not leaders of industry, government, or military; they are not in front of the camera as sports stars or entertainers; they are not artists and writers who produce work for public consumption. For the most part, the thoughts and actions of ordinary people are not a part of the public record and they seldom, if ever, have anyone tape record their words. These differences between significant and ordinary lives suggest that when we write history from the bottom up, we need to take into consideration how being "at the bottom" influences the story told and the story telling.

In this article, I examine how subordinate status shapes the life stories of white working-class women, focusing on the content as well as the language and organization of the narrative. The private lives of white, working-class women are often overlooked in the literature. Oral historians, in the mid-twentieth century took less interest in the lives of women and as a result the earlier focus on significant lives was almost exclusively a focus on men. In the 1970s, a new generation of feminist scholars began addressing this oversight. Most of the early feminist writing documented the lives of white middle-class women. Later scholarship focused more on the lives of women marginalized by race, class, nativity, and sexual orientation. Often scholars conflated race and class so that studies of white women were *de facto* studies of the middle class, and studies of women of color were studies of poor and working-class women. This bifurcation obfuscated our understanding of white working-class women. When combined with white middle-class women, the voices (and disadvantages) of white working-class women were lost. When grouped together with working-class racial minorities and immigrants, white native-born privilege was overlooked. Correcting for these two-dimensional limitations, this article focuses on white, working-class women in the more complex "matrix of domination" referred to by Patricia Hill Collins (1990) within which groups are simultaneously privileged and disadvantaged.

Another way that women are overlooked is when the gaze is on the public sphere alone. Labor scholars studying white working-class women tend to analyze women working outside the home. Their monographs document the lives of women working in factories, restaurants, and secretarial pools while ignoring the labor of women in the home. When scholars turn their focus to women at home, they usually use an exclusive gender lens for analysis and almost never include class. This is problematic because subordination is once again taken to be one-dimensional rather than occurring within a more complex matrix of domination. We cannot understand the gender experience apart from the class experience. For example, in the mid-twentieth century, middle-class women who earned college degrees and yet did not have careers outside the home were the ones most likely to suffer from the unnamed depression that Betty Friedan described in *The Feminine Mystique*. In contrast, working-class women who did not experience motherhood as competing with a professional identity were more likely to feel privileged rather than frustrated when they stayed home to raise children (Fox-Genovese 1996; Seifer 1976).

White working-class women represent a population whose private lives and unique experience of marginalization are not fully documented. Oral history, as a method for including those excluded from the social record, is a useful tool for

documenting the everyday lives of these women. When collecting their
ries, however, we need to pay attention to the ways in which their marginalization
influences both the content and form of their oral narratives. Feminist scholars,
and oral historians in particular, advocate an interpretive methodology that makes
imperative an examination of how power relations and social position, in the public sphere and the face-to-face setting of the interview, influence the construction
of a life story (Alpern et al. 1992; Anderson et al. 1990; Behar 1996; Belenky et al.
1986; Geiger 1986; Gluck 1977; Joeres and Mittman 1993; Laslett 1999; Patai and
Gluck 1991; Reinharz 1992; Reissman 1997; Romero and Stewart 1999).

## The life stories of five sisters

Between 1997 and 2002, I collected the oral histories of five sisters. These white
working-class women were born in the United States in the 1920s and 1930s.
Their stories formed the basis for my book *The Grasinski Girls: The Choices They
Had and the Choices They Made*. Four of the Grasinski sisters – Caroline, Fran,
Nadine, and Mary – are my aunts, and the fifth sister, Angel, is my mother.

All five sisters were mothers. Caroline, born in 1923, was married at the age
of 19 and after 65 years of marriage she is the matriarch of a large family: three
children, eight grandchildren, and two great grandchildren. Fran was married
in 1948 at the age of 20; she has three children and four grandchildren. Nadine
joined the Felician Order of nuns when she was 18. After 25 years as a Felician
sister, she left the convent and married. At the age of 45, she conceived and delivered her only child. Angel was born in 1936 and was married in 1956. She has
six children and twelve grandchildren. Mary, the youngest of the sisters, had just
turned 20 when she was married in 1958. She has four children. As was typical of
women in their era, the Grasinski sisters married young (except for Nadine), and
they were career mothers. They began having children soon after they were married, and except for Mary, they all remained married.

At the beginning of this project, I explained my intentions to the Grasinski
sisters by telling each one of them that I wanted to understand their lives. I began
the initial taping session with a grand-tour question: "Tell me about your life,
start from the beginning." I wanted them to construct their narratives in whatever
form or direction they chose. The interview sessions took place over a period of
several days for some of the sisters, and months for others. I recorded between
four and twenty hours of taped oral narrative for each of them.

In my initial analysis of their oral histories, I discovered that the discussions
of themselves as mothers were not lengthy or well articulated. Although their
children were central to their lives, when they told their life stories, the years

they were most likely to gloss over were those years when they were primarily occupied with the tasks of mothering. Their narratives were more detailed and descriptive when discussing those years before they were married and those years after the children were grown. In the first session, Fran talked exclusively and extensively about the first sixteen years of her life; she stopped narrating her life story at the point when she met her husband. Caroline's stories were also more detailed and vivid when describing her pre-motherhood years and her present life as compared to those in-between-years when she was raising her three children. These same years were also missing in Angel's narrative. She remembers the seven pregnancies and six births, and she tells her life in relation to the births, but there was very little in her story about those years when she was raising children. In all three cases, the mid-adult years (from about 25 to 50 years of age) were sketchy.

Nadine talked more about her child than did the others, but this still did not take up a large number of pages in her overall transcript. She talked more about the pregnancy (which was difficult at the age of 45), than about mothering her child. Only Mary, the mother who sent her children to live with her sisters for a few years after her divorce while she worked and went back to school, narrated her life story in relation to what was happening with her children. The children did not enter her narrative as central characters, however, until the divorce disrupted their lives and her motherhood had to be negotiated.

After the first set of interviews, I wrote a life history for each of the sisters based on information in the transcripts. I sent each of them the written narrative, asked them to read it and provide me with comments, and then contacted each of them individually. What I learned, unfortunately, was that they thought that I "got it all wrong," as one sister said. One particularly glaring problem with my written construction of their oral narrative was that I underestimated, underplayed, and undervalued their role as mothers. They expressed their frustrations with what they saw as my inaccurate and incomplete representations of them.

> Nadine: And then, you kind of emphasize that I was so happy being free in my apartment [this was after she left the convent], but you didn't say anything about Marie Chantal [her daughter] being, that was like, I had beautiful beautiful days of my life when I became the nun, black veil, white veil, the day I got married, absolutely beautiful, but nothing can compare to the day that I held her in my arms. That was like the most beautiful, that was my high point in my life, that was above everything and she still is. I just wanted you to emphasize that more than being free in my apartment [laughs].

Caroline also informed me that I had not written enough about how happy she was being a mother: "Most of my life was with my kids. I thought it was such a special thing to be able to mother children. I had the privilege of having children and raising them." And Fran wondered why I had not mentioned her being a mother. Despite the fact that she would not narrate her life story to me beyond her 18th birthday, she assumed that I would construct a narrative that included her three children.

As a result of these comments, I returned to collect more of their life story and this time I asked them specifically about being a mother. Through this direct probing I elicited more information about their histories as career moms; however, their "mother" narratives were still limited in the ways I discuss below.

## The hidden mother

I refer to the Grasinski sisters as career moms because their identity and behavior were dominated with the role of being mothers: as young girls, they imagined being mothers and made life choices to make this possible; as adults, they invested a significant amount of time and resources in having children and raising them; and as women, their children gave them an existential reason for being. As such, motherhood was a moral career as well as an occupational career. Yet, while motherhood was a primary identity and the tasks of mothering occupied their lives, neither the identity nor tasks appeared as prominent features in their oral histories.

To understand this absence, I analyze their oral histories using a framework first developed by Ronald Grele (1985) which focuses on: 1) the linguistic structure (grammar, phrasing patterns, and organization); 2) the relationship between the narrator and listener; and, 3) the relation between the narrator and larger society. Attending to these three levels, I note that motherhood is often missing from the oral transcripts because: 1) it is an omnipresent and ethereal identity that is difficult to articulate; 2) my relationship as a daughter and niece made me an insider and they took it for granted that I would narrate their lives as mothers; and, 3) the private sphere has less value than the public sphere, especially the activities of marginalized groups, and as a result the activities performed in the private sphere can seem mundane, trivial, and not worthy of discussion.

### The language of motherhood

When I asked Caroline to explain those 25 years in the middle of her life that she had not talked about in the initial sessions, she said, "well, then I was a mother." What does that mean? Mothering includes caring for the physical, psychological, emotional and spiritual development of family members as well as engaging in the kinship work necessary to keep the family together (DeVault 1991; di Leonardo

1987; McMahon 1995). But when I asked them to tell me what it was like to be a mother, or to talk about being a mother, they did not talk about these tasks.

Mothering is hidden in the commonplace routines that are often overlooked. Everyday chores run into each other as a bleary stream of washing, cleaning, nursing, storytelling, feeding, bathing, ironing, and vacuuming, wiping noses, wiping bums, dusting lamp shades, picking up dirty socks, and folding clean socks. Rather than being itemized, the physical tasks are lumped into a monolith of mothering, which gets spoken as: "well, then I was a mother." In addition, the years when women are engaged in these tasks – multiplied by the number of children they have – are often the years when women are most tired. Angel, who at the age of 27 was pregnant with her fifth child (and her oldest was only six years old) said, "There are whole years I don't remember." When I asked specifically about these child-raising years she said, "life was a blur."

While the physically-tiring manual-labor tasks blur into forgettable years, the emotional work of mothering can be even harder to talk about because it is less concrete. The emotional work of mothering can be done while standing in front of a sink full of dishes or driving a child to baseball practice. For example, alongside the daily chores of getting children ready for school, the mother listens to her children's hesitations and excitements and offers nurturing murmurs of fondness and gentle caresses. Unlike my "at-a-glance" schedule book that records the activities of my career as a professor, a mother's emotional tasks are not written down and often are not even spoken.

Motherhood is a *being* as much as, if not more than, a *doing*. And it is a sacred beingness. When I pushed Caroline to describe what it means to be a mother, she said, "I always thought that was such a big honour." Fran wrote: "I thank God for giving them to me." Angel also defined motherhood as a gift from God: "I like my life and I like all the people I produced, and the grandchildren. I think I'm blessed." For Angel, the six children were acts of creation that gave meaning to her life: "I realized that what I was doing was really important. I was creating little bodies, and little babies, and bodies, and more bodies, and more bodies. [laughs] But I always felt that each one child was like a real special gift." As a part of the sacred act of creation, motherhood, like all sacred things, is shrouded in mystery. The divinity of motherhood loses something when forced into words.

In sum, motherhood is a difficult identity to articulate because it involves everyday tasks that are easy to overlook and emotional work that is often invisible. Moreover, because the mother identity is ensconced to their core self, they do not have the distance necessary to see it.

Insiders already know

The stories produced and presented in this study arose not out of my separation from, but a strong connection to these women. When telling an oral history to an insider, narrators may assume a 'taken-for-grantedness' and not articulate aspects of their lives that they share with the interviewer. I was an insider in this study because I was a blood relative and I grew up with these women. Even though feminist scholars are less bothered by the necessity for distance between the researcher and the researched than are positivist traditional social scientists. It is nonetheless analytically important to examine how this closeness shaped their life stories.

As family, they took it for granted that I knew their biographies as mothers. This is one reason they were upset with their initial narratives. They expected me to write about them as mothers because I knew them, and knowing them they assumed that I saw them as mothers. Angel, my own mother, told me more about the early years when the babies were born and not as much about the years of mothering. In part, she was so tired during those years when she was raising six children that she does not remember much, but it was also because I lived those years with her, so I would already know what the household was like. When I pushed Fran to talk about the years when her children were young she said, "Well you know your cousins, you remember what that was like." The fact that Fran's initial oral history stopped before she became a mother and yet she expected me to write about her life as a mother, suggests that she took it for granted that I would write about her getting married and having children.

Only Mary's transcript had a significant number of pages devoted to her children and the problems she had mothering. This story, I believe, was an attempt to set the family record straight. Mary was estranged from the family for a long period of time because of her extramarital affair and divorce. Because of this estrangement, I did not know her story the way that I knew the others' life stories. At one point during the taping when she was describing the affair and the problems during the divorce, I said explicitly, "wow, I never knew all that was happening."

She could not take it for granted that I knew her story, nor could she take her motherhood identity for granted. Mary's motherhood identity was complicated by the divorce. Like many other women in her situation, after the divorce she had significantly fewer resources. She temporarily relinquished her motherhood tasks by sending her children to live with her sisters. She enrolled in college and worked nights. After she completed college she tried to resume her role as mother but it was more difficult; her children were scattered around the country, some were angry with her and others had moved into adult roles. Mary's pursuit of a professional career was also complicated by her mothering responsibilities. Several of her occupational career choices were made in relation to the needs of her children. It was often in describing the competing needs of school, work, and motherhood that her children entered into her life story.

None of her sisters shared those same tensions with mothering. Nadine and Caroline only worked outside the home when it did not interfere with child rearing. Fran worked only before her children were born. Angel did feel some tension during those periods when mothering and paid labor conflicted, but like her other sisters, Angel depended on her husband to provide basic needs – shelter, food, insurance, clothes. Mothering was easier for her because she was financially stable.

When an identity has to be negotiated, that is, when it becomes a problem identity, it can no longer be taken for granted. Mary's life deviated from her sisters because of the divorce. Of all of the sisters, she talked the most about her role as a mother because she could not just assume that I knew what had happened in her life, and because life events forced her to be cognizant of her mothering roles, duties, and obligations.

## Pulling the public out of the private

Narratives are constructed worldviews that include hierarchies for ranking, legitimation, routines, and value systems; they situate the narrator within this value system thereby showing their place within a moral world (Grele 1985; Linde 1986; Yans-McLaughlin 1990). People tell stories within cultural groups, as Norman Denzin notes:

> The stories that members of groups pass on to one another are reflective of understandings and practices that are at work in the larger system of cultural understandings that are acted upon by group members. These understandings contain conceptions of persons' lives, meaningful subjective experience, and notions of how persons and their experience are to be represented. (1989: 81)

In dialogue with the larger society, speakers are conscious of the value systems that underscore dominant group ideology.

In U.S. society, the public sphere holds more power than the private sphere, and these women were aware of this. They had internalized the societal belief that the public sphere is more important than the private sphere. For example, Mary said her biggest disappointment in life was, "not making more of a contribution to society. I helped a lot of people, but I think I would have liked to have done it on a broader scale." She implies that public identities have the potential to do more voluminously good work and as such they are more valued than private identities.

Motherhood is performed mostly in the home, but the identity has tremendous value in the larger cultural sphere. There is a public reward for being mothers because that is what women are expected to do (especially women in their generation). Despite this affirming social location in the larger culture, their routines are enacted primarily in the private sphere – they do not have public identities.

While mothering is private, the oral history interview itself is public, both in its immediate telling and the later retelling to a larger audience. When people tell their private stories, they are consciously or unconsciously aware of the larger value system in which their cultural and social groups are situated. It is not surprising, then, that when I pushed them to describe what they did during those child-rearing years, they talked about public activities. I asked Caroline, "So what did you do between the time you were 30 and 53?" (the missing years in her initial oral history).

> I was just, um, I was just a housewife and kids, I did a lot of things in church. I mean, I worked on bazaars; I volunteered, and stuff like that. I still do a lot at church. I volunteer at the blood bank, and I work in the pantry. I still do that, and I work at the bazaars and stuff like that. And I like to do stuff like that, I mean, what did I do? Just the doing regular stuff, I did not do anything eventful or anything like that.

She did not narrate her children's lives, nor detail the tasks of mothering (neither the concrete everyday tasks nor the emotional tasks). Instead, she described her work for a church, blood bank, and food pantry – all activities performed in the public sphere. In contrast, the events that took place in the private sphere were not described.

Fran also replied to my questions about mothering by pointing to activities in the public sector. When I asked her how she would "define herself as a mom," she talked about the importance of teaching children that Jesus "loves them" and teaching them how to genuflect in church. Then she told me how she had been an assistant catechism teacher and she had thought about becoming a kindergarten teacher but chose not to after the certification process changed.

> So, then, that's why I guess I got into Boy Scouts. [laughs] Fifteen of them in my kitchen every week. And campfire girls for nine years, about sixteen girls, going all around, to the beaches and everything with all of them. So sort of always there was children involved. And then I was a teacher's aide there for a while at Holy Spirit. That's when you did it for volunteer. And then I also went for noon hour, watching the kids at noon hour, lunch time. I did that too for a couple years, two or three years.

Like Caroline, Fran does not talk about the private tasks of mothering, but her public role as an educator, a kindergarten teacher, a scout mother, a Campfire leader and a religious instructor.

When asked specifically to describe those years when they were preoccupied with the task of mothering, the years they were not working outside the home but instead were at home with the children, they chose to focus on those activities that pulled them into the public sphere.

## Conclusion

While oral histories may be a useful method for studying women because they allow access to their private nuanced everyday world, this methodology can also create problems for the same reasons. Oral histories about public events and public identities are often anchored in action. People tell "stories" by moving from one action to another, for example: "I did this, and then I did that." The structure (or narrative) of a story is its plot; the narrative connects events and gives them meaning. In stories, something is happening. For ordinary women who have spent their lives primarily in the private sphere, everyday routines often do not have compelling story lines.

Moreover, the oral history requires a language necessary to articulate feelings and thoughts, and a belief that one's life is worth narrating. People in marginalized positions may feel uncomfortable speaking publicly because they have less education which influences their vocabulary and verbal acumen. For example, some of the Grasinski sisters repeatedly used generic filler phrases such as "watchamacallit" to stand in place for more specific words, illustrating, perhaps, that they did not have the language necessary to speak their thoughts nor the assurance that what they had to say was worthwhile. It is in the blank spaces of the oral history – the absence of content, the jumbled language – that we see the effects of subordination.    'Important'

When people cannot articulate identities, they will be hidden or missing from oral histories. Identities that represent a person's existential beingness are likely to be inseparable from an individual's core self and ubiquitous in their everyday routines. The person is usually most conscious of these identities when they become problem identities. Moreover, when the routines of the identity take place in the private sphere they can be dismissed as less relevant or overlooked for being ordinary. And finally, identities that are the basis for marginalization are the same identities that are less valued in the larger society. When this marginalization is internalized, then those "at the bottom" may see little point in articulating those aspects of their life that they do not consider "significant."

# References

Alpern, S., Antler J., Perry, E. I. & Scobie, I. W. (eds.). 1992. *The Challenge of Feminist Biography: Writing the Lives of Modern American Women*. Urbana IL: University of Illinois Press.

Anderson, K., Armitage, S., Jack, D. & Wittner, J. 1990. Beginning where we are: Feminist methodology in oral history. In *Feminist Research Methods: Exemplary Readings in the Social Sciences*. J. M. Nielson (ed.), 94–112. Boulder CO: Westview Press.

Behar, R. 1996. *The Vulnerable Observer: Anthropology that Breaks Your Heart*. Boston MA: Beacon Press.

Belenky, M. F., Clinchy, B. M., Goldberger, N. R. & Tarule, J. M. 1986. *Women's Ways of Knowing: The Development of Self, Voice, and Mind*. New York NY: Basic Books.

Collins, P. H. 1990. *Black Feminist Thought: Knowledge, Consciousness, and the Politics of Empowerment*. London: Routledge.

Denzin, N. 1989. *Interpretive Biography*. Thousands Oaks CA: Sage.

DeVault, M. 1991. *Feeding the Family: The Social Organization of Caring as Gendered Work*. Chicago IL: The University of Chicago Press.

Erdmans, M. P. 2004. *The Grasinski Girls: The Choices They Had and the Choices They Made*. Athens OH: Ohio University Press.

Fox-Genovese, E. 1996. *"Feminism is NOT the Story of My Life": How Today's Feminist Elite Has Lost Touch with the Concerns of Women*. New York NY: Anchor Books.

Geiger, S. 1986. Women's life histories: Method and content. *Signs* 11(2): 334–351.

Gluck, S. 1977. What's so special about women? Women's oral history. *Frontiers* 2(2): 3–13.

Grele, R. 1985. *Envelopes of Sound: The Art of Oral History*. New York NY: Praeger.

Joeres, R. B. & Mittman, E. (eds.). 1993. *The Politics of the Essay: Feminist Perspectives*. Bloomington IN: Indiana University Press.

Laslett, B. 1999. Personal narratives as sociology. *Journal of Contemporary Sociology* 28(4): 391–401.

di Leonardo, M. 1987. The female world of cards and holidays: Women, families, and the work of kinship. *Signs* 12(3): 440–453.

Linde, C. 1986. Private stories in public discourse: Narrative analysis in the social sciences. *Poetics* 15: 183–202.

McMahon, M. 1995. *Engendering Motherhood: Identity and Self-transformation in Women's Lives*. New York NY: Guildford Press.

Patai, D. & Gluck, S. (eds.). 1991. *Women's Words: The Feminist Practice of Oral History*. New York NY: Routledge.

Reinharz, S. 1992. *Feminist Methods in Social Research*. Oxford: Oxford University Press.

Reissman, C. K. 1987. When gender is not enough: Women interviewing women. *Gender & Society* 1: 172–207.

Seifer, N. 1976. *Nobody Speaks For Me!: Self-Portraits of American Working Class Woman*. New York NY: Simon and Schuster.

Romero, M. & Stewart, A. (eds.). 1999. *Women's Untold Stories: Breaking Silences, Talking Back, Voicing Complexity*. London: Routledge.

Yans-McLaughlin, V. 1990. Metaphors of self in history: Subjectivity, oral narrative, and immigration studies. In *Immigration Reconsidered: History, Sociology, Politics*, V. Yans-McLaughlin (ed.), 254–290. Oxford: Oxford University Press.

# Behind and beyond the stories

# Conversations with survivors
# of the siege of Leningrad

## Between myth and history

James Chalmers Clapperton
University of Edinburgh, Scotland

The following article is based upon a series of interviews conducted by the author with thirty survivors of the siege of Leningrad (1941–44). The purpose of the research was to explore the potential which oral history has in democratically repositioning our view of history away from grand master-narratives towards personal recollections. I sought to embrace various urban myths and stories which are often overlooked by historians because of a lack of supporting documentation. Consequently, it is hoped that these testimonies can illuminate our knowledge of the siege by bringing into focus the sights, sounds and smells of besieged Leningrad and the myths of everyday life. In addition, memories are examined which acutely recall the transformed topography of a wartime city ravaged by famine and without transport or electricity.

Keywords: Siege of Leningrad, myths and memories, historiography

## Background behind the project

This project originated in the late 1990's when the author visited St. Petersburg several times to perform as a concert pianist. During these visits he became acquainted with elderly relatives of colleagues in the musical community who had survived the siege of Leningrad (1941–44). The author was struck above all by the clarity of their recollections and the passion which fuelled them. These initial meetings subsequently inspired a doctoral thesis which was completed at the University of Edinburgh, Scotland in December 2006 (Clapperton 2007).

Thirty survivors, or *blokadniki* were interviewed. The testimonies were recorded onto tape and last in total around sixteen hours. Extended individual interviews each lasting at least one hour were contrasted by group interviews. The sessions took place in the centre of St. Petersburg and in outlying districts including the small town of Kolpino. The respondents came from a wide variety of backgrounds.

For example, one group comprised of retired employees from the *Elektrosila* plant situated in the south of the city while other respondents were former academics, school teachers, musicians and ordinary working people. The interviews were subsequently compared with over three hundred testimonies disseminated recently in a wide range of Russian publications. Correspondingly, an overview was ascertained of the recurring themes in published testimonies which could then be compared with the interviews conducted for this project. The actual names of the respondents have been replaced by pseudonyms.[1]

## History as story

> From the first months of the war, besieged Leningrad became what historian Pierre Nora has defined as a *lieu de memoire* (realm of memory) – one of those events that are immediately invested with symbolic significance and treated, even as they are unfolding, as if they are being commemorated in advance.
>
> (Kirschenbaum 2004: 106)

In this passage Lisa A. Kirschenbaum identifies a key challenge for historians of the siege. The blockade she asserts, "easily lent itself to mythmaking" and became an event commemorated as an evocation of personal sacrifice. At the same time "individuals wove state-sponsored images and narratives into their 'personal stories'" thereby "investing their wartime experiences with historic significance" (Kirschenbaum 2004: 106).

Svetlana Boym reminds us that in Russia the study of history does not solely concern facts and archival material. The Russian view of history is fluid and embraces literary and even poetic aspects which form an "intergeneric dialogue between fiction and history" (Boym 1994: 240). Soviet historiography forged an

---

1.   The additional testimonies were taken from numerous different sources. The most important of these was Adamovich, A and Granin, D. 1979 (rev. 2003). *Blokadnaia Kniga*. Nezavisimoe Izdatel'stvo "PIK": St. Petersburg. The journals *Druzhba Narodov, Kriticheskaia Massa, Neva, Novaia Russkaia Kniga, Novyi Mir, Oktiabr', Peterburgskii Soiuz Zhurnalistov, Ploshchad' Svobody, Smena, Znamia* and *Zvezda*. Newspapers including *Izvestiia, Komsomol'skaia Pravda, Nevskoe Vremia, Pravda*, The St. Petersburg Times and *Trud* as well as transcripts of radio broadcasts by stations such as *Radio Rossiia* and *Radio Svoboda*. Finally, various internet websites provided further examples of siege testimonies. Among these were the *agenstvo evreiskikh novostei*, <www.aen.ru>, <fontanka.ru>, <www.iremember.ru>, <www.knews.ru>, <www.megapolis.org>,<www.nv.vspb.ru>, <www.pobeda-60.ru> and <www.vesti.ru>

epic tale around the "hero city" (*gorod geroi*) of Leningrad which was portrayed both as the birthplace and defender of Bolshevism. During the Soviet period siege narratives were primarily tales charting military tactics and manoeuvres. Local patriotism was regarded as acceptable only within the parameters of the wider war effort. The concept that Leningraders were acting independently of Moscow and that their patriotic fervour was expressed predominantly as a love of their city and its unique history was often overlooked. Yet, as discussed later, surviving *blokadniki* assert repeatedly that while Leningrad was in effect cut off from the rest of Russia its populace drew their inspiration from local and spontaneous expressions of patriotism.

The problem for historians is encapsulated by the reality that even a bare statement of the facts surrounding the siege appears to belong to the realms of the mythopoetic imagination. Whether one believes the official Soviet estimate that 632,253 Leningraders perished during the siege or the Leningrad Funeral Trust's figure of 1.2 million deaths the toll of human suffering was immense (Kirschenbaum 2004:122). Therefore, it is not surprising that western historians have also been inclined to portray the blockade as a legendary tale of human fortitude. Harrison Salisbury, who was virulently anti-Soviet asserted that bickering and petty disputes between Leningrad's artists and musicians all but disappeared during the blockade. "During the worst days almost all of this had vanished. Leningrad had become one family" (Salisbury 1969:517).

Consequently, Leningraders, baptised through co-suffering or *sostradanie* became "a special breed, a special people" (Salisbury 1969:557). Even clinicians such as Svetlana Magaeva concluded that Leningraders behaved differently during the siege. "What happened in Leningrad suggests that the human organism possesses reserve capabilities unknown to science that are manifested when the situation is extremely serious" (Magaeva 2005:123, 140).

## Myth or history?

Dostoevsky once described St. Petersburg evocatively as "a fantastic vision of fairyland, like a dream which in its turn would vanish and pass away like vapour in the dark blue sky" (Dostoevsky 1841. 1972:88). The image of St. Petersburg's fragility as a city of phantoms and hallucination was intensified in September 1941 when it faced the very real prospect of oblivion. Hitler had already demanded that Leningrad be wiped "from the face of the earth" and that its inhabitants be starved to death.[2] Consequently, the later canonisation of the "hero city" was founded upon the fact that its struggle was essentially a *vernichtungsschlacht* or battle of annihilation. The difficulty for oral historians interviewing survivors of the blockade is considerable in that disentangling myth from history is potentially almost impossible. On the other hand it could be argued that veterans refer to various urban myths as a means of explaining the extraordinary circumstances which they faced on a daily basis during the 900 days. They are also part of a mechanism which helps to unravel some of the mysteries of human behaviour observed by Magaeva above. For example, the *blokadniki* interviewed for this project stressed above all the importance of a shared understanding of what it meant to "live one's death in the everyday, to confront it, and to assume it" (Wyatt 2001: 8–9). The enduring myth of a united wartime community continues to be regarded as a fundamental motivating factor behind their quest for survival. As one survivor asserted, "*Vy ne predstavlaete!*" – "You simply cannot imagine it!" (Rozanova 2003). Retired geography teacher Aleksandra Arkhipova asserted that remaining active was vital. She maintained that women tended to regard the home as a place of work and domestic chores. Men, on the other hand saw the home as a place of rest (Arkhipova 2003). It was striking that almost all of the respondents lost their fathers during the early months of the siege. Tat'iana Letenkova described the terrible day she dragged the corpse of her uncle Sasha to the cemetery. She was filled with terror as she realised it was getting dark. Suddenly, she was aware that she could either freeze to death herself or be attacked by criminals. She abandoned the body and headed for home (Letenkova 2006). These are the living nightmares of a shared past which creates a realm of unspoken understanding amongst *blokadniki*. Correspondingly, siege testimonies express a deep sense of membership of a community which is both real and imagined (Anderson 1983).

The myth of the wartime community while undoubtedly romanticised in siege testimony should not be dismissed as a means of diverting us from more factually based statements. It is an expression of that shared comprehension of *sostradanie* which created a community baptised through suffering. As Arkhipova underlined, "This was not propaganda… all you heard was who had died, who was being buried… that people were dying. We knew we had to break the blockade" (Arkhipova 2003).

The narrative of a cohesive wartime community emerged during the interviews as a topic which was also founded upon the widespread belief amongst Leningraders that being a citizen of *Piter* was inherently something special or

---

2.   Hitler issued the following directive concerning "The Future of the City of St. Petersburg" headed: 1. The Fuhrer has decided to raze the City of Petersburg from the face of the earth. See also Salisbury, H. E. 1969. *The 900 Days*…350–52 (High Command Order no.44, 1675/41).

unique. Ol'ga Rozanova portrayed the *"Sankt Peterburgskaia Intelligentka"* as a refined woman who was clearly distinguishable from other Russian citizens. Leningraders were regarded as "brighter" and "purer" than provincial citizens. "Leningraders were loved". While referring to wartime patriotism she asserted that, "Our patriotism was simply for our city. We loved our city" (Rozanova 2003). These sentiments were echoed time and again by various other respondents.

Besieged Leningrad emerges in the reminiscences of *blokadniki* as a ghostly, otherworldly place. In the absence of transport or electricity the freezing streets of old *Piter* became a place of darkness, danger and eerie silence. Veterans do not recall the siege as historians do because they view the blockade from street level. Each small journey on foot, whether to collect water from ice holes on the frozen river Neva or to collect meager rations from the bakers was a formidable challenge. In the midst of such suffering and the constant presence of death a tapestry of tales and urban myths became prevalent. As quoted below there are stories of guardian angels and community spirit but also deep seated fears expressed about the existence of cannibals. Tat'iana Letenkova recalled one terrifying encounter with a group of criminals while making her way across the ice of the Neva. She was pursued but managed to escape to safety (Letenkova 2006). While urban myths of guardian angels and lurking cannibals may not always be backed up with documentation they tell us about how *blokadniki* perceived the transformed landscape and atmosphere of besieged Leningrad. These stories often focus upon certain sights, sounds and smells. Taste also becomes a major topic in siege testimony as well as a range of improvised and unusual wartime dishes. In addition, there is a vocabulary which binds these veterans together and a range of objects whose associations retain iconic significance.

Above all, survivors are still attempting to comprehend and evaluate what happened to them during the nine hundred days between September 1941 and late January 1944. It is also important to recognise that they grew up during the Stalinist era and in many cases retain almost a quasi-religious attitude towards the Red tsar. The key difference between Soviet era historiography and siege recollections is that this group of *blokadniki* at least were less concerned now with Communist ideology itself. Certain statements certainly reflected their Stalinist education but what emerged was a sense that Stalin himself somehow possessed special powers. He was more akin in this respect to the princes of ancient Rus', a *batiushka*, or father to his people.

## Myths of everyday life

Stephen Legg wrote that, "Memory can challenge dominant interpretations of the past and stress the local and particular..." (Legg 2004: 99–107). In this regard individual memories can bring about a democratic repositioning of how history is remembered. This is certainly the case with siege testimonies which turn our attention towards what could be described as the *myths of everyday life*. These particular narratives focus upon the maintenance of mundane routines which would go largely unnoticed during peacetime. Nevertheless, after the daily ration for dependents shrunk to a mere 125 grams during late 1941 maintaining any semblance of normal life became an act of heroism in itself. As might be expected the topic of food and various improvised recipes is repeatedly discussed by survivors. Tat'iana Letenkova recalled how she survived freezing to death in the bread queues. "It was possible to wrap a blanket around yourself and tie a piece of string tightly around your body". She went on to describe the agonizing wait. "Sometimes they would come out and shout, 'delivery coming!" On other occasions there was despair when the call came out that there would be no delivery. Nevertheless, on one occasion she was ecstatic to receive a ration of black macaroni (Letenkova 2006).

Letenkova recalled that the director of the bakery was a 'gentle and wise fellow'. He was well aware of the suffering outside his shop and was revered as a kind of guardian angel. Even though the macaroni was "black, absolutely black and grey and made from dreadful flour" it was nevertheless a veritable lifeline. The tale of the kind and wise baker recalls the chapter entitled, "*U kazhdovo byl svoi spasitel*" ("Everyone had their saviour") in Ales' Adamovich and Daniil Granin's *Blokadnaia Kniga* (Adamovich, Granin 2003: 155).

It is notable that in charting the activities of their daily lives *blokadniki* often recall stories which would have been censored during the Soviet era. This is particularly true in the case of reminiscences of acts of cannibalism. Natalia Velezhova stated that, "I had to do everything. Go out and collect water and so on. My mother was a large lady. She could not go out because those people that were engaged in cannibalism might spot her". Velezhova maintained that, "Yes, the blockade is about cold, hunger and darkness but the absolute worst thing about it was the cannibalism" (Velezhova 2006).

Tat'iana Letenkova recalled that

> (...) then mama found out from a friend that a man was selling meat on the side of the street. Mama and I got two small pieces of meat from him. These were small pieces of rosy coloured meat. Possibly it was human meat. We thought it

was maybe rabbit but I don't think these pieces of meat were rabbit. Maybe it was rabbit…I don't know'. (Letenkova 2006)

Perhaps the most chilling aspect of this story is that Letenkova is haunted by the reality that completely innocently she may have consumed human meat. It should be underlined though that *blokadniki* do not regard such stories as having the potential to undermine the master-narrative of the "hero city". Therefore, crude oppositions between Soviet master-narratives and personal testimonies do not reflect the sentiments of veterans. Their stories and valedictory statements emphasise heroic themes but unlike Soviet historiography do not gloss over the sinister aspects of siege life. Therefore, it could be stated that *blokadniki* do not reject official narratives outright. Nevertheless, they continue to feel that they have something extra to add to the overall story.

During the immediate post-war period though distinct fissures began to appear between representations of the siege in Leningrad and Moscow. Harrison Salisbury and Lisa Kirschenbaum underline that the authorities in Moscow sought to erase "the scars of war and local commemorations of it". The most striking example of this tendency was the sudden closure of the "Museum of the Defence of Leningrad" in 1949[3] (Kirschenbaum 2006: 147; Salisbury 1969: 579). Interestingly, this topic still appeared to be a sensitive one for survivors. Letenkova was the most stridently anti-Communist of the respondents. She recalled a member of her family being arrested on account of his German surname. She also asked, "What did Lenin have to do with the history of this city?" (Letenkova 2006) Letenkova dismissed the name Leningrad as an alien and superficial imposition upon the former capital.

At the other extreme was the stolid patriot Valentina Kuznetsova. When asked about post-war repressions during the period of the "Leningrad Affair" the author received a firm rebuff. "I have *no* idea what you are talking about"[4] (Kuznetsova 2003). These topics do not therefore illicit a uniform response from *blokadniki*. On the other hand, even the most ardently pro-Stalinist of the respondents did not appear to shy away from the grim realities of siege life. Natalia Rudina recalled with great pride how her female classmates took up work in the munitions factory. She maintained that dystrophic children ate, worked and slept at the factory and that they toiled ceaselessly for the war effort. Yet, her most enduring and

---

3.  Salisbury maintained that "without notice or public announcement, the museum of the Defence of Leningrad was closed". The museum's director Major Rakov was subsequently arrested. Salisbury, H. 1969. *The 900 Days…* 579.

4.  *The Leningrad Affair* began in 1948 when Stalin initiated a crackdown on the cultural and political elites in Leningrad.

terrible memory was witnessing her mother's violent death after an incendiary bomb exploded.

> One day in November my mother said to me that the shelling had stopped and that we could go out. Suddenly there was an explosion… Mama was standing outside and was killed. I was left alone. (Rudina 2006)

Viktor Lodkin, a retired submariner, while emphasizing the inherent sacrality of blockade life also asserted that there was a dark side to one of its most enduring icons. The ticking metronome which replaced radio broadcasts when the announcers were too weak to speak has often been portrayed as the heroic heartbeat of a resilient Leningrad. It is a salient theme in A. Rubashkin's famous book Golos Leningrada (The Voice of Leningrad) (Rubashkin 1980). But for Lodkin its sound filled him with terror. He recalled that when the pace of the metronome's beat quickened it was a warning of impending air raids. Its pulse recalled memories of shelling and violent deaths all around. He tapped his knuckles grimly upon the table in imitation of its steady then accelerating rhythm (Lodkin 2006).

Lodkin remain deeply patriotic and defensive about the sacred significance of the struggle which he and his fellow Leningraders faced. For him, and the group of veterans who were interviewed in the town of Kolpino the stubborn image of Stalin and in particular his wartime speeches remained a source of pride. The Kolpino veterans were perilously close to the front lines. As they suffered the brutality of German shelling at particularly close quarter they clung on to Stalin's wartime broadcasts as a sign of their leader's refusal to capitulate. These narratives depict the bloody realities of life at the front and terrible personal loss. Yet their sufferings only served to strengthen their sense of attachment to *vozhd* or boss in Moscow.

Natalia Rudina began by resolutely stating that they had given,

> Everything for the front! Everything for Victory! We did this in order to have faith that we would be victorious. Life and work! That was it… Then in 1942 I fought at the front after the Germans seized a couple of houses on the outskirts. The attack was terrible. We did not give in. Not one step backwards! They broadcasted agitation from loud speakers. We were not frightened because this was just propaganda. We knew they did not have the strength to break through. We had complete faith in our victory. (Rudina 2006)

Two phrases stand out in this statement: "Everything for the front! Everything for Victory!" and "Not one Step Backwards!" Both of these slogans are striking examples of wartime propaganda while the latter recalls Stalin's infamous order no.227 which called for the immediate execution of any soldiers seeking to retreat from the front lines.

What emerges from the Kolpino narratives is a clear sense of loss, both of friends and family. Amidst the surrounding chaos which descended upon them due to the proximity of the German lines Kolpino's citizens appeared to cling onto the belief that the Soviet leadership possessed enough tactical cunning to ensure victory. Nevertheless, when asked about the importance of Socialist ideology as a patriotic source of motivation these and other veterans seemed somewhat perplexed. Purely ideological concerns appeared alien and remote yet the image of Stalin himself was apparently crystal clear.

This is a manifestation of what Stephen Kotkin has described as "socialism with a human face" (Kotkin 1995: 227). Stalin's image functions as a portal which veterans use as a means of accessing formative belief-systems. Lidiia Smirnova was adamant that, "In 1941, Stalin, that means *everything!* When you went into attack the first cry would be, *"Za Rodinu! Za Stalina!"*[5] The image of Stalin? I might be an old person but the image of Stalin is as clear to me today as it was then" (Smirnova 2006). Yet, it would be unjust to dismiss her narrative as nostalgic propaganda.

Smirnova's personal losses were immense. "Mama died. Father died of hunger. My little brother was three years old. He died as well". Many of the Kolpino veterans volunteered for youth detachments during the Spring of 1942 which entered flats and dwellings across the city. They were to discover the true cost of the blockade and all its horrors. Rudina remained haunted in particular by the discovery of the bodies of a mother and her young child. As teenagers it would be difficult for these volunteers to cope with the lasting psychological scars such sights can leave behind.

Correspondingly, several of the veterans recalled how even the sound of Stalin's voice assured them that the Soviet cause was a just one. In summary, while Soviet historiography could be criticised for glossing over the graphic brutality of this *vernichtungsslacht* the overarching theme of heroic fortitude and stubborn resistance chimes in with survivors' personal accounts.

Aleksandra Arkhipova was particularly dismissive of any suggestions that the siege story as a whole had been tainted by propaganda. She retorted, "More than a million died. Where is the agitation or propaganda in that?" (Arkhipova 2003). The tragic death of Natalia Rudina's mother and the image of the orphaned Lidiia Smirnova also remind us of the impact such a calamity had upon Leningrad's innocent citizens.

---

5.   *"Za rodinu! Za Stalina"* was the renowned battle cry "For the motherland! For Stalin!"

## Besieged Leningrad: A topography of the Uncanny

While there is little doubt that Stalin's wartime role retains a strong resonance for veterans it is arguably a much less salient theme than sensory memory. Today, there remain surprisingly few obvious traces of the siege but there are still certain locations which conjure up a "geography of *meanings*" which merge present everyday life with the everyday of the blockade (de Certeau 1984: 104).

From the mass graves in the Piskarevsky cemetery to the blue wartime sign on *Nevskii Prospekt* warning citizens about the dangers of air raids such sacred sites remind *blokadniki* that their city conceals a haunted past. During the nine hundred days Leningraders found that their focus became increasingly localised. They began to concentrate solely upon crucial journeys such as to the bakery to collect their meagre rations. For Letenkova and countless others these simple trips were fraught with danger. Not only was there the very real prospect of air raids but as stated above Velezhova feared the possibility that criminals or even cannibals lurked amidst Leningrad's frozen streets. These journeys form an essential component of the *myths of everyday life*. They also conjoin with the iconography of the siege which comprises of a range of artefacts and objects which retain a potent significance for *blokadniki*. The most emotive of these mundane icons are the *burzhuika* (a small unprepossessing iron stove), *sanochki* (small childrens' sleds which carried the dead to the cemeteries), *sto dvadsats' piats'* (the crust of black bread weighing 125 grams which represents the darkest period of the blockade) and the dreaded *zazhigalka* (incendiary bomb). Each object functions as a memory trigger which can initiate a series of snapshots recalling life during the siege.

Only a few brief examples can be cited here but the following quotations are representative of the enduring significance which these objects retain for *blokadniki*. For Svetlana Gachina, and numerous others the *burzhuika* retained a dual significance. It provided their family flat (in which she still lives) with a crucial heat source vital for survival. Yet, as woodpiles dwindled Leningraders fed the greedy *burzhuika* with furniture, books, newspapers and virtually anything which could emit warmth. Natalia Velezhova concurred that, "Warmth. All we cared about was warm air around us. Chairs, tables, shelves and books were no longer important. You just had to get warm" (Velezhova 2006).

Gachina watched in silent horror as an extensive family library went up in smoke. All that remained was the family's grand piano which still sits in her front room today (Gachina 2003). Consequently, for many Leningraders the *burzhuika* became both a giver of life yet a devourer of memories. This small stove underlined that threshold between their former lives and the realities of the siege. Ol'ga Rozanova associated the *sanochki* with the death of her father who was dragged upon the family sled to the cemetery.

> My father died on 13 January 1942. I did not go to bury him but my sister, cousin
> and mother went. He was buried deep under the ground. You had to give them
> (the undertakers) bread for this. Money meant absolutely nothing; you had to
> give them your day's ration in order to get someone buried deep in the ground.
>
> (Rozanova 2003)

Several days later she visited the cemetery herself only to witness the abandoned
cadaver of a women at the gates. A large piece of flesh had been cut from the thigh
by cannibals. *Sanochki* which would have represented childish frolics in the snow
in peacetime became signifiers of death and family tragedy.

The number *sto dvadsats' piat'* embodies what Roland Barthes described as
the "simplicity of essences". It "abolishes the complexity of human acts" through
its ability to signify the blockade as a whole (Barthes 1973: 156). For veterans the
entire nine hundred days and even the phrase *Blokada Leningrada* could almost
be replaced by *sto dvadsats' piat'*.

Aleksandra Arkhipova even referred to this daily ration when discussing
other periods of the siege. In this regard she was not being entirely factual in
her recollections but again she was utilising the symbolism of this number as a
means of depicting the entire calamity which descended upon Leningrad. In each
case, when remembering this starvation ration *blokadniki* strive through the use
of gestures to portray the black rectangular crusts of bread and recall how difficult
it was to digest their bricklike consistency.

Finally, the *zazhigalka* represents the unpredictability of siege life and the reality that death could come at any moment. Arkhipova witnessed a women being killed on the opposite side of the street. "*Bukh!* (Bang!) and she was gone!"
(Arkhipova 2003). Viktoriia Ruslanova walked past the corpse of a women lying in
the street. Moments earlier she had heard the whizzing sound of a falling incendiary. She continued onwards not out of malice but with the thought that, "Well, at
least this time it was not me" (Ruslanova 2006). These and other similar recollections conjoin with enduring visual memories of wartime Leningrad. The city descended into an all consuming silence interrupted rudely by air raids. Snowdrifts
piled up untamed in the streets which concealed thousands of frozen corpses.

In addition, the impact of the searing temperatures cannot be overestimated.
*Natalia* Velezhova stated that, "'I was born in Leningrad. I have lived here all
my life but I never have seen such cold as during that winter" (Velezhova 2006).
Velezhova, Gachina and countless others huddled around their family *burzhuiki*.
Yet, for them it was both a giver and a taker of life. Each icon has a dual meaning and functions in the memory as a constantly shifting metaphor. *Sanochki* no
longer represented the joy of childrens' play but became hearses. Even food itself, the most prized possession of all also represented human flesh. Each image

is both sacred and defiled becoming emblematic of a tale which embodies both guardian angels and lurking phantoms. The St. Petersburg of today with its hidden geography of meanings therefore still alerts *blokadniki* to the hauntology of the past (Derrida 1994:4).

Within the wider context of historical research emphasis has usually been placed upon archival based findings. Our view of history emerges generally from the analysis of documents contained within libraries and both public and private collections. In comparison, the study of oral history has often been regarded as a questionable exercise due to the perceived unreliability of personal recollections. It can be argued however that oral history within the context of siege of Leningrad testimonies democratically repositions the overall story away from military strategies and Communist ideology towards the *myths of everyday life*. This is a particularly valuable exercise in a society which was hitherto strictly monitored by the Stalinist state. As *blokadniki* enter their final years they also appear eager to relate their memories while time allows. Correspondingly, there remains only a short window of opportunity before the last veterans finally pass away. Siege discourse may also be mythic discourse but it does not entail a journey away from reality. For survivors, the myths of everyday siege life make the past *more* not less real to them. Above all, they are describing to us what it was like to "confront one's own death in the everyday" (Wyatt 2001:8–9). They are merging the sacred and the real. Margaret Hiley states that, "The message of the myth is: *This really happened*" (Hiley 2004:849). In essence, that is the message that *blokadniki* are striving to convey. As Aleksandra Arkhipova stated, "It was a unique era. We survived for nine hundred days. More than a million people died. That is a fact. You just cannot get away from it. No one, not anyone should be allowed to forget it" (Arkhipova 2003).

## References

Adamovich, A. & Granin, D. 2003. *Blokadnaia Kniga*. St. Petersburg: Nezavisimoe Izdatel'stvo PIK.

Anderson, B. 1983. *Imagined Communities: Reflections on the Origin and Spread of Nationalism.* London: Verso Editions & NLB.

Barthes, R. 1973. *Mythologies.* London: Paladin.

Boym, S. 1994. *Common Places: Mythologies of Everyday Life in Russia.* Cambridge MA: Harvard University Press.

Clapperton, J. 2007. *The Siege of Leningrad and the Ambivalence of the Sacred.* PhD dissertation, University of Edinburgh.

de Certeau, M. 1984. *The Practice of Everyday Life.* Berkeley CA: University of California Press.

Derrida, J. 1994. *Specters of Marx: The State of the Debt, the Work of Mourning, and the New International*. P. Kamuf (trans). London: Routledge.

Harrison, H. E. 1969. *The 900 Days. The Siege of Leningrad*. New York NY: Harper & Row.

Hiley, M. 2004. Myth and mythology in Tolkien. *Modern Fiction Studies* 50(4): 838–60.

Kirschenbaum, L. A. 2004. Commemorations of the siege of Leningrad: A catastrophe in memory and myth. In *The Memory of Catastrophe*, P. Gray & K. Oliver (eds). Manchester: Manchester University Press.

Kotkin, S. 1995. *Magnetic Mountain: Stalinism as a Civilization*, 227. Berkeley CA: University of California Press.

Legg, S. 2004. Memory and nostalgia. *Cultural Geographies* 11(1): 99–107.

Rubashkin, A. 1980. *Golos Leningrada: Leningrad Radio v Dni Blokady*. Leningrad: *Iskusstvo* Leningradskoe Otdelenie.

Wyatt, N. 2001. The mythic mind. *Scandinavian Journal of the Old Testament* 15(8–9): 13–61.

## Interviews

Aleksandra Arkhipova, interview with the author, Edinburgh, April 2003

Svetlana Gachina, interview with the author, St. Petersburg, July 2003

Valentina Kuznetsova, interview with the author, St. Petersburg, July 2003

Tat'iana Letenkova interview with the author, St. Petersburg, September 2006

Viktor Lodkin, interview with the author, St. Petersburg, September 2006

Ol'ga Rozanova, interview with author, St. Petersburg, July 2003

Natalia Rudina, interview with the author, St. Petersburg (Kolpino), September 2006

Viktoriia Ruslanova, interview with the author, St. Petersburg, September 2006

Lidiia Smirnova, interview with the author, St. Petersburg (Kolpino), September 2006

Natalia Velezhova, interview with the author, St. Petersburg, September 2006

# Women soldiers and women prisoners

## Oral testimonies of Ruta Czaplińska and Elżbieta Zawacka

Anna Muller

Ph.D. Candidate at Indiana University, USA

In this essay I present the stories of two women soldiers, Elżbieta Zawacka and Ruta Czaplińska, involved in the Second World War struggle who stepped out of the roles traditionally attributed to Polish women. Both were soldiers, both engaged in the anti-Communist activities after the war, and both suffered imprisonment for their actions. In the essay, I try to show how differently these two women constructed their life stories. While Zawacka saw herself as a soldier who was always determined, Czaplińska's story is full of doubts, sadness, and reflection. I hope that these oral stories reveal how within one culture and similar set of values, defined by devotion to Poland, there is space for various models of women's engagement.

Keywords: women soldiers, Polish women, the Second World War, life stories, anti-Communist activities

When I began my dissertation research on the experience of women imprisoned for anti-state activity in post-1945 Poland, I knew that there are two institutions which gather women who could become principal informants for my dissertation: the Association of the Women Political Prisoners, called *Fordonianki,* and the Foundation of the Pomeranian Archive and the Military Service of Women, called FAPAK.[1] In the archives of these institutions as well as among people affiliated with them, I hoped to find documents, such as letters and memoirs, and make contact with women who were involved in the pre and postwar conspiracy. I indeed found everything I had expected and more. What I unexpectedly found was the extent to which these two groups of women with similar life stories and

---

1.   The name Fordonianki refers to Fordon, the prison where most women served their sentences.

backgrounds differed in the ways in which they understood the meaning of their experiences and the nature of women's involvement in Polish history.

Motivated by the fear that the predominant, male-centered public discourse would sweep the women's experience away, both FAPAK and *Fordonianki* bring together women with similar life stories, many of whom were politically involved then repressed as a consequence of this involvement. There are clear differences between them. While FAPAK is mostly focused on women's involvement in the struggles for independence from the 19th c. through WWII, Fordonianki deal with post-1945 women political prisoners punished for their anti-Communism. These differences find further reflection in their public activities and the political profile of both groups.[2]

To give just one example, in April of 2007, FAPAK finalized its biggest project and unveiled a monument of Maria Wittek, the first Polish woman General and a commander of PWK (*Przysposobienie Wojskowe Kobiet*), an organization training women for military service. The monument was erected in front of the Museum of the Polish Army and unveiled at the 10th anniversary of Wittek's death. A month later, in May of 2007, *Fordonianki* organized a meeting with the President of Poland, Lech Kaczyński, during which they gathered prison mothers, women who either gave birth to their child in prison or, due to the imprisonment, were separated from their children.

The image that FAPAK supports is that of a brave woman soldier, regardless of her political affiliation. Consequently, the women that FAPAK gathers represent the spectrum of political stances – from women affiliated with the Home Army to women from units trained in the Soviet Union. The emasculated woman soldier that FAPAK promotes contrasts *Fordonianki*'s more traditional image of a Polish woman who, seeing her home in danger, got involved into a struggle that eventually led her to prison. Endorsing an image of a suffering mother (or a potential mother) in prison, a symbol of women's commitment to Poland, *Fordonianki* are open to women who at least since 1945 have been anti-Communists.

In order to probe these differences further and ask about the individual experience behind the stories and ideals that these two organizations support,

---

2.  While Fordonianki publish mostly memoirs or documents, testifying to women's life in prison, in its publishing activities FAPAK mostly publishes articles and bios of women soldiers. Examples of Fordonianki's publishing activies are: Otwinowska, B. (ed). 1995. *Przeciwko złu. Wiersze i piosenki więzienne 1944–1956*. Warszawa: Akces, Otwinowska, B. (ed) 1999. *Zawołac po imieniu: księga kobiet więzniów politycznych*.vol. 1–2. Warszawa: Vipart. The examples of FAPAK 's books are: Zawacka, E. and Biernacka, M. (eds.). 2004. *Słownik biograficzny kobiet odznaczonych Orderem Wojennym Virtuti Militari*. Toruń: FAPAK and Kabzińska, K. (ed.). 2003. *Sylwetki Kobiet Zolnierzy*. Toruń: FAPAK, Zawacka, E. (ed.) 1998. *Służba Polek na frontach II Wojny Swiatowej*, vol. 1–V. Toruń: FAPAK.

I look closer at interviews that I had with Professor and General Elżbieta Zawacka and Second Lieutenant Ruta Czaplińska. Zawacka is the founder and, despite her age (99), the key figure behind all FAPAK initiatives. Czaplińska was one of the first to begin organizing former women prisoners, which eventually led to the establishment of the Association of *Fordonianki*. The interviews I had with both women were not structured around a pre-prepared questionnaire; rather, my plan to gather answers to questions had to change since both women preferred telling me their life stories rather than answering questions. In the end, my intervention in their narrations was minimal.

Investigating the interviews I conducted with Zawacka and Czaplińska entails drawing from their memory, which is in turn filtered through their present. Their memory is not a passive depository of facts, but an active process of creation of meaning. Describing in detail the people and events they wanted to remember and passing in silence the rest, both women re/created their life stories for me. These stories, thus, became unique not because of the "logical, casual sequence of the story," but because of "the way in which the story materials are arranged by narrators in order to tell the story" (Portelli 1998:67). Following Alessandro Portelli's suggestion to pay attention to the ways through which people recreate their coherent life stories, I attempt to look into how both women make sense of the past: how they organize their narratives, what modes of story-telling they choose, and how they intersect the larger historical framework with their personal stories.

## Elżbieta Zawacka – a Soldier[3]

It is difficult to meet with Elżbieta Zawacka. I called her four times before she finally had enough time to meet with me. At the end of our long telephone conversation, Zawacka, in a General-like voice, told me what I should read before the meeting and told me what questions I should and should not ask. In the end, she said: "Call me a day before you come to make sure I am alive. At my age, you never know…"

The beginning of our conversation was difficult. She tested my knowledge of military history, the laws concerning women's military service in European countries, etc. I barely passed. And here my role ended. From this point on, it was only Elżbieta Zawacka who spoke, paying no regard to my questions or remarks. It was her meeting with her life not with me. Gazing at the wall, she began

---

3.   All the citations of E. Zawacka are taken from my interviews with her. Elżbieta Zawacka, interview by author, Toruń, March-April, 2007, Toruń.

telling me about her childhood when she was raised in a German-speaking Polish family in Toruń in the middle of the German part of partitioned Poland. Every once in a while she paused, looked at me and said: "I need to make sure you understand. I was raised in the Pomerania region. It was natural that we did not speak Polish. My mom was very ambitious. She wanted all her children to be educated, and to do this we had to speak German." She began learning Polish in 1918, when she was 9 years old and Poland regained independence. Zawacka finds it difficult to narrate this moment; she begins with a lot of energy, but as she proceeds I see increasingly more tears in her eyes as emotions take her breath away. She narrates:

> And imagine that 1918 is coming. There is a rumor that Poland exists. Nobody knows that for sure. Poland for us was only this small area with Warsaw. But there are rumors – Poland, Poland... My father, neighbors, people who speak only German see all those beautiful horses, uniforms, the posture... Polish soldiers of General Haller. They are so beautiful... And they scream for the first time: "Poland hasn't died yet...." And the tears of these adult men.... as if they were children... Nobody ever saw them crying... And they woke up to Polishness. Everything became Polish... strangely Polish...

Zawacka tells her story in an epic mode. She recalls her absorption in the historical events and her treatment of those events as having a fundamental meaning for her life is overwhelming. Her life is framed by 1918, the year Poland regained independence and Zawacka recognized her Polishness and the commitment to the organization that became the essence of her life – PWK, an organization training women for military service. "PKW was so important for us that my friend added the words of the PWK pledge to her daily prayer." Interestingly, this is the only time Zawacka mentions religion during our conversations.

When she talks about PWK, her fragile voice becomes stronger, more rhythmic and her narrative is punctuated by the commands that she received as a woman soldier. There are no more tears, she is regrouped and focused. Regardless of how difficult her life became after, the decision to become a soldier had been taken and her new life began. There is no more space for an ordinary life and doubts coming with the unknown. As a soldier, aware of the coming war, she was devoted to two causes: the defense of Poland and the will to equalize women soldiers with men soldiers. She narrates:

> When I went to my first PWK camp, my ordinary life ended and there was only PWK in my life. I worked and studied. I was a teacher and even liked it. But first of all, I was the instructor of PWK. Then 1939 came. The work for PWK was the most important. You don't know this feeling when the motherland (*ojczyzna*) is

in danger. I was a soldier. We knew that a war is coming and we knew that we had to prepare women as part of a regular army. I have been growing with the thought of war since December of 1930, since I was part of PWK.

For Zawacka, a PWK instructor in the Silesia region at that time, the beginning of the war was marked by an order to participate in the defense of Lviv. With a group of fifteen PWK instructors it took her several nights and days to travel to Lviv. She recalls this trip almost day by day with a map, showing where they passed a bridge which was soon after blown into the air, where they caught a bus, etc. Once in Lviv, she organized an anti-airplane and anti-tank defense. Her story of the defense of Lviv is rhythmic and fast. Every time she mentions PWK, she repeats the full name of the organization, not the acronym, twice or three times to make me realize the importance of the women soldiers. The pace of her speech changes when she reaches the moment of October 17th, the invasion of Poland by the Soviet Union. Once again, she cries and has difficulties catching her breath.

> There is a meeting of officers. Lviv is giving up. What are you choosing? We had to choose something. The choices are – Russian captivity, escape to civilian life, or escape through Hungary and France. You have to decide… the end… there were so many suicides, so many… because they did not know what to do. What is going to happen to us? What to choose? What is the right choice? Can I handle it?

After Lviv surrendered, Zawacka decided to travel to Warsaw. It was the real beginning of WWII, and as a soldier Zawacka had to be where soldiers were needed – in the middle of the war, in Warsaw. The tone of her voice and the pace of her speech changes again; there is no more space for weakness. She speaks fast, with her regular confidence in the importance of her role as a soldier. In late fall of 1940, Zawacka as "Zo" joined the Polish anti-Nazi resistance, specifically the headquarters of ZWZ (*Związek Walki Zbrojnej*, the Association of the Military Struggle).[4] Soon after, she became one of the most active liaisons in the Department of Foreign Communications, so-called *Zagroda*. She served as a courier for the Home Army, organizing trails for other couriers and carrying letters and other documents from Nazi-occupied Poland to the Polish government in exile and back. She remembers:

---

4.   *Zagroda* is the name for the Department of Foreign Communications. Its role was to maintain the roads of communication via land for mail and people from Warsaw to the headquarters of the Main Commander in exile in London and other offices in Europe. See Minczykowska, K. and Sziling, J. (eds) 2004. *Z dziejów Wydziału Zagranicznej Komendy Głównej ZWZ – AK "Zagroda,"* Toruń: FAPAK.

> I have always been Elizabeth: in France I was Elise Riviere, to Denmark I went
> as Elizabeth von Brauneg, and in England I was Elizabeth Watson or Elizabeth
> Kubica. I knew my legend so well, it grew on me so strongly that I ceased being
> Elżbieta Zawacka. I had been a liaison since the beginning of the conspiracy.
> I knew how to behave. I knew various tricks indispensable while crossing the
> border illegally.

When she plunges herself in her past trips as a liaison, she begins romanticizing
her narrative. She talks about places she saw, beautiful nature, foreign cities, etc.
She relishes narrating a trip through the Pyrenees to London to the Polish government in exile in February of 1943. Her narrative becomes more personal and yet
there is still no place for stories that would go beyond her defined role as a soldier.
Regardless of where she was and what name she carried, Zawacka stresses that
she always knew her place and role. She was to inform others about the situation
in Poland and request full soldier rights for women who served in auxiliary units.
"It was important," she stresses. "Our volunteers were only members of auxiliary
units. We had to give women full rights as soldiers of the Polish Republic, soldiers….," she repeats. In September 1943, she was parachuted back to Poland. "A
wonderful flight," she remembers. "I was not approaching the earth, but the earth
was approaching me."

After the war, Zawacka was imprisoned and sentenced to ten years in prison
for treason and espionage. She dismisses my questions about prison. "There is
nothing to be proud of. This was not important." The epic narrative of her active
life prior to prison contrasts with her inactivity in prison, and as such is not worth
discussing. She is a soldier and the essence of her life lies in constant struggles
and achievements: the training of soldiers within PWK, the defense of Lviv, the
struggle for recognition of women-soldiers, etc.

According to Daniel James, the epic mode "implies the individual's identification with the community and its values, and leaves little room for the expression
of individual identity" (James 2000: 162). Zawacka's narration, though a seemingly intense personal performance, is closely interconnected with the Polish 20th c.
military struggle, with one significant difference – this time it is told by a female
soldier. In a sense, her individual story resembles the professional historical discourse which, for example, FAPAK adapted – the organization that Zawacka
heads. Perhaps Zawacka's autobiographical memory became the foundation of
the public memory of brave women soldiers that FAPAK espouses. This brings us
to one more issue: the way Zawacka tells her story and the sense of entitlement of
women soldiers that she expresses creates the impression that she does not dwell
in the past, but the issues she raises concern the present. Her narrative has a very
political nature and touches on the issues of the role of women in Polish history.

At the end of our conversation, she switched to her favorite topics – her current projects and the prospect for new ones. The official opening of the Monument of Maria Wittek is a fulfillment of one of Zawacka's dreams – official recognition of women soldiers' contribution to Polish national struggles. Currently, she is gathering information on women soldiers who died during the Second World War. We engaged in an interesting discussion, or rather I was questioned who should be considered a war hero; should everybody who died in the war be remembered and celebrated? Commitment to Poland and activism is the answer to her every question.

### Ruta Czaplińska – a Soldier in Prison[5]

Ruta Czaplińska is unlike Elżbieta Zawacka. Quiet, focused, and withdrawn, she constantly comes back to her past, her involvement in the anti-Communist resistance, and finally her prison experience. She analyses and reanalyzes the situations she experienced and people she met, asking herself over and over again about the meaning of her experience. A conversation with me gives her another chance to ask the questions that she has been pondering for years. While Zawacka does not want to talk and be interviewed because this takes her away from her various life projects, Ruta Czaplińska's return to her life experience gives her another chance to come to terms with unresolved issues of her past. Weeks after our interviews she still calls me with new or partially modified answers to issues we discussed. In the middle of one of our long conversations, Czaplińska says that half of her remained in prison. The more time I spent with her the more I realized how correct she was.

Ruta Czaplińska was born in 1918 in the patriotic home of a landowning Polish family with a long tradition of participating in national upheavals. The father of Czaplińska's mother participated in the January Uprising of 1863 and was the Godfather of Józef Piłsudski. In March of 1945, a friend of Czaplińska's brother, Leszek Roszkowski, from the right-wing anti-Communist organization NZW (Narodowe Zjednoczenie Wojskowej, National Military Unity) asked her to join them. She agreed and became the head of Communication for NZW. In this function, she was imprisoned in April of 1946 and sentenced to ten years in prison. When she begins narrating the story of her imprisonment, her narration adopts a clearly romantic mode, which Daniel James defines as "a quest for values

---

5.   All the citations of R. Czaplińska are taken from my interviews with her. Ruta Czaplińska, interview by author, Wrocław, March-May, 2007 and January 2008.

in a degraded world, whereby the individual's moral career is established through her ability to overcome obstacles and difficulties" (James 2000: 162).

> When they arrested me, they took me to a room with an open window. For a moment, I even considered jumping… I think I thought they would kill me, but I didn't know what death is. Did I have a chance to better prepare myself for a prison and interrogations? I thought my friends are imprisoned, I don't know in what kind of danger they are, I am not going to try to save myself… I admitted that I was the head of communication and this was the worst thing I could have done. It was a mistake because as the head of communication I know much more. What should have I done?

The moment of Czaplińska's trial is one of the most painful for her. And yet at the same time it fills her with the joyful certainty of a moral victory over those who imprisoned her. Almost all the men from her case received a death sentence. After the trial, when the court members left, the lawyer who defended them gave them holy bread he had brought illegally. With a trembling voice and tears in her eyes, Czaplińska recollects this moment,

> They took holy bread facing a window. They had already absolutions. Those who sat in a cell next to a priest received them via tapping on a wall, and those who did not have this opportunity at a given hour looked out a window and a priest from the outside gave them an absolution. And one of my boys, Leszek, asked not to have a mourning mass for his soul, but a joyful one, because he is dying for his motherland (*ojczyzna*).

After the trial, Czaplińska was moved to Fordon, the central prison for women, where she was kept for two years, from 1948 to 1950. In August of 1950, she was moved from Fordon to Inowrocław, the prison where women were kept in almost total isolation from the outside world. The story about her life in prison is very detailed, especially with regard to her female cell mates. Similarly to Zawacka, she feels like a repository of knowledge and memories of her late friends. For years she wrote short recollections of people and special moments of life in prison, which work as triggers for her memory. Her stories are different than Zawacka's. She talks less about heroic deeds and more about daily survival, death, ethics, God, etc. What was right and what was not? What could she have done for those who faced a death sentence? Can she now forgive the communist authorities for what was done to people who received a death sentence?

For Czaplińska, the time of imprisonment was not lost in passivity, contrary to how Zawacka sees it. It was an extension of prisoners' former struggles, perhaps even its most important part. In prison every single word or act had to be thought through, because the responsibility for those inside as well as outside of the prison walls was much bigger. From this point of view the most significant for Czaplińska was the time she spent in Inowrocław, an isolation prison. No people meant having no references to her thoughts and actions; only her, her thoughts, and God to whom she often prayed. "I did not have anybody to share my thoughts with. It was painful to think without having any support, any response, or any possibility to talk to others. Am I right or not? Why am I here? These questions troubled me. I cannot live in negating everything."

Her narrative is interrupted by anecdotes through which she tells me little oddities in people's behavior, jokes, etc. Anecdotes are "morality tales with both a social and individual register: they are about proper and improper behavior, responsible and irresponsible actions, about the way the world is and the way it ought to be" (James 2000: 172). In one of her anecdotes, she narrates,

> At some point, there were Germans in a cell neighboring ours. At first we didn't want to talk to them. They asked us if we have bread and we began leaving bread for them in a toilet. But we still did not want to talk to them. Our first impulse was not to help Germans, but then what can we do – they are asking for bread. Could we say no? Later, they tapped to us to say thank you.

This anecdote expresses not only the moral dilemmas prisoners faced, but also conforms to the image of Czaplińska and women prisoners she wants to maintain as moral women who were able to face the obstacles that lie outside the normal quotidian experience. The questions that Czaplińska keeps asking herself and her interlocutors play a similar role. She never welcomed war as Zawacka did. Her involvement in the anti-Communist conspiracy was more a result of her debt to family traditions and a sense of wrongs that affected her friends and family than a challenge that she took with enthusiasm. Although framed by historical events, her story is intensely personal, questioning over and over again her role in what happened to her and lessons from the experience she can draw for the future. *Fordonianki*'s activities, which she in part initiated, correspond with issues that Czaplińska constantly ponders upon.

Czaplińska finished our last meeting telling me about her attempts to get in touch with families of her cell mates. New questions appeared – how to pass on knowledge to children not interested in the deeds of their parents and how to make the next generations understand the value of this experience. We read out loud a letter by Monika Dymska, a member of the anti-Nazi resistance, who was hung in Germany during WWII. Just before her death, Dymska wrote a letter to her family. Czaplinska stored a copy of this letter as one of her most valuable documents. We talked about Dymska's mental strength in the face of death and the perseverance in our ideals despite the circumstances.

## Marcysia – a Soldier and Prisoner

One of the topics that emerged during my conversations with both women was Emilia Malessa, called Marcysia. Marcysia was the head of the Home Army's Department of Foreign Communications, which was responsible for organizing courier routes linking the leaders of the resistance with the Polish government in exile. After the war ended, Marcysia remained in the underground resistance structures in WiN (Wolność i Niepodległość, Freedom and Independence). According to people who remember her, already in the spring of 1945 Marcysia considered withdrawing from the conspiracy. Tired of the double life she led, she welcomed the call of the WiN leader, Colonel Jan Rzepecki, for a slow return to a normal life (Mietkowska and Przewoźnik 1996: 12).

Marcysia was imprisoned in October of 1945, six days before finishing her work for WiN. During the interrogations, she trusted the promises and the word of honour of the secret police officer Józef Różański and decided to disclose the people involved in the work of the Home Army section she headed. Before she decided to do it, Marcysia talked to Rzepecki and received guarantees from the Minister of Public Security (MPB), Stanisław Radkiewicz, that after the investigation all the people revealed would be released from prisons. In 1947 Marcysia was released. The people she disclosed were not. In a desperate attempt to have the guarantees of the MBP realized, Marcysia went on a hunger strike outside the prison walls. In June of 1949, Marcysia committed suicide (Mietkowska and Przewoźnik 1996: 12).

In Fordon, Czaplińska was imprisoned in a cell next to Marcysia. She communicated with other women from Marcysia's cell via tapping, but not Marcysia herself. Marcysia did not tap on the wall. During our meetings, Czaplińska talks about Marcysia with a big dose of compassion and gratefulness. For Zawacka, Marcysia, as head of *Zagroda*, the organization where Zawacka worked, was a boss and a friend. Recollecting her last meeting with Marcysia, she says,

> While walking I noticed a woman whose gait I recognized. Her coat had a big stain. She looked like Marcysia, but it could not be her. Marcysia has always been so elegant. She always took good care of herself. She considered it to be important in her service. And here with a stain… We welcomed each other. She asked me if I revealed myself. "No? We have to reveal who you are, it is necessary. I will go with you," she said. When I heard that, I said goodbye to her. She was completely confused. I don't know how it could have happened. She was such a smart woman. When she realized what she did she committed suicide.
>
> (Mietkowska and Przewoźnik 1996: 13)

After a moment of hesitation, she continues: "I don't know how it could have happened. I don't know how a person like her could have believed the Russians. She should have known better. After her release from prison she could have become a Colonel. Obviously, she did not become one."

For Czaplińska, Marysia's tragedy epitomizes the problems and tragedies of life in prison and the issues that one had to resolve in one's heart – to trust an officer's word of honour and perhaps help people from the resistance or not. Marcysia is a symbol of prisoners' torment, the sense of responsibility for those who stayed outside the prison walls, and sometimes perhaps even the lack of knowledge about the danger of the system. At stake were the lives of many people, but also one's honour and dignity. According to Czaplińska, Marcysia behaved the way she did because honour was the main value in her life. "I think it was this respect for the word of honour of an officer, engrained in all of us, that became the reason why Marcysia revealed the people she worked with. Her suicidal death was the highest protest against the lie committed against her."

Zawacka's slight disappointment with Marcysia's action contrasts with the compassion and understanding that Czaplińska presents. For Zawacka, Marcysia is a person who got confused, hence did something that soldiers are not supposed to do. For Czaplińska, Marcysia's death was the evidence of her struggle, while for Zawacka it was her acquiescence to committing a mistake. Marcysia's doubts and struggles do not fit the epic narrative of Zawacka, and at the same time they correspond with Czaplińska's moral dilemmas and the belief in the need to overcome individual weaknesses. The question, though, remains to what extent these differences can be extrapolated on the attitudes of both women towards the role of women in Polish history.

Zawacka has been engaged in different battles her entire life: from military battles to battles for recognition; from attempts to receive permission from Polish authorities to grant women full rights of being soldiers to a fight for the recognition of women soldiers in history. Narrating her life story, she is still engaged in one of her battles. As she mentions throughout her struggles, one of the most difficult obstacles was gender relations. According to Zawacka, men are reluctant to understand the value of women as soldiers; they tend to depreciate women in their work and find it difficult to work with women supervisors. She continues,

> I had a very good life. Sure, there are moments when I regret that I don't have my own family. But that is how things worked out. Other things were more important. I still have missions to fulfill. I need to pass the stories about women soldiers to the next generations. Women constitute half of Poland. What I have in mind is the constant service to the nation. It also means devoting a family for the service to your nation. Understanding this will enrich coming generations.

In her attempt to go beyond the stereotypical image of women as mothers and wives that contradicted her own story, Zawacka created her own model of a woman's service to nation, something that represented her own life well. It is a person with clearly defined goals and roles, either an involvement in public life or a devotion to private life. Partially for this reason, in the bios of women soldiers, she often stresses the fact that these women never married. Women soldiers that she admires are equal to men soldiers in commitment, decisiveness, and strength; they have a clear focus, which is often combined with a lack of family of their own. In this light, Marcysia's doubts and hesitations despite her knowledge about Communism are difficult to comprehend.

Ruta Czaplińska talks little about the role of women. Similarly to Zawacka, she is single; not out of choice, but rather a result of circumstances and the fact that she spent most of her youth in prison. The need to recover memory about imprisoned women is more a result of a sense that her entire generation of post-war resistance fighters has been pushed to oblivion than of a feeling of women being marginalized. The lives of various women – her cell mates and friends from the prison – take a lot of her attention, but she equally speaks about the men she met as a resistance member. She worries about them and their families. They and their families became her family and fulfill her need to complete the social roles that she as a woman is supposed to fulfill. When compared to Zawacka, Czaplińska's views on gender and female-male relationships are more traditional. Soldiering and the armed involvement in the struggle for Polish independence is not her calling, as in the case of Zawacka, but rather a sort of obligation and the natural consequence of women's tendency to sacrifice. Czaplińska is a woman who combines a sense of responsibility for people surrounding her with a commitment to a more abstract idea of a nation that these men support. Finally, she is someone who experiences Polish history in an especially painful manner, in auxiliary positions to men, supporting them in combat, but also in words and prayers.

Elżbieta Zawacka and Ruta Czaplińska are both unusual women who stepped out of the roles traditionally attributed to Polish women. Both were soldiers, both engaged in anti-Communist activities, and both suffered for their actions. Zawacka's narrative is epic and romantic and as such fits the image that FAPAK promotes. It is the story of a woman who grew into her role as a soldier, always active, determined, and convinced that the path she has chosen is the best one. From her fascination with Polish officers she saw in Toruń in 1918 through her participation in the organization training women for military service to her war service, she organizes her story to show that she is determined to be a soldier and serve Poland, seen as a great collective duty. In contrast to her narrative, Czaplińska's story is full of doubts, sadness, and reflection. It is the story of a victory over the debasing conditions of unjust imprisonment, and yet a story full of melancholic realization of the price paid for this victory. Occasional anecdotes in a sense play the role of a counter-narrative to the more serious version of her life, pointing to a "lighter side" of her stay in prison without abandoning the main idea that life is full of ethical questions and there are no easy choices in life. These oral stories help understand how within one culture and similar set of values, defined by devotion to Poland, there is space for various models of women's engagement.

To end this paper, I would like to add a little bit about the subjective nature of oral testimonies. According to Katherine Borland, a personal narrative is a performance that creates meaning on two levels simultaneously. "It constitutes both a dynamic interaction between the thinking subject and the narrated event (her own life experience) and between the thinking subject and the narrative event (her assumptions of responsibility to an audience for a display of communicative competence)" (Borland 1998: 320). The narrative changes once a context changes and a narrating person starts renegotiating a sense of self. Additionally, any interpretation of interviews results from an encounter between the historian aware of the subjectivity of the research method s/he is pursuing and the person who is interested in telling her/his story. As a result, the interpretation of any oral interviews is a profoundly personal issue of reading, involving intellectual and emotional elements that both sides bring to a meeting.

My conversations with Elżbieta Zawacka and Ruta Czaplińska raise similar issues of the subjective nature of interpretation. During our meetings a specific form of relationship emerged between me and them. In the case of Zawacka, my contact was less emotional and more professional and detached. There was a formula that Prof. Zawacka chose because, as I assume, it allowed her to keep a distance, become less personal in her narrative, and in a sense maintain the epic mode of her narrative. My engagement with Ruta was quite emotional and with time evolved into friendship, or perhaps into a set of friendships: between a teacher and a student, between a grandmother and a granddaughter, between two women of different ages, one older and wiser and the other younger, eager to learn from the other.

Ruta Czaplińska died two days before I finished this essay. She called many times while I was working on it, asking to read it. Unsure how she would react to what I wrote, I kept postponing sending her a version of this paper until it was too late. This only strengthened one question that lingered with me while I interviewed both women: to what extent the relationship I had with these two women added an additional layer to my understanding of them and as such should be included into the process of interpretation? Or perhaps, to what extent did our relationships already color my view of these women and deepen the differences I see between them?

## References

Borland, K. 1998. That's not what I said. Interpretative conflict in oral narrative research. In *The Oral History Reader*, R. Perks & A. Thomson (eds), 320. London: Routledge.

James, D. 2000. *Dona Maria's Story. Life Story, Memory, and Political Identity*. Durham NC: Duke University Press.

Kabzińska, K. (ed.). 2003. *Sylwetki Kobiet Żołnierzy*. Toruń: FAPAK.

Mietkowska, M. & Przewoźnik, A. 1996. Kapitan Marcysia, *Magazyn Gazety Wyborczej* 21: 12–14.

Minczykowska, K. & Sziling, J. (eds). 2004. *Z dziejów Wydziału Zagranicznej Komendy Głównej ZWZ – AK "Zagroda"*. Toruń: FAPAK.

Otwinowska, B. (ed.). 1999. *Zawołac po imieniu: księga kobiet więzniów politycznych*. Warszawa: Vipart.

Otwinowska, B. (ed.). 1995. *Przeciwko złu. Wiersze i piosenki więzienne 1944–1956*. Warszawa: Akces.

Portelli, A. 1998. What makes oral history different. In *The Oral History Reader*, R. Perks & A. Thomson (eds), 67–69. London: Routledge.

Zawacka, E. (eds). 1998. *Służba Polek na frontach II Wojny Swiatowej*. Toruń: FAPAK.

Zawacka, E. & Biernacka, M. (eds). 2004. *Słownik biograficzny kobiet odznaczonych Orderem Wojennym Virtuti Militari*. Toruń: FAPAK.

# 'The stranger within my Gate'

## Irish emigrant narratives of exile, tradition and modernity in post-war Britain

Sarah O'Brien

Department of History Mary Immaculate College, University of Limerick

This essay discusses the use of oral narrative in interpreting the Irish migrant experience in post-war Britain and reveals the extent to which oral methodology challenges established norms about the Irish Diaspora. Informing the essay is an oral history project carried out with Irish migrants in Birmingham between 2005 and 2008 and extracts from these interviews illustrate, amongst other factors, migrants' struggle to balance the demands of the 'homeland' with the opportunities of modernity, and their contestation of an exile identity. Essentially, this paper demonstrates how textual analysis of oral narrative illuminates the process of identity reconfiguration that occurred in Irish enclaves and determines the significance of gender, class, religion and nationalism in informing the migrant experience.

**Keywords:** Irish migration; Identity reconfiguration in post-war Britain; Catholicism; Birmingham Bombings

Ireland until1960 was a country defined by its nationalist romanticism, pastoral fundamentalism and Catholic devotion. Éamon DeValera, a key figure in Ireland's struggle for independence, dominated Irish politics from the 1930s until 1959 and sought to retain the young nation's integrity by preserving a monolithic, self-sufficient culture, independent of Western capitalism. This resistance to industrial innovation inhibited post-war economic growth and forced thousands of young Irish people to vote with their feet in protest against the frugal comfort that its government forced upon Irish society.[1]

---

1.  For further discussions see Brown, T. 2004. *Ireland; a social and cultural history 1922–2002.* London: Harper Perennial. Also MacLaughlin, J. 1994. *Ireland; The Emigrant Nursery and the World Economy.* Cork: Cork University Press.

Despite emigrants' disillusionment with the policies of the Irish government many retained an anti-colonial outlook which portrayed the home-land as a pastoral idyll, still crippled by the effects of British colonialism. This outlook was, in some sense, a ploy that helped potential emigrants to justify leaving, and facilitated emigrants to portray themselves as victimised exiles rather than voluntary emigrants who were seeking out a better life in England. Twentieth century Irish songs and ballads popularised this notion of forced Irish exile and painted nostalgic images of the lone Irish man, desolate and helpless because of England's corrupting capitalist influences, with his dreams of returning home in tatters. *The Navvy* exemplifies the emotional and negative portrayal of life in England;

> My hands are scarred, my back is bent
> I'm writing in my diary in this worn out tent
> The whisky tastes like water and the soup it tastes the same
> And I know the grass is greener from where I came (McLarney)

This essay shows how oral narrative reveals, uniquely, the imbalances in this emotional and negative perception of emigration. Informing the paper is an oral history project that was carried out with Irish immigrants in Birmingham, a large industrial city in England's West Midlands that received a substantial influx of Irish immigrants after World War II. The thirty interviews recorded for this project reveal that not all immigrants perceived emigration as exile and many embraced the new experiences that were opened to them in the liberal British landscape. However, tension is evident in the narratives between the immigrants' desire to transcend their past and integrate into the host society and their guilt at diluting their inherent ethnic and cultural traditions by associating with British modernity (Harte 2004: 233–251). During the 1950s the Irish clustered together in inner city parishes and the constant visibility of fellow country men reminded migrants of the indelibility of their origins.[2] While this ghettoisation was, for some, a comforting and familiar force in Britain, for others it inhibited social mobility and economic success. The body of this essay will employ extracts from recorded interviews to illustrate how these cultural, political and ethnic tensions were manifested in the immigrants' consciousness. Conclusions will suggest that immigrants who perpetually looked back to the homeland for cultural affirmation became stranded in a liminal space, unable to return to an imagined past and unwilling to immerse in a modern future.

---

2.  In 1957, 51% of Irish immigrants lived in the middle rings of Birmingham. Irish immigrants clustered particularly in Sparkbrook, Sparkhill and Balsall Heath. Irish immigrants made up between ten and twelve percent of these wards populations. Censuses of Great Britain. 1955. 1961.

A study of the Irish in Birmingham was sought out for a number of reasons. Of primary interest is the significance of the Irish population in Birmingham. Although a presence of Irish immigrants existed in the city from the post-Famine years, it would not host its greatest influx of Irish until the 1950s, during the development of the British Welfare State. The Censuses of Great Britain illustrate the proportions of the mid twentieth-century exodus to Britain and the relevance of Birmingham as an Irish immigrant locus. Between 1946 and 1971 531,255 people emigrated and roughly three quarters of these went to Great Britain. 51,000 of these Irish migrants arrived in Birmingham, yet the social and cultural impact of this Irish influx has been largely underestimated by historical research to date (Smith 1969: 26). Most studies of the Irish in Britain centre on nineteenth century migration rather than the migration of the mid-twentieth century which in some way explains this dearth in research (Swift and Sheridan 1999). As well as this, studies of the Irish have been broad-sweeping and document-based. Consequently they overlook the individual struggles of Irish migrants to balance their cultural and ethnic traditions with the modern, progressive environments that they encountered (Jackson 1986: 125–139). In contrast, the use of oral methodology, as employed in the study upon which this essay is based, illuminates the unrepresented in the migrant experience, by collecting the conscious and unconscious memories and recollections of immigrants who are unaware of the generalisations that academia has placed upon their experiences and outlooks. This results in a refreshing and reinterpreted view of Irish migration and Irishness in the twentieth century.

## Narratives of leaving- a myth of exile?

Interviewees' recollections of leaving Ireland in the 1950s encapsulated a grand-narrative of exile and loss, that Irish society expected them to internalise. Three quarters of the interviewee's emphasised that economic depression *forced* them to leave, which showed the perpetuated instincts of Irish emigrants abroad to justify their absence from the homeland. Patricia recalled getting on the train to Dublin "with tears in her eyes" having left her native Galway because no suitable employment existed (Patricia 2005). Similarly, Kathy recounted the bleak economic climate in the 1950s that allowed her no option but to go to England:

> [Q. So why did you initially decide to go to England?]
> A. Well because there were no jobs here. None whatsoever. You just couldn't get a part time job. Things were so bad that you just had to go to England whether you liked it or not. (Kathy 2007)

Economic nationalism from the pre-World War II years until 1958 implanted an aversion to self-progress and individualism in Irish society. Self-ambition proved an obstacle to the ideals of communal pastoralism that were advocated both by successive governments and the Catholic Church, which was aware of the damage that modernity and materialism had done to established churches in Britain and Western Europe. This resistence to self-progress was recognised by Inglis, who argues that self-denial was so ingrained in the Irish body and mind that it became an essential part of its social character (McKenna 2006).

Considering this socio-cultural climate, it is of little surprise that immigrants played down the personal ambitions and aspirations that influenced their decision to leave, thereby allowing the narrative of exile to reign in the national consciousness. Consequently, the oral history project discussed here and carried out approximately fifty years after the participants had emigrated, provided an important opportunity for immigrants to express the personal rather than economic decisions that influenced their departure from Ireland, without fear of vilification from a moribund tradition-bound society (Harte 2004: 239). Liam articulated in plain language his memories of growing up in rural Ireland in the 1950s which contradicted popular images of an organic, self-sufficient society:

> Yerra, 'twas desolate in Ireland, you know. There was nothing there. Really there was just nothing there. We were small farmers; there was ten of us there. Sure what would ten of us do in a small farm? As our school-master used to say to us, 'Another one for John Bull'. (Liam 2006)

The last sentence in this extract refers to the national personification of England, 'John Bull' created in 1712. John Bull was characterised as a sturdy, conservative, rational figure and explicitly contrasted with contemporary caricatures of the irrational, simian-like Irish Paddy that abounded in English print media. The narrator's reference to the figure reveals two underlying layers in the Irish migrant psyche. Firstly, it shows the immigrants' internalisation of traditional stereotypes of Irishness and Britishness that are derived from a colonial past. The position of the Irish as subordinate 'others' in England's colonial empire did not disappear after Irish independence was achieved. Interviewees' narrations confirmed that Irish immigrants in post-war Britain retained an inferiority complex that was derived from colonialism and perpetuated by negative stereotypes of Irishness that re-surfaced frequently in the 1960s and 1970s in British newspapers.[3] Raymond recalled that 'in this country [England] you were always perceived in a certain way' though he did not elaborate on what form these perceptions took (Raymond

---

3.  For examples see *Birmingham Mail,* 19 September 1973, 8 March 1977.

2006). The way in which interviewees spoke humbly of themselves, their quiescent manner in the interview and indeed their initial reluctance to be interviewed collectively illuminated the inferiority complex that pervaded Irish enclaves in Britain. Patricia exhibited this quiescence when she discussed her employment in Birmingham:

> We were living in Birmingham and it was very easy to find out about jobs. You could opt in and out of jobs in those days quite easily, you know only these mediocre jobs. Jobs that people with qualifications wouldn't take.
> (Patricia 2005)

Secondly, Liam's last sentence illustrated Irish society's passive acceptance of emigration in the 1950s. He recalled, though did not criticise, the school master's mild cynicism but ultimate acceptance that Ireland was an emigrant nursery for Britain (MacLaughlin 1994). The fact that those in positions of power perceived emigration as a natural evil in Irish society also impacted on potential immigrants who would carry with them a fatalistic attitude to emigration and a pre-conditioned hankering for a homeland that they were destined from birth to depart from.

Kathy's narrative gives insight into some personal reasons that influenced female Irish emigration. She recalled many memories of her dynamic social life in England and articulated the sense of self-identity that her career in London's hotel industry provided. These recollections contradict stereotypical images of the lonesome down-trodden migrant, as exemplified in *The Navvy*. Furthermore, they illustrate how the interview acts as a process of self-actualisation for the narrator, where past events are re-evaluated in a desensitized light. Such revelations rarely emerged at the beginning of interviews. Kathy inaugurated her interview by stating that 'you just had to go, there was nothing, *nothing* here. And if it wasn't for the money sent over from England the people would have starved here' (Kathy 2007). This captures, once again, the extent to which immigrants feel obliged to justify their absence from their birthplace. However, half-way though the interview she seemed to take stock of the positive experiences that she had encountered in England and the negative one's that she had fled from in Ireland (she had dyslexia and was bullied during her child-hood) and she admitted, in an almost confessional manner, that she was eager to leave and embraced the opportunities that England had to offer, thereby refuting a history of exile:

> Oh I was never sorry to go and when I got there I liked it. 'Twas a lot more lively than this [referring to Ireland]. And you had loads of friends, especially the Irish, they'd ask you out for tea... (Kathy 2007)

The incongruence between the immigrants somewhat hopeful attitude to leaving and Irish society's fatalistic treatment of its emigrants was also articulated unconsciously by Bridie. She recalled a sense of bemusement at the scenes of mourning that she witnessed as she boarded the boat to England;

> As I was getting in on the boat there were two fella's there and the one was playing the accordion and singing [narrator sings] 'When you return to the land of your birth there'll be no one to welcome you home' and I thought 'Oh God'! And here I am all these years later... (Bridie 2006)

One can deduct from this statement the oppressive claims that cultural nationalism placed on potential immigrants. In the closing sentence of the extract Bridie expressed a sense of validation ('and here I am all these years later') at her settlement in Birmingham, despite the fatalistic attitude of the home-society which conditioned immigrants to perceive emigration as a force that severed their identity.

## Tradition vs. modernity in post-war Britain

The claims of tradition did not disappear from the immigrant's consciousness on arrival in Britain. Indeed nostalgia for a familiar homeland intensified as immigrants struggled to come to terms with the insecurities that confronted them in England. Their heightened awareness of the 'otherness' of their dress, accent and educational/occupational experience in England influenced them to associate within exclusively Irish networks. This further facilitated the creation of an idealized memory of a utopian past. These idealizations were strengthened by the unwritten code that immigrants should not criticize the home-land in English company, a point made clear in MacAmhlaigh's memoirs of life in England in the 1950s: "The Paddies over here are very much against that kind of thing- that anyone should pretend in front of the English that things are not good in Ireland" (Iremonger 2004: 86).

Thus, the hangover from a colonised past and immigrants' self-conscious inferiority influenced an unrealistic image of home to emerge. Immigrants lodged, worked socialized and drank together as they became more convinced of the idealizations of Ireland that abounded in their consciousness. Liam reflected proudly on the ten years he spent in a lodging house with neighbour's from his hometown. He did not recall this as a peculiarly backward situation but rather stated it as an indicator of his authentic attachment to Ireland: "When we came here first we all stayed in our own living surroundings. The Irish were renowned for that. Sparkbrook, Sparkhill we came in, to an old London woman in Sparkbrook and we were with her for ten years in digs" (Liam 2006).

These close-knit associational networks enabled Irish men to transplant the social characteristics of their home-town to England's largest cities. Gaelic sports and 'manly drinking' kept old provincial rivalries and macho posturing alive in England (Harte 2004: 240). Hugh, who was unusual in that he did not subscribe to these norms of Irish masculinity, recalled working with an Irish man in England who personified these traits. He immediately joined an Irish football team on arrival in Britain and this gave him a sense of continuity and familiarity.

> I was very friendly with this one chap. And he took his whole value from being a member of the Meath football team. And I think he would be very typical now. Because he was obviously playing football for Meath. And when he went over he had this network and he continued that, which gave him a whole identity. And I know he came back to Ireland afterwards and probably just slotted back in to where he was. (Hugh 2006)

In essence, football and hurling clubs helped emigrants to forget their distance from the homeland and their outsiderness from both the home society and also minimised the need for contact with British culture. The GAA fought hard to preserve the Irish language and Irish culture in Britain and frowned on players who were seen to admire or patronise English cultural forums (O'Brien, forthcoming). The Irish language became particularly important as an ethnic indicator in Britain and interviewee's articulated their preoccupation with its preservation. Tom voiced his disgust that European languages were more popular in Ireland than the Irish language, stating that 'in Ireland now, they're doing so many languages now but they seem to be losing their own" (Tom 2006). MacAmhlaigh, a native Irish speaker, also articulated his ferocious determination to preserve an undiluted Irish dialect in England. He recalled with anger that "you have fellows coming over here and they are only a couple of days in the country and they have an English accent. There's no gob like an Irish gob" (Iremonger 2004: 86). These insights show that Englishness was perceived by Irish immigrants as a dark, corrupting influence that had to be resisted at all costs. Ironically, in Ireland, doubts about the necessity of the Irish language were being expressed in the 1960s, as the new government sought to modernise the country through the Education system to attract foreign investments and industry. The reflections of male interviewee's particularly reveal how Irish traditions could become congealed and distorted by immigrants' efforts to retain an uncorrupted, organic, and authentic Irish identity.

Irish immigrants tendency to marry and associate only with Irish people were also made clear by interviewee's (Hornsby Smith 1985). While male interviewees were traditionally more vocal about their desire to preserve their ethnicity, female interviewee's also said that they could not really contemplate marrying a foreigner, despite the fact that many of these girls had left Ireland because few marriage choices existed there. Only one of the twelve first generation Irish women that were interviewed during this project married a non-Irish partner. Bridie articulated her awareness that this ethnic exclusivity was irrational. Nevertheless, she seemed resolved to preserve this outlook; "I never think of anything only Ireland and I never mix with anybody only the Irish. That's me though, that's not good…" (Bridie 2006).

Marrying an Irish partner was not just an expression of sameness but also reflected immigrants' personal insecurities and lack of confidence in British society in the 1950s. Hugh implied this fear of forming a relationship with an English partner in the extract below:

> Funnily enough I wouldn't have gone off with English girls. I think its something to do with the unknown. I did go out with English-born girls but they were of Irish extraction. But, others I didn't, I would have met them now… and even had some opportunities but I didn't take them because I probably felt amm, a little bit, maybe insecure? I'm not too sure now… (Hugh 2006)

The claims of tradition were most strongly channeled through Irish music and Irish pubs in Britain. A spectacular abundance of songs dealing with emigration emerged during the 1950s. These were sung in pubs, clubs and dances alongside ballads that glorified Ireland's struggle for freedom and lamented the martyrs of past rebellions. Tom reflected that these nostalgic forums were essential to his survival in Britain:

> The thing that kept me going was the Irishness. You know, the music and you mixed with Irish people. I met my wife to be, Bridget, a Galway woman, on our way to mass. That's how a lot of the Irish met people, you went to Irish pubs, anything with an Irish connection. You know, you listened to the results from Ireland, listened to the Irish music because that was a part of your life and you felt safe then in your own environment. (Tom 2006)

Though immigrants were comforted by the sameness and continuity that these forums evoked, they did little to help them adapt to the realities and demands of British modernity. Pubs, music and song also influenced an unrealistic ideology of Ireland and Irishness to be created in Britain. Harte identifies how Irish immigrants in these exclusive ethnic arenas filtered the past through a benign lens so that the impoverished, claustrophobic society that they fled from was transformed into a peasant arcadia (Harte 2004: 242). This myth of Ireland has harmful repercussions for immigrants returning there in their retirement years. Several returned immigrants were interviewed during this oral history project and their shock at the reality of life in post-Celtic Tiger Ireland resonates emotionally during the interview. Patricia's narrative showed her disappointment at discovering that her most cherished memories of Ireland's open door, communal society had disappeared while the suppressive features of rural Irish life which she had filtered from her memory still existed and suffocated her once again:

> Oh I missed home terribly even when I was in England I missed Ireland. Even right up to, what am I now, seventy six, I miss Ireland. You'd always be listening for things about Ireland. You never get Ireland out of your system. But now that I'm back here I miss England because having lived there for fifty-six years I miss the shops, the buses, not the people. I miss the variety in the supermarkets and the easy access, being able to look around the shops.
> (Patricia 2005)

Essentially, Irish emigrants were never fully able to embrace the traditions of the past or the possibilities of the future. That Patricia stated 'I still miss Ireland' in this extract is extremely relevant, as this interview was recorded in her home in Ireland which she had been living in for almost two years after returning from Birmingham. Clearly the Ireland that she misses is the place that was created in the collective consciousness of the Irish in Birmingham when they arrived in the 1950s. They neither discarded nor updated this model and so rejuvenate their ethnic identity through memories of childhood and traditions of yester-year. Moira also noted her realisation that the Ireland that she recreated in Birmingham no longer represented a cultural reality. Consequently she stated that she preferred to stay in Birmingham and cling on to this dream rather than return home and admit that Ireland had moved on without her:

> The Ireland that we knew is no longer there...for those who like to go back to the way it was now this [referring to the pub in Birmingham where the interview took place] looks more Irish than Ireland now. They've got rid of things and thrown things out. (Moira 2007)

Inward-looking Irish associationalism also gave the false impression that the Irish were a homogeneous, supportive and intensely proud community in Britain. This idea was quickly shattered by interviewees' oral narratives. Many interviewees recalled the resentment, jealousy and violence that pervaded these Irish circles:

> To be truthful, and you might as well call a spade a spade, they'd shoot one another down quicker than they would pull together...If the Irish see one with less than him- no cooperation. The best people I met in the buildings were the English people, because they were fair. You'd want to watch your back with the Irish people and, like, it's an awful thing to say but that is a fact like. (Liam 2006)

Tom too related this internally destructive dynamic within Irish associationalism when he stated that "we have a very mistrusting- that may be harsh- community. To try and get people to trust, they always think you're after something for yourself. All the other ethnic groups here stand solid. We seem to fight among ourselves and lose out on the benefits" (Tom 2006).

Rudyard Kipling sums up this desire for ethnic sameness despite internal adversities in *The Stranger within my Gate*:

> The men of my own stock,
> Bitter bad they may be,
> But, at least, they hear the things I hear,
> And see the things I see;
> And whatever I think of them and their likes
> They think of the likes of me. (Kipling, Jones, Orwell 1994: 574)

## The pull of modernity

While many interviewees adhered to the norms of what Harte describes as tribalistic, sociopathic Irish networks, a minority of interviewees expressed their struggle to escape from this closed-minded Irish clique-ness on arrival in Britain. Female interviewees particularly reflected their desire to absorb the personal, economic and cultural opportunities that they encountered in the urban metropolis. Ireland in the 1950s promoted self-sacrificing mother-hood as an idealized role for women and this was also endorsed in parishes of high Irish concentration in England, where the Catholic Church continued to inform the choices of Irish immigrants Nevertheless, alternatives to this identity presented themselves to the Irish immigrant woman who absorbed the opportunities that working in the public sphere in Britain provided her. In Ireland employment opportunities for women were extremely limited in the post-war years and were generally low status tributaries of the domestic sphere such as farm servants, shop assistants and house staff. On arrival in Birmingham, women found themselves working in a varied public labour market, in buses, trams, hospitals, factories and offices that often provided opportunities for promotion. Kathy's testimony showed that carving out a successful career in a chain of London hotels changed her perspectives of her duties as a woman and led her to challenge the obligations that were placed on her, and other Irish women, in Britain:

> There was two girls, I think they were sisters, their salaries were little enough… and they used to send three pounds a week home. And sometimes, when we were going out somebody would say 'Should we ask them out as well?' and

you'd go down and ask them and they'd say 'I can't . I've no money left. I sent three pounds home.' And I said 'Do you do that every week? And I said 'Well you shouldn't, there's a big family of you there, let the others do it for a while'. But no. I thought 'twas wrong. (Kathy 2007)

Miriam, a returned emigrant, also depicted how financial independence and a career gave her the confidence to socialise in a wide variety of networks that allowed her to express her middle-class aspirations.

> You were usually asked out. To a good place for a good meal. You were there for a while before you got established. But once you were established you *were* established. People got to know you and we had an awful lot of regulars. We'd go down to Peter's Bar and you'd know everyone in Peter's Bar. There was loads of places, there was about six or seven in the area and we'd go there, 'twas great… You'd never go into a pub here (in Ireland), you'd be talked about.
> (Kathy 2007)

The associational tapestry and public profile of the Irish woman in England shifted her acceptance of her pre-destined role as wife and mother. While studies of Irish emigration attribute economic reasons as the principle factor influencing emigration, the narratives of Irish women reveal more personal reasons:

> I began to get bored of my life outside, there was nothing really there for me, I 'didn't want to settle down and then I came over here and I really enjoyed my life. The old buses were open at the back so we collected the fares, 'twas great company and we had clubs and we used to go to dances and all that, it was lovely. (Margaret 2006)

An increased awareness of personal desires was inadvertently expressed by Margaret when she stated that "It was hard when I had kids young and I couldn't afford, like, make-up, or I couldn't go to the hair dressers like other people or couldn't go out 'coz there was no one to mind the children…" (Margaret 2006).

The Irish woman's observations of British peers and their cultural norms also influenced a growing realization and criticism of the illiberal attitudes that existed in Ireland toward relationships, sexuality and marriage. Career opportunities, financial independence and a broad and varied social life, where men from all walks of life could be accessed, corroded the Irish female psyche that accepted without question a marriage of convenience and domesticity, in which profit and function, rather than love and compatibility, were the crucial components. A young Irish female author illustrated this awakening in a letter sent to the *Catholic Pictorial*:

> Unless a girl can produce a farm, business or dowry her chances of matrimony
> are pretty slim. The marriage stakes in Ireland are unjust and unfair. Whilst
> a girl liked to be married before her looks start to fade, an Irishman knows
> very well he can still find a wife when his hair is grey and his face looks like a
> contour map of West Cork.[4]

Hugh was one of few male interviewees who responded to the pull of modernity
rather than tradition in England. He was particularly drawn to the educational
and cultural activities that abounded in London and expressed frustration at his
Irish friend's indifference to these opportunities.

> Well I went to these dances and I quickly found that it wasn't the place for
> me. It was too incestually Irish. And the thing that struck me when I went
> to England was this whole different culture that I didn't know about. For
> example, access to music. I'm talking about classical music. I thought this
> was astonishing, living in North London, you could take a bus down and you
> could be in some of the major concert halls of the world and the only problem
> that I had was companionship... (Hugh 2006)

Despite Hugh's criticisms of 'incestuous' Irish associationalism he simultaneously
expressed his struggle to balance the appeals of British modernity with the expectations of his Irish peers. Though he was enlightened by new cultural possibilities
in London he was also afraid that these personal interests would alienate his Irish
peers. Consequently he hid his interest in art and music in Irish company:

> I was sketching that time. And I remember sitting out up in High Gate village
> sketching in the pub. Now if I saw any of my friends, if they were passing by,
> who were working on building sites, I would have probably ran up the nearest
> alley! (Hugh 2006)

It is then reasonable to conclude that the claims of tradition were not discarded
lightly by Irish immigrants, no matter how determined they were to benefit from
progressive British modernity. Hugh revealed the feelings of self-division and
self-doubt that he confronted as he struggled to balance these new experiences
with his own unique heritage in Britain. "I wonder", he asked at the close of the
interview, "are you losing your Irishness by being influenced by these things?"
(Hugh 2006).

Immigrants who sought economic success and social mobility through British
capitalism were also subject to the criticism of their ever-watchful Irish co-work-
ers. An aversion to self-advancement was internalised by potential immigrants

---

4.  *Catholic Pictorial,* 17 March 1963.

in the 1950s and this attitude permeated the Irish enclaves in Britain. To attain economic success was a symbol of adaption to English culture and for inward-looking migrants, this translated as a rejection of Irish culture. Consequently, immigrants were forced to disguise or limit their personal achievements and aspirations. Hugh recalled a male nurse whom he befriended in London and described how he used to deny that he was a nurse in Irish company because "it wasn't the done thing". Hugh himself admitted that "secretly I was very proud that I was now getting up a rung of the ladder" showing how self-pride was treated with contempt by Irish peer groups (Hugh 2006). Consequently, the inherent inferiority complex in the Irish enclaves and immigrants' resolve to reject English culture in favour of tradition inhibited thousands from achieving any level of economic or residential stability.[5] The interview performance showed, in real time, the programmed response of Irish immigrants to play down their personal achievements. Most interviewees emphasised their peasant backgrounds rather than their current class identity, though several discussed their children's occupations to inadvertently express their success in Britain. This rhetoric revealed, once again, the perpetuated struggle of Irish immigrants to retain the traditional values of the home society at the cost of a modern and plural identity.

In conclusion, it seems pertinent to address the influence that I, as an Irish interviewer, had on these immigrant's oral transmissions. I became conscious during the project that my ethnicity probably influenced these interviewees to exaggerate their Irish accents and regard for Irish traditions. If they did so it nevertheless reasserts the basic thesis of this chapter which argues that the Irish in Britain struggled, and still struggle, to reconfigure their ethnic identities to survive in Britain. I have discussed how the Irish struggled to fit in to Irish peer networks but of course they also had to create an identity that was acceptable to the host society. The women that I interviewed admitted that they hid their accent in public to avoid being perceived differently, though Irish men seemed less capable of plasticizing their ethnic identity. Hiding the Irish accent became a particularly important survival mechanism for the Irish in Birmingham after 1974. On 21 November of that year two bombs attributed to the I.R.A exploded in pubs in Birmingham, killing twenty one people and injuring hundreds more. These events crudely and abruptly resolved the immigrant' struggle to maintain the

5.   A number of social and economic papers discuss the disproportionate economic and social disadvantages that Irish immigrants experience in contemporary Britain. See Hickman, Mary J. and Bronwen Walter. 1997. *Discrimination and the Irish Community in Britain*. London: Commission for Racial Equality. Also Mac an Ghaill, Mairtín. 2000. The Irish in Britain: the invisibility of ethnicity and anti-Irish racism. In *Journal of Ethnic and Migration Studies* (Vol. 26) 1: 137–147, January. pp. 127–132.

nostalgic traditions of the homeland in Birmingham. Republican songs that had been popularly sung in Irish forums took on a sinister tone and migrants realised the dangerous consequences that republican idealism and indulgent cultural nostalgia could foster. Interviewee's articulated the burden of guilt and shame that was adopted by the Irish in the city following the events of November 1974. Many immediately severed links with Irish associational networks, thereby weakening the regressive tug of attachment to the home-land.

> Those days you were up in the pub and you'd sing Kevin Barry and you had the bit of banter, that all went. Oh Jesus it did, no way…the [St. Patrick's Day Parade] took a long time to come back and it never went around the city again. You had to be so careful. (Tom 2006)

Moira similarly recalled her outright rejection of any symbols of Irish nationalism after the Bombings, indicating the lengths that Irish immigrants took to avoid being linked with republican sectarianism:

> We didn't even want to know about anything like that, especially at Easter Time, they had these kind of lilies or something, little emblems, but we didn't want anything, we didn't want any trouble, we didn't really want to know at all. We had to live here and we didn't know what we'd be letting ourselves in for. (Moira 2007)

> Irish people were pleased that there was somebody arrested for it. And that it wasn't anybody belonged to them. And it did, undoubtedly, serve as a safety valve. (Raymond 2007)

As these extracts show, the 1974 Birmingham Bombings called the shared consciousness of the Irish in the city into question. Suddenly immigrants became anxious to differentiate themselves from a blanketed Irish identification and began to attribute more importance to their gender, regional background and religious devotion to avoid vilification from the host society. The 'stranger' that Kipling refers to in his poem had, in the Irish immigrant context, terrifyingly transformed from the English colonizer to the Irish terrorist and Kipling's verse echoes Irish immigrants' insecurities about what to expect next from this threatening Irish stranger:

> The Stranger within my gates.
> He may be evil or good,
> But I cannot tell what powers control –
> What reasons sway his mood;
> Nor when the gods of his far-off land,
> Shall repossess his blood. (Kipling, Jones, Orwell 1994: 574)

The ability of oral narrative to capture these moments of emotional turmoil and identify sudden processes of identity reconfiguration is testament to its relevance to modern Irish history and to the study of culture and migration in general. The narrative of exile and simplistic image of Irish immigrants humped over *The Kerryman* in an English pub has existed too long without interrogation.[6] Contemporary Irish society should be aware of the sacrifices and pressures that Irish immigrants suffered to fulfill the ideological expectations of the homeland. Oral history will, undoubtedly, become the vehicle that will channel these messages.

## References

Harte, L. 2004. 'You want to be a British Paddy?' In *Ireland in the 1950s, The Lost Decade*. D. Keogh, F. O Shea & C. Quinlan (eds). Cork: Mercier.

Hornsby Smith, M. P. 1987. *Roman Catholics in England*. Cambridge: Cambridge University Press.

Iremonger, V. 2004. *An Irish Navvy, The Diary of an Exile*. Cork: Collins Press. translated from MacAmhlaigh, D. 1964. *Dialann Deoraí*. Routledge and Kegan Paul.

Jackson, J. A. 1986. The Irish in Britain. In *Ireland and Britain since 1922* [Irish Studies 5], 125–139. Cambridge: Cambridge University Press.

Kipling, R., Jones, R. T. & Orwell (eds) 1994. *The Works of Rudyard Kipling*. Ware, Hertfordshire: Wordsworth Editions.

MacLaughlin, J. 1994. *Ireland; The Emigrant Nursery and the World Economy. Undercurrents*. Cork: Cork University Press.

McLarney, A. *The Navvy*, www.celtic-lyrics.com.

McKenna, Y. 2006. Embodied Ideals and Realities: Irish nuns and Irish womanhood, 1930–1960. *Eire-Ireland*. 41(1/2): 40–63.

O'Brien, S. Forthcoming. Irish Associational Culture and Identity in Post-war Birmingham. PhD dissertation, Mary Immaculate College.

Smith, R. J. 1969. Migration in post war Birmingham. *History of Birmingham Project Studies in Birmingham's Population* 1, Paper 9.

Swift, R. & Sheridan, G. (eds.) 1999. *The Irish in Victorian Britain, The Local Dimension*. Dublin: Four Courts Press.

## Interviews

Note: all names have been changed to protect the identities of interviewees.

Bridie, interview with the author, 24 August 2006
Hugh, interview with the author, 16 November 2006
Kathy, interview with the author, 24 May 2007

---

6.  *The Kerryman is* a provincial Irish newspaper.

Liam, interview with the author, 23 August 2006
Margaret, interview with the author, 19 January 2006
Moira, interview with the author, 1 February 2007
Patricia, interview with the author, 21 December 2005
Raymond, interview with the author, 24 August 2006
Tom, interview with the author, 24 August 2006

# Public space challenges

# Painting in sound

## Aural history and audio art

*Look up this some of this guys stuff.*

Charles Hardy III

West Chester University, Dept. of History, USA

Placing aural history practice in the context of natural and electro-acoustic sound communication, this paper explores the intersection of audio art and aural history. It includes an analysis of the creative opportunities that electroacoustic and digital media offer aural historians, a brief introduction to pioneering works on the borderland between aural history and audio art, and a short history of the author's own works in this field. The article concludes with an explanation of the benefits of creative work in audio art to oral historians, including a greater sensitivity to the power and wonder of sound communication, expanded audiences, and an enhanced appreciation of the tools of the aural historian's craft.

**Keywords:** public history, aural history, audio art, digital media

I am in the United States what is known as a "public historian". I have spent most of my career authoring histories for the listeners and viewers of public radio and television, for museum visitors, heritage tourists, K-12 teachers and students, and the general public. So one of my constant challenges has been to devise ways to bring the riches to be found in history, its lessons and morals, its conundrums and wonders, whatever select pieces of the great blooming mess that I am able to grab hold of – to folks who are free to walk past or turn the channel because something more interesting attracts, or promises to attract their attention.

A few weeks ago I attended the National Folk Festival in Richmond, Virginia, and there heard the Madison Hummingbirds play.[1] To look at them standing around you wouldn't think much: a group of close to twenty young African-American men dressed in khaki slacks and white shirts. But then they

---

1. The 69th National Folk Festival, held from October 12–14, 2007, included a broad offering of folk music from around the world.

began to play. For the first song, the American gospel classic "What a Friend We Have in Jesus", they were joined by a large woman who sang slowly and quietly with the trombones. As the tempo and volume slowly built, the singer began to exchange verses with the lead trombonist, who preached through his horn, until everyone was on their feet. Next thing I know, I am smiling and laughing in utter delight. The trombones – whose sound is impossible to capture on CD – filled the tent, drove out all fleeting thoughts and emotions, and transported us into a world of amazing joy.

As the song built in energy and tempo, the singer put on a virtuoso performance. Driven on by the band and audience, she used every ounce of her physical strength, emotion, and breath to carry us along with her. It was an amazing performance: an inspiring and uplifting musical experience.

The Madison Hummingbirds are a trombone shout band from a Sweet Daddy Grace Church in Norfolk, Virginia.[2] They are Pentacostalists, part of an American evangelical movement famous for its members speaking in tongues, snake handling, and other ecstatic forms of worship. Taking literally the Biblical injunction to "Make a joyful noise unto the Lord" (Psalm 98:4) the Daddy Grace church trombonists play their music to share God's love with the world.

Now this made me wonder, who are these people? And how do they do this? Where did they learn about these joy vibrations, and how did they figure out how to animate and sustain these transporting sounds? I suspect that none of them are rich, nor do they ask payment for their music, and as African Americans living in Norfolk they have, no doubt, their share of tribulations and sorrows. But they carry in the sound of their horns and their voices this extraordinary history and spirit.

### A sound event becomes sound history

Now I did not record that performance, but I did purchase other Madison Hummingbird sound waves on CD. That recorded sound event is now a piece of sound history, a close facsimile of their vibrations captured by electro-acoustic technologies. My memory, narrated through the sound vibrations of my voice, is another piece of history animated through sound. And as an aural historian I can use both

---

2.   Bishop C. M. Grace (1884–1960), known to his followers as Sweet Daddy Grace, was born in Cape Verde Islands, Portugal. He came to America in 1903, settled in New Bedford, Massachusetts, and in 1919 founded the United House Of Prayer For All People. In 2000, his church, headquartered in Washington D.C., had about 3.5 million members. See Dallam, M. 2007, *Daddy Grace: A Celebrity Preacher and His House of Prayer*, New York: New York University Press.

**Image 1.** Beulah Collins

to make historical sense of the Madison Hummingbirds. To further document and explore the origins of their vibrations I could record interviews to hear them tell me the history of their church, and how they make their sounds. And to amplify and contextualize the spoken words of their personal histories I also could record their sermons, rehearsals, and performances.

By making music or playing someone else's music we fill space with sound waves, and if successful, we entrain others to those vibrations; we bring to life that joy, or sorrow, or lust, or anger, or hope. The human voice conjures remembered events acoustically in the same way. This is part of the magic of language. Those memories may be sung or spoken; they may be laughed or cried, shouted or whispered. They may invite you in or warn you to stay outside (Schafer 1977).

In conducting oral history interviews, I have always delighted in people's voices, the sounds of which as much as the content of the words spoken, have engaged and enriched and informed me. Through our unique instrumental bodies, like God's trombones, we add our own voices to the great vibrational symphony of the world.

One memorable instrument, for me, in that great aural symphony is the voice of Beulah Collins, who was eighty-eight when I first interviewed her in a senior centre in West Philadelphia in 1983. Hers was a humble but valorous story. Understated in appearance, she told me of her move to Philadelphia from the eastern shore of Maryland after the death of her husband during the influenza epidemic of 1918; of placing her young son in another's home while she worked as a live-in maid so that "my boy could get an education"; of her never remarrying for fear that a stepfather "might not be good to my boy"; of his success – learning to read, he became a school principal – and of her intention to be buried "back home" beside her husband in a graveyard in rural Maryland, a place she had not seen in more than sixty years. Beulah died more than twenty years ago; but I still have her voice, laughing and singing, questioning, and telling the story of her life, however partial, disguised, and shaped during her encounters with the nice young white boy from the radio station.

I interviewed Collins again in 1984 for "Goin' North: Tales of the Great Migration", an oral-history based radio documentary series on the history of African-American migration from the American South to the city of Philadelphia during the early decades of the twentieth century. From her two interviews I also produced an 8-minute autobiographical vignette, "Beulah Collins", which aired on National Public Radio in 1986.[3]

Now in producing her condensed autobiographical vignette, I edited close to three hours of reminiscence into a compelling narrative from the life story that she provided me, and in doing so I took some artistic license. The sound of crickets that I used as an ambient bed I recorded in Goochland County, Virginia, some eighty miles from the eastern shore of Maryland. But those crickets, that natural soundscape, is also part of the sound history of rural America and of Beulah's life. I used the sound of a vacuum cleaner, a sound marker associated with domestic work, as punctuation to denote a change of scenes. I didn't use much of it. Like a good spice, a little goes a long way and too much, by drawing attention to itself, can spoil the dish. So the audio producer, like a chef, must have good ingredients and use them skillfully. To cook in sound we need the human voice, natural and human soundscapes, sound markers, music, and other sound events.

Oral history interviews, as we all know, are performative, and each person's vocalizations – language, accent, intonation, sonority, cadence, tonality, vocabulary – the whole complex symphony of verbal expression, is living history, a

3.  Excerpts of her interviews I also included in *Goin' North: Tales of the Great Migration*, an oral-history based radio documentary series, available on the Talking History website, <http://www.talkinghistory.org/hardy.html.> 1 March 2008.

historical artifact, a vessel of culture forged over centuries of communal expression that then emerges from the unique form of each of our bodies and lives. Listen to your grandparents, to any nonagenarian, to recordings of Jean Harlow, or Mussolini, or Martin Luther King, or Marilyn Monroe; there is no way for the imagined world of the written word or the best of actors of stage and screen to touch the authentic voices captured by aural historians.

## The call to audio art

In the early 1980s I was producing ½-hour oral history-based sound documentaries for public radio in Philadelphia, and feeling increasingly imprisoned by the standard radio documentary formula that alternated continuity (narration) and actuality (recorded events), transitioned by music and sound effects. I also was fascinated by how the interviews that I and others were conducting contained within them deep truths and beauties in the sounds of interviewees' voices as much as in their words; ineluctable qualities that were suppressed and muted in audio and video documentaries. And I was thrilled by how combining a recollection with a related archival recording related to that memory amplified its meaning and brought it to life in what were to me magical ways.

The electromagnetic capture and reproduction of sound is truly one of the wonders of the modern world. Because of its ubiquity, we tend to forget that sound recording and electric-acoustical communication are still, from the perspective of human history, in their infancy; that not until the late 1800s did we have the ability for the first time to capture, store, and call back into existence facsimiles of sonic events that had until then existed only at the moment of their creation. One of the first uses Thomas Edison imagined for his phonograph was capture of the words and voices of the great men and women of his age for the benefit of future generations (Hardy III & Dean 2006).

Less than a century ago, radio-telephony was "the riddle of the ages", an invisible Aladdin's lamp that swept aside the barriers of time and space, ending the isolation under which humankind had labored since the dawn of time – or so the media utopians wrote. Hindered neither by mountains or oceans, walls or weather, electromagnetic signals sped out in all directions, and could be plucked from the air with little more than some copper wire and a crystal. Imagine the thrill of listening for the first time to the jumble of voices and music; to the words of presidents and kings, to the fiery crash of the Hindenburg, and the imminent consequences of the Martian invasion – a radiophonic narrative some Americans

L ong awaited and eagerly anticipated, **Mordecai Mordant's Celebrated Audio Ephemera,** a world renowned revivification of the sounds of the past resurrected through the magic of radio studio production, is now available for broadcast.

Dedicated to the proposition that the long since abandoned and all but forgotten is as good as anything on the contemporary scene, **Celebrated Audio Ephemera** is a series of 5 minute audio curiosity cabinets; past pastiches composed of only the very finest audio detritus selected carefully from the rugged survivors of a turbulent ocean of sounds washed up upon the shores of the arch preservationist, Mordecai Mordant.

∎

Listen to rasping recrudescences of sound as hard steel grinds its course through grooves of shellacked bakelite spinning at dizzying speeds of 70, 75, 80 revolutions per minute!

Wonder at the wizened vocalizations of hoary octa - and nonagenerians as they resurrect transient moments from previously unrecorded youths!

Marvel at Professor Mordant's unparalled skills in the esoteric science of audio-studio production.

Return to the days of wonder, when radio telephony was a dream, horses pulled fire engines, America was America, and nothing was impossible!

∎

Yes, **Mordecai Mordant's Celebrated Audio Ephemera,** programs for the ages, present incontrovertible, living proof of the proposition that the tried and true and forgotten is at least as good as the all new and improved. And they come to you either seamless or fully self-contained.

∎

Make a note of this vital information! Audio Ephemera is available by satellite over the NPR system on: Tuesday, November 11th, 1986 13:00-13:59 hrs., Channel 8 and Tuesday, November 18th, 1986 13:00-13:59 hrs., Channel 8

Program Titles:
EXERCISE 6: FIRE
NOTHING IS IMPOSSIBLE
EXERCISE 8: AMERICA IS AMERICA
ETHER ORDER
VIRGINSKA
IT'S JUST LIKE ANYTHING ELSE.
EXERCISE 7: THE PUGILISTS
AND our feature presentation, THE PRODIGAL SON.

∎

Lengths: This special introductory edition of **Mordecai Mordant's Celebrated Audio Ephemera** is composed of seven, 5 minute modules, and one, 8 minute feature piece.
Mode: mono (of course)
Use: Unrestricted — upon return of response card.

∎

W ho is Mordecai Mordant? Professor Mordecai Mordant, M.R.P., grand purveyor of the passe and dedicated doyen of dotage, is the noted originator and pastmaster of audio archeo-frottage. This edition of **Celebrated Audio Ephemera** he fashioned with the able assistance of Mr. Charles Hardy of Overbrook Farms at **Toucan Productions** in Philadelphia, a state-of-the-art production facility which enabled expression of the full wizardry of Professor Mordant's skills at audio-legerdemain.

∎

**Mordecai Mordant's Celebrated Audio Ephemera** was made possible through the wisdom and foresight of the **Pennsylvania Council for the Arts** and the **National Endowment of the Arts,** a federal agency.

∎

For further information about this unique offering, please contact Toucan Productions in Philadelphia. **(215) 732-3784.**

∎

**Image 2.** Brochure, "Mordecai Mordant's Audio Ephemera

briefly mistook, on the eve of the Second World War, for the unfolding end of extraterrestrial destruction.[4]

When conducting aural history interviews we all hear and experience such memorable moments. Sometimes they stand out because of the history they reveal, sometimes because of how they advance our scholarly agenda; sometimes, too, they stay with us for reasons that are hard to articulate – because they speak to us in more mysterious and personal ways. Now what might happen, should the aural historian take those memorable words spoken about the past and then combine them with other sonic artifacts – like a Madison Hummingbird's musical sermon – and create a narrative or poem or sculpture or montage not for the purposes of historical scholarship, but instead, to paint with sound; to sculpt through speakers or headphones? What might it sound like if the aural historian became a bricoleur of audio ephemera and treated sound artifacts as ends in themselves; as God's trombones?

Having grown bored with the standard form of radio documentary, I received grants in 1985 that enabled me to produce a series of six, five-minute oral history-based audio montages and one eight-minute piece, "The Prodigal Son", that I titled "Mordecai Mordant's Celebrated Audio Ephemera". Here my objective was to re-animate the lost worlds revealed in the interviews and old phonograph recordings by weaving together snippets of sonic artifacts into "past pastiches" short enough – I hoped – not to wear out their welcome, and long enough to take listeners into far off places.

I built the montages around life transforming moments, symbolic events, and magical tales. In "It's Just Like Anything Else" I combined a septagarian's recollection of his own rite of passage when he had crossed the threshold from childhood to maturity by leaving his house – by the back door – for the first time in a pair of long pants with an octogenarian's still empowering account of having the local barber cut off her long, beautiful hair in the early 1920s against the wishes of her father, and three octogenarians laughing recollections of their first rule-bending applications of lipstick and rouge. In "Ether Order," three elderly men return to boyhood as they describe the process of capturing disembodied voices and music from the air with copper wire wrapped around a Quaker Oats box, which I combined with novelty records from the 1920s to reconjure the thrill of radio in its early days. "Exercise 6: Fire," I built around the tale of a retired fire horse pulling a milk wagon at breakneck speed down a city street without his driver in pursuit of fire bells in

---

4.  Orson Welles' radio play of H. G. Well's novel *War of the Worlds* is one of the most famous radio broadcasts in American history. Performed as a Halloween special on October 30, 1938, the broadcast's first half hour was presented as a series of news bulletins that suggested that an actual Martian invasion was in progress.

**Image 3.** Virginia Bartow, circa 1934

the distance and an exercise instruction record from the 1920. In "Nothing is Impossible," a Jewish nonagenarian who had grown up in a rural Russian shtetl shares his delighted rumination on the marvels of electric lights, automobiles, and other modern inventions before concluding that "nothing is impossible". In "Virginska," octogenarian New York concert singer Virginia Bartow evokes the Russian romanticism of American high society during the 1920s through her loving reminiscence of how her Russian voice teacher – Andrew Salama, a member of Nikita Balieff's

Chauve Souris – introduced her to a fantastical world of timeless love, transcendental beauty, and agonizing yearning that had filled the great emotional void of her own life, and that she gave voice to more than a half century later by singing the Russian folk songs she had mastered before the Second World War ended her hopes of a professional career.[5] These were some of the disembodied and iconic fragments of sound and recollection that my alter ego Mordecai Mordant layered with fragments of voices and instruments and sounds fossilized on ceramic discs in the early 1900s; acoustical vibrations and electromagnetic signals reanimated and combined through analog open reel electrical-acoustic technologies and the legerdemain of audio collage.

In the final feature piece, "The Prodigal Son", I animated eighty-eight-year-old James Plunkett's account of how he had been led astray by the "bright lights", when as a young man he had moved from rural Virginia to Philadelphia during the First World War, by interweaving his story with verses from a phonographic recording of James Weldon Johnson's famous 1928 poem "God's Trombones". This combined narrative I then embedded in recordings of African-American sermons, jazz bands, and spoken word routines from the 1920s and early 1930s.[6]

Now these pieces may not be to your liking. Listener response was mixed. Here, however, is where I encourage that you listen to any oral history interview and piece of audio art with an ear towards what you might create as the universe speaks to you in response to your own purposes. And here, I propose, is another value of audio art to the aural historian: it has a good chance of holding its value. I cannot read my own scholarship without hearing disembodied censoring voices; critiques of weak or obtuse writing, of dated interpretations and methodology, and all manner of other faults and shortcomings. Listening to Audio Ephemera, on the other hand, still makes me smile, and carries me back into those worlds of wonder.

---

5.  A variety show that had its beginnings in Moscow in the early 1900s, the Chauve Souris in the 1920s attained international success with its mix of dance, theater sketches, folk music, and comedy. After arriving in New York in 1922, the troupe appeared on Broadway throughout the 1920s. For an introduction to its history see Sullivan, L. 1986–1987. Nikita Baliev's Le Theatre de la Chauve-Souris: An Avant-Garde Theater. *Dance Research Journal*, Vol. 18, No. 2 (Winter): 17–29.

6.  Distributed as an independent series over the National Public Radio satellite, "Mordecai Mordant's Celebrated Audio Ephemera" was carried by more than 30 stations but has never been released on CD or published on the web. "The Prodigal Son" and other pieces can be heard on the Talking History website. <http://www.talkinghistory.org/hardy.html.> 1 March 2008. To learn more about its history see Hardy III, Ch. 2001. Prodigal Sons, Trap Doors, and Painted Women: Reflections on Life Stories, Urban Legends, and Aural History. *Oral History: Journal of the Oral History Society* 29(1): 98–105.

### From painting to sculpting in sound

"Mordecai Mordant's Audio Ephemera" was an experiment, some of the short-comings of which I became acutely aware of even while producing the pieces. One of the biggest problems, to my ears, was sound quality. Determined to be true to the early days of sound recording, I produced Audio Ephemera in mono.

Image 4

Once in the studio, engineer Len Perskie and I quickly discovered that the limited dynamic range and noise of archival recordings restricted our ability to layer sounds.[7] The montage of sounds I wanted people to hear became unintelligible when layered monaurally. The solution was obvious: instead of painting with sound on a flat, one-dimensional monaural surface, why not sculpt? This I could do by increasing the number of channels. Stereo was the obvious choice, but what, I wondered, would happen if I had four separate channels of audio to work with instead of two?

So in 1987 I received enough grant money to produce "This Car to the Ballpark", an 18-minute quadraphonic audio arcade produced from oral histories, archival recordings, contemporary music, and sound manipulations created on a digital sampler. My engineer this time was Jay Allison. After placing a speaker in the each corner of the studio, we laid the tracks and experimented moving sounds around and through the room. The effect, for me, was magical. Four channels opened the space, and the movement of sound – a train moving diagonally through the room from the left rear to right front corner, a voice moving slowly around us as it passed from one speaker to the next, volleys and cascades of instruments and voices bursting around us from four different directions, one voice in the left speakers and the other in the right conversing across the room, and the constant movement of sounds made this "star-lit world", the Ballpark's concluding words, come to life.

I built "This Car to the Ballpark" around four voices: 100-year-old William Robinson's account of how a white landlord threatened to put him on a chain gang for stealing three peaches in the 1880s, ninety-five-year-old Louise Smith's account of resisting peer pressure to become a prostitute and her own desire to kill her philandering husband in the 1920s; seventy-eight-year-old George Baker's reminiscence of fire engine horses in the 1910s, and eighty-year-old Virginia Bartow's recollections of the tragic life of her Princeton educated husband (class of 1922), who "never learned to dance".

The piece begins with a disoriented phone message, left on an answering machine by Virginia Bartow just days before her death in 1987, then sequeways to an excerpt from an oral history interview in which she recalled the thrill of running down a hill as a child to greet a train after she was released from a rope to which her parents had tied her in the early 1900s. It then moves to montages built around interview excerpts with elderly African Americans' William Robinson and Louise Smith, white-working class Philadelphian George Baker, and then

---

7.   My engineer on "Mordecai Mordant's Celebrated Audio Ephemera" was Len Perskie of Toucan Productions in Philadelphia. A painter turned audio engineer, Perskie was a perfectionist who brought an artist's sensibility to radio production.

back to Virginia Bartow, each animated with period phonographic recordings. Transitions from one montage to another I threaded together with excerpts from a 1930s' novelty recording of a conductor calling out stops along a street car ride to "the Ballpark". In effect, the featured pivotal memories of each person's life become stops on an imaginary trolley ride. In the final montage, the voices and sound artifacts of Bartow and Smith – of the world of wealthy Anglo-American and working-class African-American culture – are combined, and the piece ends with Smith reciting the lyrics of a gospel song composed by her minister, Charles Albert Tindley, over Bartow's playing of a Russian folksong, "The Nightingale".

The expense of presenting quadraphonic audio in the 1980s and 1990s – it required four speakers, a four-track open-reel analog tape deck, two amplifiers, and a mix board – the logistical challenges of moving and setting up the hardware, and the acoustical challenges of performance spaces restricted playback of "This Car to the Ballpark" to a handful of venues. These included *Earfest: The Theatre of Sound*, a national juried festival of audio soundworks, and the 1988 Oral History Association annual meeting in Baltimore, during which the audience was invited to move around the room. The denseness and movement of sound thrilled some people and disquieted others. Both "Mordecai Mordant's Audio Ephemera" and "The Car to the Ballpark" made extensive use of low-fidelity 78rpm recordings, which pose an additional challenge to novice listeners. Digitally recorded live sounds and digitally remastered archival recordings eliminate the sonic challenges of working with low-fidelity recordings in the production of audio art and aural history documentaries.

## Oral history and audio art

The rapid development of affordable digital technologies since the 1980s has both simplified and democratized our ability to author in sound, and the Internet, wireless transmission, and portable receivers have shattered radio, phonograph record, audio cassette, and CD into an expanding option of new media for dissemination into the ever-growing global docuverse. The last few decades have also witnessed the emergence of the related fields of sound studies and sound histories (see Bull and Les Back 2004; Erlmann 2004; Smith 2004; Sterne 2002).

Multi-channel audio art and aural histories are now a viable option for oral historians, museums, and others. In recent years, a number of artists-turned-aural historians and oral historians-turned-artists have begun to turn to audio art (see Kahn and Whitehead 1994; Kahn 2001; Labelle 2006; Hardy III 2006).

Audio art and oral history have a natural affinity. Storytelling and reminiscence, as we oral historians repeatedly intone, are by their nature aural forms.

Scholars exploring their performative nature continue to change the way that we think about the oral history interview and its uses. That the intersection of theater and oral history has become a vital subfield of oral history practice is demonstrated both in papers presented at this conference and in *Remembering: Oral history and Performance,* a fascinating collection of nine essays on "oral history-based performance", edited by Della Pollock and published by Palgrave Macmillan in 2005.[8]

Oral historians, however, have devoted far more attention to radio documentary and to theatre than to audio art or other media arts. Sound documentary producers are comparatively numerous, and many of them highly skilled. But most documentarians' interest in oral history interviews is for the information contained within them; not their physical properties – both psycho-acoustic and electroacoustic – their aesthetic qualities, or the deeper truths about the human condition that can be found within them. A handful of folks, however, have begun to explore in the borderlands between audio art and aural history, and to identify their work as "audio art".[9]

The new edition of *The Oral History Reader* includes an article on artist Graeme Miller's "Linked" project in London. This public art installation, which opened in 2003, represents a fascinating hybrid of public history and audio art (Butler and Miller 2006). Miller and other researchers interviewed local citizens and road protesters who bear "witness to the disastrous impact the M11 link road has had on his local neighbourhood since its construction in the 1990s". Miller then mounted twenty transmitters high on lampposts along a six-lane motorway in east London that continuously broadcast the audio montages he created from these interviews and other sound elements. Billed as "a landmark in sound, an invisible artwork, a walk", Linked takes listeners on an audio Easter Egg hunt for recordings that use musicality, including repetition and silences, "to build in space for thought both within the broadcasts and between the receivers". To bring the past to life, Miller also instructed some of his narrators speak in the present tense, viewing the past in their mind's eye as if it were happening in front of them.[10]

The co-author of the article on the Linked project is Toby Butler, who in 2005 produced "MemoryScape Audio Walks: Voices from the hidden history of the

8.   In her introduction, Pollock notes that the telling of oral histories, the making of history in dialogue, is inherently performative. Each interview is a heightened encounter with each other and the past, performance existing in that liminal space between then and now. For Pollock, the oral history interview as "an ignition point" for people who use oral history in theater.

9.   I must apologize in advance for only mentioning British and American projects; my knowledge of those working in other countries and languages is sorely lacking.

10.   See Miller, G. *Linked.* http://www.linkedm11.info/.; Lavery, C. 2005. The Pepys of London E11: Graeme Miller and the Politics of Linked. *New Theatre Quarterly* 21: 148–160.

Thames": two fascinating and pathbreaking riverside audio walking tours that use sounds, oral history interviews, and archival recordings to explore the hidden history of twenty-three stops along the Thames River in London. Butler supplemented his own oral history interviews with others housed at the London Museum, then set these in binaural soundscapes that he recorded with bud mikes.[11]

Both of these fascinating projects place their oral histories back into the physical worlds they document. And they demonstrate the expanding opportunities that new digital media tools provide us for doing so. Both place their audiences in the actual physical locations of the history, and permit browsers to chart their own way through the programming. Smith equips visitors with wireless receivers that capture the programming from strategically placed transmitters. Butler's tours can be purchased on CD, with maps, at the London Museum or downloaded to an MP3 player from the MemoryScape website – along with a full printed transcript. Both, too, have created websites that include interactive maps, photographs, and other complementary documents. On his, Graham embeds the location of the transmitters in a satellite map of his tour area.

### Conclusion: On the ease and advantages of audio art to the oral historian

These tours are but two examples of the many new forms of aural history/audio art enabled by digital media. They also highlight aspects of the digital revolution's impact on oral history practice, which include the following.

Audio art improves oral historians' technical skills. When one authors in sound, a poorly recorded voice and soundscape is like a beautiful portrait, once alive with detail and color, and now obfuscated irreparably beneath layers of dirt and old varnish. Once one thinks of the interview as a sound event, as a precious sonic artifact, as a dramatic performance, the tools that one uses to capture sounds – and moving images – as accurately as possible, become very important. The components of one's field recording kit – field recorder, microphones, headphones, and so forth – become essential tools of one's art and craft. This makes perfect sense to a documentary photographer, painter, sculptor, musician, or scientist. Oral historians whose objective in the use of their field recording hardware is limited to the intelligibility of spoken words, lack the artist and musician's concern for the physical properties of the materials by which they create.

---

11. See Memoryscape Audio Walks, http://www.memoryscape.org.uk/ and the February 12, 2007 interview with Butler published online at ReadySteadyBook, http://www.readysteady-book.com/Article.aspx?page=tobybutler. 1 March 2008.

The move into aural history and audio art broadens oral historians' responsibilities. It requires, for example, that oral historians record the historically specific and historically endangered soundscapes, sound objects, and sound artifacts of a narrator's life and community, all of which are important historical documents, and all of which are needed by authors in multimedia.

The tools for audio art production are affordable and comparatively easy to learn and use. The basic requirements are a good field recorder and microphone, laptop computer, and digital audio workstation shareware.

Digital scholarship and audio art are collaborative endeavors. The digital revolution presents wonderful opportunities for aural historians work with people who have the technical skills and training in the arts, especially digital media arts, that most oral historians' lack.

Audio art can enhance oral historians' abilities to hear and to listen.

Audio art, by the nature of its focus, can enhance, open, and deepen oral history scholarship.

Audio art can broaden aural historians' audiences. Sound and thought both emerge out of silence; they are energy events. We as a species take in and experience the world as much through our ears as though our eyes. Moving from the written word to sound enables aural historians to reach those who spend little time reading and a great deal of time listening.

Audio art is a realm of open exploration in which one can use memories and sound artifacts to compose, sculpt, fabricate, reveal–insert the verb or verbs of your choice – to make sense of the human condition through recorded sounds.

# References

Bull, M. & Back, L. (eds). 2004. *The Auditory Culture Reade*. Oxford: Berg Publishers.

Butler, T. & Miller, G. 2006. Linked: A landmark in sound, a public walk of art. In *The Oral History Reader,* R. Perks & A Thomson (eds), 425–434. London: Routledge.

Erlmann, V. (ed) 2004. *Hearing Cultures: Essays on Sound, Listening and Modernity*. Oxford: Berg Publishers.

Hardy III, C. 2006. Authoring in sound: Aural history, radio, and the digital revolution. In *The Oral History Reader,* R. Perks & A Thomson (eds), 393–406. London: Routledge.

Hardy III, C. & Dean, P. 2006. Oral history in sound and moving image documentaries. In *Handbook of Oral History*, T. L. Charlton (ed.). Lanham MD: Altamira Press.

Kahn, D. 2001. *Noise, Water, Meat: A History of Sound in the Arts*, Cambridge MA: The MIT Press.

Kahn, D. & Whitehead, G. 1994. *Wireless Imagination: Sound, Radio, and the Avant-Garde*, Cambridge MA: The MIT Press.

Labelle, B. 2006. *Background Noise: Perspectives on Sound Art*. London: Continuum.

Pollock, D. (ed.). 2005. *Remembering: Oral History Performance* [Studies in Oral History]. New York NY: Palgrave.

Schafer, M. R. 1977. *The Tuning of the World*. New York NY: Random House.

Smith, M. M. 2004. *Hearing History: A Reader*. Atlanta GA: University of Georgia Press.

Sterne, J. 2002. *The Audible Past: Cultural Origins of Sound Reproduction*. Durham NC: Duke University Press.

## Appendix

"This Car to the Ballpark" (1988)
A 14 minute, 49 second, stereo memento mori.
Producer: Charles Hardy III
Engineer: Jay Allison, Woods Hole, MA.

"This Car to the Ballpark" was first created as a quadraphonic audio montage produced from oral histories, archival recordings, contemporary music, and sound manipulations created on a digital sampler. This annotated transcript is for the shortened stereo remix of the original 18-minute composition.

## Introduction: "The phone call"

MUSICAL OPENING (Untitled composition, Charles Hardy, 1987, performed on Oberheim Matrix 6 synthesizer)

ANSWERING MACHINE MESSAGE, VIRGINIA BARTOW (Virginia Bartow to Charles Hardy, March 1987): Charlie this is Virginia. I seem to be ill and I want you to come and get me Deary, I – you've got to come and get me. They're keeping me here. They're supposed to be on a picnic, but I'm not myself and I want you to come and get me. I must see you. Charlie. I must see you. I've got to, I've got to see you Deary, I've got to see you, I'm alright, but I was sick last night. See you dear –

RECORDED OPERATOR (Recording a telephone operator, 1987): If you'd like to make a call, please hang up and try again. If you need help, hang up and then dial the operator –

BARTOW: That's it dear, he's out. Operator did you get that, and I must get him in. But I've got to speak to Charlie, there's something the matter with me. Please the number is 879 –

RECORDED OPERATOR: If you'd like to make a call please hang up and try again. If you need help, hang up and then dial the operator.

SOUND OF DIAL TONE

SOUND BRIDGE: DINNERTABLE CONVERSATION: (Hardy Family Reunion, private recording, 8 October 1983.)

BARTOW (Interview with Virginia Hardy Bartow, 26 August 1985.) And father was very serious about me being a musician. He wanted all his children to be something.

MUSICAL BRIDGE: "The Nightingale", private recording OF Russian folk song transcribed by Andrew Salama and sung by Virginia Bartow, circa 1962.

I was put out in a field in a place where there were trees and I was tied to a little doll carriage. And any time my doll freed itself I rushed after it and picked it up, and tied myself back up to the tree again. Wasn't that a funny reaction. And the family used to laugh at me. But then one day they let go of the ropes and I went flying down millions of stairs to the railroad tracks. I loved the railroads so.

SFX: TRAIN and WHISTLE (Recording of B&O locomotive)

BARTOW: We were another world; a starlit world.

## Scene 2: "Three peaches"

STREET CAR CONDUCTOR, from novelty recording, "Ballpark" produced by Helen Meyers, Blue Bird, B-644-B: Ding ding. Ballpark this car goes to the ballpark. Fares please. Ten cents lady. Transfer sir? Where to? No lady, this car goes to the ballpark, ballpark car here, fares please.

SOUND BRIDGE: "Rosie", Negro Prison Songs, Tradition, 1958. Soundscape recording of crickets, Goochland County, Virginia

WILLIAM ROBINSON (Interview with William Robinson, 25 July 1983): I was born December the 11th, 18 and 80. And therefore the Lord has brought me safe this far and no marks against me. Nothing like that. Everything I did, I tried to do it and if I saw it, you done something and if I knowed it was wrong, I'd run and get away from you cause them white folks was strict.

SHORT MUSICAL BRIDGE: "Rosie"

ROBINSON: I had done something one time and that was this. I didn't go into the orchard, but I received three peaches. Well, the man said "The receiver is just as bad as the rogue". See, that's why – I didn't go into the orchard and I listened right in the man's face when he said if I was just a little older – I wasn't but 8 years old – that resented it just a little bigger, "I'd put him on the chain gang". I listened right at him. And I was scared because I heard them working on it. I was never on it. But I heard them working, heard singing on that and working on the roads.

MUSICAL BRIDGE: (chain gang singing) "Hot Summer Days", Negro Prison Songs, Tradition, 1958.

THUNDERSTORM SFX (Recorded in Goochland County, Virginia, summer 1983)

ROBINSON: My father had to pay $21 for three peaches. He had to pay it because I received the peaches there. And the white man was the one that looking right at him just like I'm looking at you and I heard him say if he was just a little bit bigger I'd put him on the chain gang, and I was scared to death. But them three peaches learnt me a lesson. It learnt me a lesson that don't take what isn't yours.

FOUR-CHANNEL AUDIO MONTAGE, includes:
"Why I'm a Klansman", The 100% Americans, KKK Label, Indianapolis, Indiana, circa 1924.

"Special Demonstration Double Disc" Columbia, 1912.
William S. Hart, Promotion for the 1925 motion picture, "Tumbleweeds".
"Explanation of the Objective of the U. N. I. A.", Marcus Garvey, See Bee G453.
Promotion for the 1929 Motion picture "Innocents of Paris". Reminiscence with Irving Kauffman, The Recording Pioneers Phonograph Record Enterprise, LP101, 1974.

## Scene 3: "I kicked over the table"

BARTOW: They were lost and the girls too were lost, the debutantes. And I remember thinking I was glad I was studying while I was a debutante. I was a very poor debutante. I wasn't like the girls and they didn't care for me.

MUSICAL BRIDGE: "Sitting on Top of the World", circa 1930.

BARTOW: But the girls who made the hits those days would dance with the man, then move away and dance with another man and just raise hell. They thought they were terrific, those Cabots and Lodges that only speak to God, you know. That was a terrible era in New York and Boston.

STREET CAR CONDUCTOR ("Ballpark"): Blabber Street, watch your step. Watch your step there, watch your step. All right, step up. Fares please, fares. This car goes to the ballpark, ballpark car here. Fares please.

MUSICAL BRIDGE: "The Charleston is the Best Dance of All" Charlie Johnson's Paradise Ten, Victor 21491, 1928.

SFX: (Sound of people at a party, recorded 1984)
"The Prodigal Son", James Weldon Johnson, Musicraft 1084, circa 1937.

LOUISE SMITH (Interview with Louise Smith, 24 September 1984.): They used to go in these places where the girls used to dance and they throw out money on the floor at them on the stand at them. And they would be dancing and wiggling and carrying on. Well things like that, my mother never raised us that way. So therefore I didn't go in for that. And my mother taught us when we was at home to keep out of bad company and then you would keep out of trouble. And so, that's the one thing, I never – a person that I know would go to this place or that place – I may have gone with them once, but after I found out what they were doing, I quit. I didn't go no more.

SHORT MUSICAL BRIDGE: "The Charleston is the Best Dance of All" Charlie Johnson's Paradise Ten, Victor 21491, 1928.

SFX: (Woman moaning, recorded 1987)

SMITH: In Atlantic City there was a bunch from Virginia that I knew, and they said we are going out tonight and having a big time. And I didn't know what they meant. And they went to a beer garden and they were drinking beer and they were singing. They tried to make me drink beer. That's the night that I kicked over the table. One girl had a hold of my hand and the other was trying to pour the stuff in me. And I yanked that and and [SFX: TABLE CRASHING, GLASSES

BREAKING] kicked the table and kicked the whole thing over. And then I broke away from them and never went with them no more.


## Scene 4: "And he showed how the devil pranced"

STREET CAR CONDUCTOR: Kindly move back in the car please, there's plenty of seats in the rear. Move back. Next stop Clancy Street, Clancy Street. Transfer for Hoodoo Heights. Transfer for Hoodoo Heights here....

SFX: Railroad Train interior rumble slowed down on a Roland Sampler.

BARTOW: And Ned was always very polite, but you know when it came to things like making the family punch, he would fuss and fuss and fuss. They were fussers the Bartows. And he'd never do it and get mad and finally I'd do it and he just never could be graceful. And he wouldn't learn to dance. See how he suffered. Wasn't that awful. A boy who wanted to dance and be a jolly boy. He had no chance. He went to the wrong boarding school and went to Princeton, a terrible place in those days. So he never found himself.

SFX (Cows mooing manipulated on a Roland Sampler to sound like long, low moaning).

SMITH: One night I attempted to kill my husband. I went to the store on South Street and bought the gun and had taken the money out to pay the man to kill him and as true as I would have bought that gun he would have been dead and I'd be pulling time. But something spoke to me just as plain and said "Vengeance is mine. And I will repay sayeth the Lord". [SOUND BED OF AFRICAN-AMERICAN PREACHER BUILDING IN BACKGROUND: "The Downfall of Nebuchadnezzar", Reverend J. C. Burnett, Columbia 14166-D, 1926.] Instead of buying the gun I came on to church on a Tuesday night's prayer meeting. Dr. Tindley got up that night and he told how the Devil gets you in trouble but he never knowed nobody who the devil got out. And after the Devil gets you, he showed how he pranced. And when he got through I went to him like a child and cried on his shoulder and told him he was talking to me, cause I had just attempted to get a gun.

BRIDGE: Reverend J. C. Burnett, "The Downfall of Nebuchadnezzar".

SMITH: I went home that night right around at 1522 Catharine Street, I got down on my knees and I prayed to the Lord. I cried. I prayed. I cried. Every time I went to get up it was like somebody pushed me right back. I stayed down there until the burden was lifted and when the burden was lifted I felt like I had wings, I could fly.

MUSICAL BRIDGE: "Certainly Lord", Deacon A. Wilson & Choir, (Webster Hotel in Chicago), Victor 20423, 1926.


## Scene 5: "An American Tragedy"

STREET CAR CONDUCTOR: Clancy Street. Watch your step now getting off. Let the passengers off please. This car goes all the way to the ballpark. Fares. Ten cents lady. Fares, put them in. Plenty of seats in the rear of the car. Move back please, lots of seats.

MUSICAL BRIDGE: "Slumming on Park Avenue", Ray Noble & his Orchestra, Victor 25507-A, 1937.

BARTOW: He had an Uncle who was a partner of J. P. Morgan, but Nevett was never popular. He was awkward. He was terribly awkward. His father did nothing about it. He used to look at him. "What is this boy saying?" And I think Ned's life was an American tragedy.

SMITH: Cause that's where all crimes begin at, home. If you don't train a child – because my mother taught us that book, "Train a child in the way he should go and when he grows old he won't depart from it". And I'm a witness. I've lived past ninety years and I know what it is. And I tried to follow her teaching and my father's teaching.

FOUR CHANNEL AUDIO MONTAGE, including:
"The Warbler's Serenade", Arthur Pryor's Band, Victor, 17380-B.
"The Steamer Trunk", Party Records, circa 1934.
"Sounds of the Forest", Charles Kellogg "The Nature Singer", Victor 55092-A.


## Conclusion: "A Star-lit World"

STREET CAR CONDUCTOR: Raidy's Ballpark. Last stop. Raidy's ballpark, all out. Ballpark, last stop here

SFX: Crowd noises

MUSICAL BRIDGE "The Nightingale", private recording, Virginia Bartow, circa 1962.

SMITH: A Better day is coming. No more shall Lords and Rulers their Heavy victim pressed, Shall bar the door against the poor and leave them in distress. But God the King of Glory who hears the Raven cry, will give command that every man have plenty by and by. A better day is coming.

BARTOW: We were another world, a starlit world.


## "The Car to the Ballpark" featured performers

Virginia Hardy Bartow, (1902–1987) began her life as the daughter of a wealthy New Englander. When she proved uncomfortable in "society", her parents in 1919 sent her to Paris to study music. She became a concert singer, gave well-received performances in Carnegie Hall, Bermuda, and abroad, and then starred with the Blue Hill Troupe in New York City. In 1928 she married Nevett Steele Bartow Jr., a young stock broker from South Orange, New Jersey. The Bartows moved into an apartment on the upper East Side in Manhattan. Nevett worked for a Wall Street brokerage until the onset of the Great Depression ruined his career and his self-confidence. In 1938 Mrs. Bartow became a student of Andrew Salama, a classically trained musician and performer in Balieff's Chauve Soiree, who had fled Russia during the Revolution. She became Salama's benefactress and entered into the life of a community of Russian émigré artists whose romantic sensibilities and "oriental melancholy" appealed deeply to her artistic temperament. After a divorce from her husband in 1945, Mrs. Bartow cut her remaining ties to society, and "went Russian". To help finance her son's musical education she turned her Manhattan, West Village apartment into a student pensione and led the life of a gilt-edged Bohemian. A strong willed, loquacious, and attractive woman with a flair for the dramatic, Mrs. Bartow drew generations of musicians and artists to her residence "Salamovka", a former hunting lodge on a wooded mountainside above the Delaware Water Gap in New Jersey until her death in 1987.

William Robinson: (deceased) Born on December 11, 1880 in rural Georgia, Robinson left school at the age of fourteen to work full time on the family farm. At the age of forty-eight he "just got a notion" and, upon the advice of friends, came to Philadelphia. Robinson worked briefly as a longshoreman, became a barber, and eventually owned a barbershop on Poplar Street in North Philadelphia. Throughout his life he remained a devout churchgoer and holder of many church offices. When I interviewed Mr. Robinson in July 1983, he was 103 years old and in frail health. He appeared not to hear or understand many of my questions and to be unclear about who I was or why I was questioning him. But amidst his generally disjointed and incomplete recollections, he returned repeatedly to one recollection: an incident that had taken place ninety-five years before, when at the age of seven he had been unjustly accused of stealing three peaches by a neighboring farmer, who threatened him with imprisonment and forced labor on a chain gang. The twenty-one dollars the supposedly aggrieved farmer forced Robinson's father to pay for the theft of the three peaches was well over a year's wages and bound the family even deeper into peonage to the plantation owner whose land Robinson's family sharecropped. As the interview proceeded, I began to wonder if the tale of the three peaches was not just a story about the Jim Crow South, but Robinson's way of protecting himself against me, a young white man disturbing his peace for unclear reasons. Soon, Robinson stopped answering questions altogether and fell into a Bible verse-laced monologue on the importance of honesty and minding one's own business.

Louise Smith (deceased) was born in 1893 on a tenant farm outside Granville, North Carolina, up near the Virginia border, where her mother raised the white landowner's children. A precocious student, she left school after her father broke three ribs lifting railroad ties, then came to Philadelphia in 1910 to help support her family. There, she worked as a live-in domestic, a job that she engaged in off and on for the next seventy years. Although never attracted to the "Bright Lights", trouble seemed to keep finding its way to her door. In 1914 Louise was almost forced into prostitution in Atlantic City by an older friend of her sisters under whose protection she had been placed. That winter a young man who wanted to marry her followed her back home. Against her better judgment, Louise allowed her mother, who always thought that a boy who was good to his parents makes a good husband, to persuade her to accept his proposal. Her husband turned out to be a philanderer with a fondness for dice, a penchant for travel, and a predilection to violence. During the course of a stormy ten-year marriage he threatened and harassed her, at one time attacking her with a razor "to mar [her] good looks". Mrs. Smith joined the Calvary Methodist Church soon after her arrival in Philadelphia. Calvary's pastor was the renowned Charles Albert Tindley, one of the city's most influential ministers and also one of great black gospel songwriters of the early twentieth century. When Louise's mother died the same day as his wife, Tindley took her under his wing and became her protector and confidante. When interviewed in September 1984, she still lived in the apartment that he had obtained for her more than sixty years before.

"This Car to the Ballpark" was funded by a fellowship from the Pennsylvania Radio Theatre, the Philadelphia Independent Film/Video Association Subsidy Program, and the Pennsylvania Council on the Arts.

# Oral history as a dialogue with the Polish-Jewish past of a local community from the perspective of social pedagogy

Marta Kubiszyn
Maria Curie-Skłodowska University, Lublin, Poland

The article is a part of the author's broader project researching multicultural education in Poland. It presents oral history as a form of social activity which can help partly reconstruct the memory of the Polish-Jewish past and reinforce the re-building of the formerly multicultural identity of local communities. Oral history is analysed here within the theoretical and methodological framework of social pedagogy. The paper also presents the efforts aiming at introducing oral history into the educational activities of the Grodzka Gate – NN Theatre Centre in Lublin, a local cultural institution which focuses on the history and heritage of the city's local community by restoring and re-reading its Polish-Jewish past.

**Keywords:** social pedagogy, public history, oral history, Polish-Jewish memory

The goal of this article is to present oral history as a form of communicative social research, which can help partly reconstruct the forgotten Polish-Jewish memory of the past in Poland as well as reinforce the process of (re-)building the identity of local communities in the context of their former multicultural character. Oral history will be analysed here within the theoretical and methodological framework of social pedagogy, where examining the condition of the local community is accompanied by activities focused on solving current problems by its members. The paper shows oral history in the wider context of a social and cultural environment, and treats it as a method of restoring the intergenerational dialogue and transmitting local tradition. The environmental framework for this paper is conditioned by the current situation of Lublin, a city in south-eastern Poland, whose former ethnic, religious, and national diversity, together with the history of the destruction of that multicultural world during the Second World War, determines the character of the city as a life- and educational environment. The concluding section will present the efforts aiming at introducing oral history into the educational and artistic activities of the Grodzka Gate – NN Theatre Centre in Lublin, a local cultural institution which focuses on the history and heritage of the local community by restoring and re-reading the forgotten Polish-Jewish past of the city.

While the term "social pedagogy" is present in many languages (social pedagogy, *Soziale Pädagogik, Sozialpädagogik, pédagogie socjale, pedagogika sredy*), there are many important differences as to how it is understood in particular countries. The sources of these differences go back to the process of forming social pedagogy as an academic discipline. It is derived from a practical social activity, and in the first half of the 20th century, its development was influenced by a number of non-academic factors. There are basically two, wide and narrow, ways of understanding the term "social pedagogy" in Polish scholarly literature. In its narrow meaning, "social pedagogy" is defined as a theory and practice of social work. This meaning is close to the definitions present in western literature, where "social pedagogy" is usually understood as a discipline that pertains to the relationship between an individual and society, with this relationship seen usually as a sphere of potential conflict. On the theoretical level social pedagogy analyses the relationship between an individual and society, and examines the position of an individual in a social group. In practice, social pedagogy undertakes some activities to prevent potential conflicts, to relieve existing ones, and to reduce their social consequences through planned socio-pedagogical intervention. In its wider meaning, typical of Polish scholarly literature, social pedagogy is a discipline which refers to mutual influences between the environment and individual. In its open methodological attitude, social pedagogy refers both to social and biological sciences and to cultural studies. At the same time it emphasizes the importance of the environment (understood widely as a set of biological, social, and cultural factors) in the process of socialization and education. In this wide context, social pedagogy can be defined both as a theory and practice of the environment, in the sense that it treats all social institutions as a life-environment. It analyses potential and actual educational influences of different factors existing in the environment, and, at the same time, it aims at rearranging and integrating the environment, aiming to transform it into an educational environment oriented at certain values, such as: tolerance, dialogue, partnership, freedom, responsibility, openness, solidarity, and empathy. Activities of this kind are crucial in the process of building a modern society, whose members have cultural and social competence that enables them to participate in both local and national culture, and, at the same time, to adopt an open attitude towards other cultures. The formation of this kind of social attitude requires a rejection of standardised forms of education in favour of individualisation of the educational process and developing critical thinking skills and communicative abilities.

Educational goals of this kind can be achieved through local (community) education. Referring to the local culture and heritage, and to values that play an important role in the process of forming the identity of local community members, local education is also a method of organising the local community around social and educational activities. By supporting processes of discovering and activating local community potentials, it can also support the process of deeper social changes (Theiss 2006: 12). Additionally, it can help in forming pro-environmental attitudes among young people. Defined as a positive approach toward local environment, these attitudes can appear in the form of the active reception and creation of local culture, and in the form of working for the benefit of the community by its members. An important element which, through educational curricula, can form such attitudes is developing interest in local culture, tradition, and heritage, consisting of such elements as: physical space, history, social memory, and local and family traditions. If the social and cultural heritage of a local community has been formed with the participation of people of various ethnic and religious backgrounds, local education can be in the form of historically-oriented multicultural education. Studying the culture of a certain ethnic group, and learning about other cultures and their interactions in the past, a student can not only build his/her own cultural identity but also become more accepting of diversity. In this way local education can be regarded as a starting point of European and Global education.

Lublin was inhabited for several centuries by people of different ethnic origins and different religions. Since the beginning of the 15th century, Jews constituted the most important among all its minority groups. For a few centuries the Jewish community lived in a separate district, situated around the Castle, outside the city walls. During the Second World War, thirty-eight thousand Lublin Jews were exterminated by the Nazis, who also destroyed the Jewish district to a great degree. Not only was the demographic and urban structure of the city changed, but an important part of the city's material and spiritual heritage was destroyed as well. After the war, under the influence of communist ideology, Lublin's Polish-Jewish past was ignored. Both academic and popular literature passed over in silence the issues concerning minorities that once used to live in the city. These issues were also dismissed from educational curricula and school handbooks. The purpose of this neglect was to incorporate into the local community's consciousness a false feeling of national and ethnic unity in Lublin, the Lublin region, and the whole Polish People's Republic, in order to indirectly foster ethnocentric and xenophobic attitudes among young generations. As a result, major changes in individual and social memory took place, which also brought important transformations into the identity of local community members.

The nationalist ideology implemented by communist authorities to deform the history of the country is still partly present in the Polish educational system. Although these issues have yet to be examined systematically, this observation can be confirmed by the results of research that has been conducted in different parts of the country. Although interesting curricula concerning history and culture of minorities are being conducted by individual teachers in many schools all over the country (Nasalska 1999: 81–82), incorporating such projects into the educational system on a large scale is hindered not only by external structural limitations, but also by a low level of knowledge and competence of teachers, who are mainly unaware of these issues. Research shows that most of the examined handbooks touch upon multicultural issues only at a basic level, and often present an ethnocentric attitude. Moreover, research confirms the shortage of multicultural-profiled curricula, well-trained teachers, good handbooks, and other educational materials (Ambrosewicz–Jacobs 2003: 17; Kubiszyn 2007: 64–70). Therefore, since public and private schools are not able to fulfil their duties concerning multicultural and local education, their efforts have to be supported by public and non-governmental cultural and educational institutions of a different kind. From the perspective of social pedagogy, reinforcing educational institutions by other institutions from the local community is a crucial element of the process of transforming the local life-environment into the educational environment.

Political and social changes that occurred in Poland after 1989 caused national, ethnic, and religious minority groups to enter both the public and political scene, claiming their aspirations to social and cultural emancipation. Since 1989, different kinds of activities focusing on the pre-war multicultural character of the country have taken place. The past is being used as an important element of political discourse in a new way: recollecting private memory discourse and, at the same time, rejecting the official historical discourse concerning multicultural issues. At the same time projects of this kind can also be analysed in the wider framework of a growing interest in autobiographies, which appeared on an international scale in the eighties, when it became obvious that the generation which personally experienced all the most important historical events of the twentieth century was passing away.

Oral history seems to be one of the most valuable methods that can help restore and inspire re-reading the private and collective memory of local communities, especially if this memory is not homogeneous and contains multi-plot narratives. Institutional and spontaneous activities that are being held in this area lead not only to the discovery of some new facts but also help develop an understanding of history and social processes in a local context – from the perspective of an individual, whose life-story is connected with a given place and time. At an academic level, oral history provides an opportunity to find out about the structures of social memory patterns and to re-read individual interpretations of the past, which have been constructed from the perspective of certain social and cultural categories.

While oral history can be briefly defined as a form of historical research which goes back to the source of historiography by referring to individual memory, there are many ways of understanding this term in scholarly literature. For the purpose of examining the social and cultural heritage of local communities, oral history can be defined as a research technique that can be applied within different kinds of theoretical and methodological frameworks. At the same time it can also be defined as a separate research method that refers to the humanistic paradigm – not only providing the rules of gathering material but also offering certain solutions concerning its analytical methods (Theiss 1988: 133). Referring to the self-educational dimension of this kind of project makes it possible to put oral history in a methodological perspective of action research, which emphasizes the fact that the process of changing the local environment by individuals can be the result of academic activity (Theiss 1996: 138). By focusing attention on given issues concerning, for example, problems of the ethnic identity of a marginalised minority group, an oral history research project can be an important element of the wider empowering process, connected with (re-)building the agency of a given group.

From the perspective of social pedagogy, local education, which refers to oral history and concentrates on (re-)interpreting the current images of the past in the context of a certain social and cultural background, is quite important for educational curricula in Poland. Historical perspective and the nationalist vision of a one-nation country, strong before 1939, is one factor which, due to family and social transmission, shapes attitudes toward minority groups among young people in the present day. Referring to different kinds of historical sources, including individual memory of local community members, enriches the image of the past and extends the historical consciousness of the young generation, while helping to protect social and individual memory against external manipulation (Kula 2002: 148). Social pedagogues agree that this kind of activity seems to be a key factor in restoring the continuity of understanding social and historical processes, but also in changing social attitudes.

Since 1997, the Grodzka Gate – NN Theatre Centre in Lublin has been collecting and displaying documentary materials of different kinds that refer to the history and heritage of the city in the interwar period. Oral testimonies help in the process of recognising the image of Polish-Jewish Lublin from before the Second World War, which no longer exists yet is present in the memories of its former citizens. Individual fates linked together with the history of the city are reflected in the recorded testimonies of several dozen Catholic and over a dozen Jewish inhabitants of pre-war Lublin. Thanks to these materials, it was possible to reconstruct some elements of the urban structure of the former Jewish district.

Oral testimonies, which include information concerning some sensual memories connected with colours, sounds, smells, and tastes, helped to restore the "muliti-sensoric landscape" of the pre-war city. It was also possible to reconstruct some patterns and forms of individual experiences of people living in the multidimensional cultural space (Lowenthal 1998:6–18).

Together with the recording and editing of oral testimonies, various kinds of educational and artistic projects that focus on oral history have been carried out in co-operation with other local cultural institutions, secondary schools, and universities. They are not necessarily academic projects, but rather activities aimed at the idea of sharing oral history materials with the local community in pursuit of reintegrating the forgotten or rejected part of memory with the well-known and accepted one.

Long-term educational oral history projects held by the Centre embrace not only recording testimonies by participants of the projects themselves, but also analysing them in order to solve certain research problems. In the act of communication, participants can both acquire knowledge and gather some individual experience. Recording and editing oral testimonies helps them develop critical thinking and interpersonal skills, while forming an openness to different kinds of narratives and sources providing diverse visions of the past. Being a participant in such a project also requires some theoretical skills and helps develop such features as empathy, patience, openness, honesty, tolerance, respect, and tactfulness, which are necessary in humanistic research. The projects launched by the Centre often take the form of short workshops whose participants work on previously-edited oral history materials. In both cases, participants experience a confrontation of two discourses of different kinds. The "historical discourse" – known from historical books and school education, which aspire to objectivity – can be confronted with the subjective "memory discourse". There is dissonance between the "historical discourse", which can be identified with modernism, imperialism, and scientism and the "memory discourse" identified with post-modernism, humanism, and emancipation. This can be observed at the level of: (re-)constructing facts, differences between the oral and written tradition (which is considered to have a higher status), and understanding and explaining the background of certain events.

Opened in May 1999, the permanent multimedia exhibition entitled "A Portrait of the Place" introduced oral history into an unconventionally arranged exhibition space of the labyrinth of narrow corridors of the Grodzka Gate itself and its two attached buildings. Displaying the exhibition in this kind of space transforms a visit to "A Portrait of the Place" into a "walking-tour" around the former Jewish quarter. The main element of the scenography is a wooden construction.

Slide projectors and loudspeakers were installed into this construction, and some enlarged pre-war pictures were attached. Visitors can watch pictures and slides showing streets that no longer exist as well as particular architectural objects and silhouettes of the former inhabitants of the area. Oral testimonies constitute the key element that co-constructs the space of the exhibition. While watching pictures, visitors can listen to memories and to the specially prepared (re-)construction of the "sound-scape" of the pre-war Jewish district. A similar way of constructing the space of the exhibition can be observed in "The Primer", displayed in one of the barracks of the former concentration and death camp at Majdanek. It was prepared in 2002 by the Centre together with the Majdanek Museum, and it refers to the fate of the youngest prisoners of the camp. In order to present, in a symbolic way, their fate, the life-stories from the Museum's archives of four children were used: two Polish-Jewish, one Polish-Catholic, and one Belarusian-Russian Orthodox. The idea that lies behind this project was to show the life of young prisoners through basic words and categories that turned out to be helpful in understanding the cruel reality of this place. The symbolic "survival primer", which in 1942 replaced the real, beautiful, and colourful primer – the first book that accompanies children starting school – was presented through such words as "roll-call", "barrack", "cyclone" or "crematorium". Just as in "A Portrait of the Place", the whole space of the exhibition consists of archival pictures, documentary materials, and oral testimonies together with different sounds recalling images of certain places and events. The purpose of using human voices and pieces of audio art as key elements in both exhibitions was to transform them into a form of theatrical performances, where the space itself tells its own story. Not only does it make both exhibitions more attractive for the visitors, but it seems to affect them on an emotional level by stimulating their imagination.

Oral history materials have also been used by the Grodzka Gate – NN Theatre Centre as an integral part of Memory Mysteries. Conducted in public space, these performances refer to the symbolic meanings connected with the past of the city. They attempt to answer the question which is often posed by both historians and artists, as to what forms of artistic activity can help in restoring, protecting, and passing on the history of a local community, and how artistic activity can defeat intolerance, prejudices, and resentment. The sound-sphere consisting of recorded oral testimonies, sounds recalling memories of certain places and events, together with some recollections delivered on the spot by participants, were an integral element of almost all the Mysteries produced in the years 2000–2006. Replacing conventional forms of theatrical narrative with individual testimony, although known in the documentary theatre tradition for almost a hundred years, once again leads us to the conclusion that only documentary material showing individual perspective can bring us closer to the truth, defined as the subjective truth of historical experience of an individual. At the same time, this form of activity reveals the understanding of history as a continuing process of constructing and re-constructing narratives by members of a given group, according to the interpretation and re-interpretation of the past events. From the perspective of social pedagogy, the educational dimension of this process concentrates around understanding how those constructed narratives and interpretations of the past shape our thinking and attitudes in the present day.

The Mystery entitled "A Poem about the Place", produced late in the evening on October 12th, 2002 in Lublin's Podzamcze (the area at the bottom of the castle), referred not only to the history of the Jewish district once situated in this area but also to the history of the local castle, which during the Nazi and Soviet occupations served as a prison and a place of torture and murder for many people. The original public space was transformed by visual and sound scenography. All the wells of the sewage system in the area were opened, and several loud-speakers and powerful lights were installed inside. At 8:00 P.M. street lights in the area were switched off, and the shafts of light coming from the underground appeared. While the participants followed the trail marked by shafts of light, the narrative of the Mystery containing oral testimonies was delivered. Coming from the underground and quietly resonating in the darkness, the narratives concerned the pre-war life in the Jewish quarter, the deportation of Jews from Lublin to the Bełżec death camp, and the destruction of the Jewish district, intertwined with the stories of the prisoners of the Castle from the '40s and '50s. The trail ended at the empty place where the famous Maharshal Synagogue once stood. There the participants found a huge black curtain hanging across the street symbolizing silence: the untold part of the narrative, which can never be expressed by those who survived and which can never be understood by those who never experienced those events personally.

Although very interesting as a form of theatrical performance, "A Poem about the Place" can also be analysed as a unique example of displaying oral history materials on location. Again we deal with a theatrical situation when, through oral testimonies, the public space itself shares with the visitor-participant its own history, becoming a witness of the traumatic memory that has been rejected and forgotten by the local community.

By referring to oral history, the exhibitions "A Portrait of the Place" and "The Primer", together with the Memory Mysteries constitute an artistic situation with an important educational dimension, building up a space for social dialogue that touches upon the most painful topics for the local community. Referring to various narratives in the pursuit of reconstructing different images of the past, which are present in the consciousness of living people, made it possible to expose the tension between the linear narrative typical for traditional historiography and the non-linear narrative that reflects the structures of human memory. Comparing these two narrative forms helps re-create the image of Lublin as a Polish-Jewish city, while at the same time stressing the epistemological distance between different forms of documentary materials and showing their documentary and constructed character.

Oral history, defined as a form of communicative research which helps to examine relationships and influences in the local environment, can diminish the distance between the language of social communication and historical reality, at the same time building space for interaction and social communication between members of a local community. If the participants of that dialogue belong to different national, ethnic, or religious groups, oral history becomes an element of multicultural education, helping at the same time to restore natural intergenerational communication. According to Wiesław Theiss, oral history can be defined widely as a humanistic idea, as an alternative source of knowledge about the past, and as a factor reinforcing social activity (Theiss 1998: 38–40). While providing an opportunity to restore the alternative narratives of the past of a local community, it can also support the process of building democracy and civil society, and at the same time help in gaining social and individual agency. Referring to the theory and practice of social pedagogy, we can assume that local education oral history projects regarding the humanistic concept of an individual as an active creator of his/her own environment may, as American and Western European experiences show, serve as the starting point for social change (Thompson 2000: 173–189).

## References

Ambrosewicz-Jacobs, J. 2003. *Me Us Them. Ethnic Prejudices Among Youth and Alternative Methods of Education. The Case of Poland*. Kraków: Universitas.

Kubiszyn, M. 2007. *Edukacja wielokulturowa w środowisku lokalnym. Studium teoretyczno-empiryczne na przykładzie Ośrodka Brama Grodzka – Teatr NN w Lublinie*. Toruń: Adam Marszałek.

Kula, M. 2002. *Nośniki pamięci historycznej*. Warszawa: DiG.

Lowenthal, D. 1998. Fabricating heritage. History and memory. *Studies in Representation of the Past* 1: 6–18.

Nasalska, E. 1999. Edukacja międzykulturowa w polskiej szkole. *Kwartalnik Pedagogiczny* 1: 73–86.

Theiss, W. 1988. Badania biograficzne: Przypadek dzieci syberyjskich. *Kwartalnik Pedagogiczny* 1: 133–146.

Theiss, W. 1996. *Zniewolone dzieciństwo. Socjalizacja w skrajnych warunkach społeczno-politycznych*. Warszawa: ŻAK.

Theiss, W. 1998. Oral History in Poland. *Words and Silence Bulletin of the International Oral History Association* 3: 38–40.
Theiss, W. 2006. Edukacja środowiskowa – wprowadzenie. In *Edukacja i animacja społeczna w środowisku lokalnym*, W. Theiss & B. Skrzypczak (eds), 12–34. Warszawa: Centrum Wspierania Aktywności Lokalnej CAL.
Thompson, P. 2000. *The Voice of the Past: Oral History*. Oxford: Oxford University Press.

# Sharing oral history with the wider public

## Experiences of the Refugee Communities History Project

Zibiah Alfred

University of Essex, United Kingdom

The Refugee Communities History Project has sought to share refugee com-munity oral history life story material with refugee communities but also with the wider public, school groups and tourists visiting the exhibition "Belonging" held at the Museum of London from October 2006 until February 2007. This paper will explore issues that may arise when sharing material with audiences "outside" of the community from which material is collected. Issues to con-sider when making material accessible to audiences who feel negatively about, prejudiced against or hostile towards the communities from which material is collected will be discussed.

Keywords: oral history, refugees, community, informed consent, audience

## The project

The Refugee Communities Oral History Project (RCHP) has been led by the Evelyn Oldfield Unit in partnership with the Museum of London, London Met-ropolitan University and fifteen refugee community organisations in London. Its aim has been to highlight the diverse contributions that refugees have been mak-ing to London life from 1951 to the present day. Oral history interviews carried out with 150 refugee interviews over a two year period have been permanently ar-chived at the Museum of London. Elements of these oral history interviews have featured in a high profile public exhibition "Belonging" at the Museum of London (October 2006 – February 2007), on websites and in multimedia resources such as *childhood landscapes* (2005) and *Crossing Borders* (2005). Detailed background information can be found on project website www.refugeestories.org and www. museumoflondon.org.uk/belonging. The author of this paper has been involved, as one of fifteen RCHP Oral History fieldworkers, in collecting, archiving and disseminating RCHP oral history material to wider audiences.

The RCHP has sought to share refugee community oral history material with refugee communities but also with other audiences, for example the wider public, UK school groups and tourists visiting the exhibition "Belonging" at the Museum of London. This paper will explore issues that may arise when sharing material with audiences "outside" of the community from which material is collected. Issues to consider when making material accessible to audiences who feel negatively about, prejudiced against or hostile towards the communities from which material is collected will be discussed.

## With whom do we share?

Oral history projects may be set up for different purposes. Projects may be undertaken on the initiative of an individual pursuing a personal interest, to record material for sharing within a very small circle of people known to interviewees. For example, members of a family might record each others' life stories without any intention that material recorded be shared beyond the family circle.

Other projects may aim to share material with a larger number of people or with a specified community familiar to project participants. This may be an audience group to which interviewees already feel a sense of belonging, for example other members of a sports association to which interviewees have membership.

Alternatively, the target audience may be a group to which interviewees feel no sense of belonging but with which they are familiar, as might be the case for example in a project where older people record life stories for pupils from a known local school community. In some cases, the specific group targeted may not be known to the interviewees initially, but be, rather, a group that interviewees get to know through involvement in an oral history project. For instance, projects may involve youth group members interviewing older people in their locality from a different faith group. Groups might initially take part in joint activities which facilitate the building of relationships of trust, prior to oral history interviewing. Relationships between people from "teller" and "listener" groups may be built over a series of oral history interview meetings and continue beyond the lifespan of the oral history project.

However, in other cases, an oral history project may from the outset be concerned to share material with audiences beyond the groups or communities to which interviewees feel a sense of belonging or connection. Some projects aim to share material as widely as possible, making material accessible to people of all walks of life and political persuasions from all over the globe, in both present and future time. This may raise ethical questions around informed consent, discussed later within this paper.

## RCHP aims

The RCHP had, from the very beginning, a clear and explicit aim to highlight, to people from diverse backgrounds from refugee and non-refugee communities, the diverse contributions that refugees have made to London life from 1951 to the present day. This aim was not, as happens with some projects, something which emerged after interviews had commenced and interest in the interviewee community had grown. Rather, the RCHP, from the outset, set out to collect oral history material which could be shared within particular cultural refugee communities, with other refugee community audiences and with the wider public, within the project area of London and across the UK. The project did not specifically aim to make materials available beyond the UK; this was beyond the remit of the project's key funders Trust for London and the Heritage Lottery Fund. Nevertheless, project team members were open to the idea of making material available to people in all parts of the globe and communicated this possibility to interviewees from the outset.

The RCHP team sought to make material accessible to people of all ages and backgrounds, from school children to elderly community groups. Material was collected in the preferred spoken languages of interviewees with the intention that it would be accessed by people of different mother tongues and translated into English where necessary. From the outset, material was collected to deposit safely in the permanent archives at the Museum of London for posterity.

## Why share oral history material?

Oral history project participants may wish to share material with personal interest for personal gain, for example in fame, or wealth, or respect, or political advantage. Participants might also have the welfare of others in mind and, share material with the hope of informing people about a particular topic or issue, promoting learning and provoking thought, sparking academic discussion, triggering community debate, prompting social action, eliciting emotion, encouraging empathetic understanding between people, connecting communities, emphasising a social message, or simply to entertain.

RCHP participants aimed, through sharing refugee life story material in the public realm, to educate the general public about the life situations refugees may face in London and challenge prevalent negative stereotypes about refugees. There was a socio-political intention to give a public platform to the voices of the marginalized in society. The RCHP team hoped that people prejudiced against, or hostile towards, those labelled "refugees" would also engage with material, as well as people already willing to empathise with people in refugee situations. One of the deep aims of the RCHP was to engender social change by presenting refugee voices in a way that might dispel negative tabloid myths about refugees and deconstruct negative public discourse through promoting understanding, empathy and respect for refugees.

Unlike some other types of oral history project, the RCHP team intended from the outset to court debate. RCHP participants were open-eyed to the controversies that sharing materials might cause amongst the general public and aware that some people might display continuing hostility towards refugees beyond exposure to RCHP material.

### How RCHP Oral History Material was made accessible to people of diverse backgrounds and communities

RCHP oral history material was initially recorded onto minidisk and then transferred onto CD and into a format where the whole interview could be stored as a computer sound file. With interviewee consent, the RCHP team presented material in a variety of formats to maximize accessibility to diverse audiences. Interviews were transcribed verbatim, making their content more easily accessible to people unable to spend the hours and hours that would be needed to listen to all interviews individually to discover their content. In an ideal world, with more funding available, interviews would have been transcribed in the language of the interview and then translated into other languages to promote their accessibility to speakers of different languages. As it was, whilst interviews were recorded in English and mother tongue languages, funding available permitted the team to produce transcripts of all interviews in English, or translated into English, only.

In oral history interviews, meaning and emotion may be ascertained by tone of voice and pauses, as much as by word content that might be captured in a written transcript; project team members were keen to encourage people to listen to the voice recordings of original interviews as much as possible, in preference to simply gleaning meaning from written transcripts. Interview sound files were divided into short ten minute segments for storage within the Museum of London's oral history digital data collection, enabling people to scour transcripts for keywords and then dive in to listen to relevant interview sound-clips.

The RCHP team recognized that there was much more that could be done to share material than simply depositing it in the public archives of a Museum. With interviewee consent, the relevant refugee community organizations were given CDs of whole interview recordings and encouraged to devise creative ways of sharing material.

Material was edited into digestible audiences. For example, selected interview extracts were recorded onto DVD, such as *Life Journey: Afghan Community Oral History* and *childhood landscapes,* with accompanying music and images for distribution to schools, libraries and colleges. These promoted general interest in the RCHP, signposting people to access whole interviews by visiting the Museum. Materials were presented in ways that took into account the needs of different audiences. For instance, material selected to be shared with school children was presented in a child-friendly format, with engaging interactive activities designed to encourage children to explore the meanings behind oral history extracts. Material presented to people from "outsider" communities was accompanied with explanatory contextualizing notes which, where possible, were made by the oral history interviewer in consultation with the interviewee. Practical measures were taken where possible to find ways of making material accessible to those with visual and hearing impairment; for instance, care was taken to choose suitable font sizes and colours for people with visual impairment, following guidelines of websites www.webcredible.co.uk and www.disability.gov.uk.

Material was edited for display in local exhibitions, at local community centres and local libraries as well as for the large public exhibition entitled "Belonging" at the Museum of London, which ran from October 2006 to February 2007. Displays of sound material were enhanced through visual displays of objects lent by interviewees, by artwork, photography and visual displays of text and interactive museum exhibits. Talks, workshops and a range of artistic performances such as dance, drama and music, were coordinated to take place in the exhibition space to complement exhibition materials. Such a programme promoted public access to material, drawing into the exhibition people, who might not otherwise have entered the exhibition space to engage with oral history material.

Placing interview extracts on project website www.refugeestories.org.uk and the Museum of London website, enabled people with internet access from all around the globe to explore material.

## Ethical issues: The possibility of excluding people from participation by aiming to share material widely

Oral history projects influence ongoing processes of creating, building and shaping communities. Project designs seeking to make material accessible to as wide an audience as possible may deter some individuals from participation. Oral fieldworkers may play a role in excluding people from communities through setting up project conditions that disable some individuals from participating in projects and having visibility as community members.

A number of people declined the invitation to be interviewed for the RCHP. Not wishing to pressurise nominees to participate, project staff did not oblige nominees to explain their personal reasons for declining the invitation, beyond simple probing to ensure any worries nominees might have were not founded upon misunderstandings about the project.

However, of the nominees who declined, some volunteered explanation. Besides practical reasons such as lack of time, concerns about personal life story material being shared with others were voiced. In some cases, the concern was about personal life story material being accessible to people within communities to which nominees felt belonging. Often people were aware that sharing their own life story would involve disclosing something of other peoples' life stories from their own perspective. Some people were concerned that this might create difficulties for their own relationships with the people whose stories they in part disclosed where, for example, perspectives on events differed, or where perspectives concurred but might cause others discomfort if revealed. Many people were aware that simply avoiding mentioning others by name might not protect anonymity where "inside" community members might be able to detect other clues to identity.

However, for others, the real concern was sharing material with strangers, people whom they would never know or meet, or with people whom they knew but as members of communities to which they did not feel belonging. Much of this concern centred around safety. Some refugees had very real concerns about the persecution they, or their family members, might face if personal stories in which individuals could be identified were exposed in a public realm. Some refugees feared being traced by people from the countries from which they had fled persecution; some had real fears that sharing a personal life story might prompt trouble for themselves, their family of friends, trouble from their former country's secret police or other agents.

Rather than exclude people with such fears from the project, the RCHP team sought to find ways to accommodate people with such worries and needs. The possibility of identity being recognized from the distinctive sound of an individual's voice was pointed out to potential interviewees. People were offered limited anonymity through the option of choosing a pseudonym. Opportunity to listen back to recordings and request for identifying information to be cut was offered to everyone. People were encouraged to supplement oral history interviews with personal photos, but willingness to do so was by no means a criterion for participation in the project; it was recognized for some sharing photographs might jeopardize personal safety or conflict with religious or cultural beliefs about the use of the human image.

Some interviewees explained that they felt far more self-conscious and anxious about sharing material with unknown and possibly "refugee hostile" audiences and being exposed to the eye of potentially negative tabloid media, than about sharing material with families or known refugee communities. Project interviewers sought to listen to and address interviewee concern about the possibility of facing mockery or ridicule. For instance, interviewees were offered an opportunity to attend training in handling media interest and courting the media to their own advantage. The knowledge that they were participating in a group project, taking some risks as a group with the support of community organizations, rather than as isolated individuals, dispelled some interviewee anxiety about exposing personal material to potentially hostile listeners.

Some interviewees explained that whilst they did not mind sharing personal life story material with people they knew, or with strangers, they considered participation in the RCHP to be an overwhelming responsibility which carried expectations they personally felt unable to fulfill. Understanding that the RCHP had a grand aim of challenging negative stereotypes about refugees, some interviewee nominees felt their life story would not sufficiently support such an aim and preferred to give their opportunity to other nominees whom they felt had stories that would better evoke support for refugees. The challenge here for the oral history fieldworkers was to enable each nominee to see that her personal stories might indeed be valued by others, without pressurizing the nominee to take part against her own personal judgment. This was done in part by encouraging nominees to have a go at telling their stories with the reassurance that would be free to pull out of the project at any time. Nominees were assured of the opportunity to listen back to recordings in the privacy of their own homes, and with family or friends if they wished, before having to decide about giving consent for material to be shared with others. Nominees were all assured of the option of requesting parts of their interviews to be edited out if they wished. At the choice of interviewees, editing out was done either permanently, or in a way where it could, under some conditions be retrieved. For example, some interviewees had concerns about material being heard by others within their own lifetimes but were quite happy for material to be removed from the public domain for fifty years after which they did not mind if it was heard by others. Here the project benefited greatly from the special support of the Museum of London which has the understanding, economic power and technical ability to be able to offer interviewees the possibility of putting such conditions on material usage.

### Protecting the welfare of interviewees when presenting interviewee material to a wider unknown audience and the issue of informed consent

Where an interviewee is able to gain insight into the nature of the intended audience with whom her material will be shared, informed consent about the sharing of material may be given. Of course people granted access to recorded life histories may develop an interest in sharing material with a wider audience unknown to the interviewees at later stage; material might find its way to other audiences, with newly acquired permission from the interviewee, or without interviewee knowledge. This is a risk that can be explained to the interviewee; it is not a certainty.

Where material is placed in public domains, such as public libraries, archives and museums, or on websites accessible from all around the world, it is likely that material may be accessed by people from communities unfamiliar to the interviewee. Indeed, the range of communities from which people may access material may span well beyond the imagination of any individual and stretch into the future beyond all the communities that exist in the world within the interviewee's lifespan. An elderly person from a Welsh village for example, may never in his wildest dreams imagine that an anthropologist from Ghana would be interested in his life story material, or that his material may be stumbled upon and explored by a stranger surfing the net.

Negative consequences of sharing material widely, albeit with good intent, may arise. The oral historian who foresees the possibility of various negative consequences arising from the sharing of material faces dilemmas with ethical dimensions. To what extent should she protect the interests of interviewees and their families, and her own interests as an interviewer, over and above the interests of the general public, or wider humanity? By what criteria can such interests be measured? To what extent is she responsible for ensuring that interviewees understand the risks they take in agreeing for their personal material to be shared widely? What constitutes interviewee "informed consent"? To what degree should a good oral historian take pains to carry out practical steps to protect her interviewees from future harm?

Take the dilemma of obtaining informed consent from the interviewee for the sharing of personal stories. Whilst an individual may rationally understand that giving permission for his personal material to be placed in a public domain, such as a website, means that it can be accessed by people all over the world, it does not mean that all the implications of this are grasped at the time of signing a consent form. Placing personal material in open access domains means that material may be accessed by people who may have, or develop in the future, malicious intent towards that particular individual, or whom may have good intent but act with bad consequences. At the time of giving consent for material to be placed on a website for example, an individual may have no thought that he might in the future have resulting problems with stalkers, or with identity theft, or with someone turning his personal life story material into a book or play without permission for profit or writers' glory, or with defamation of his name.

Placing material on the web may leave an individual prone to problems in the future on account of the particular communities with which he identifies, or might be identified by others, within his interview. One cannot always predict ethnic war or guess the ways in which groups may divide against each other. Refugees from former Yugoslavia and Rwanda attest to growing up in communities without awareness of anyone wishing them harm, before later, in a changing socio-political climate, finding the need to conceal personal details linking them to certain groups for fear of being caught up in ethnic persecution.

Of course the possibility of material being accessed by people who may use it to cause harm to the interviewee also exists when material is shared within a circle of people known to the interviewee. However, arguably, the better the understanding of the audience with whom material will be shared, the better position the interviewee is in to calculate such risk and weigh this risk up for against the potential benefits of choosing to participate in the project. Identifying the profile of the audience with whom material will be shared may also make it easier to identify any culprits misusing material and to put a stop to any harm should problems arise.

A good oral historian will seek to follow an ethical code of practice in interviews, such as that of the Oral History Society (www.ohs.org.uk/ethics) and obtain informed consent from interviewees about the storage and usage of personal life-story material. To what extent does this require the oral historian to spell out cautions about possible material usage? How many oral historians for example, think it important to point out the possibility of stalking to individuals from whom they are requesting permission to place material on a website? To do so might appear to be raising concerns bordering on paranoia. The interviewee often looks to the interviewer for strength to share their story in public realms. An interviewer warning interviewees to consider worries that they have not already thought of herself may inspire little confidence in hesitant interviewees and deter them from signing consent forms to share material.

Yet since stalking is a possibility that increases when personal material is made widely available, for example on the internet, it is perhaps a consideration that interviewers should point out to interviewees. In a study conducted at Leicester University between October 2004 and September 2005, 1300 victims of stalking, aged 10–71, of which 60% resided in UK, volunteered to complete an online questionnaire (Sheridan, www.stalkingsurvey.com). One in ten stalkers were said to have "begun their campaigns as total strangers to the victim"; one finding of this study was that "before they were targeted, victims simply did not believe stalking could happen to them". Stalkers employed a diverse range of tactics including defamation of character and identity theft (http://www.le.ac.uk/pc/aa/stalking/keyfindings.pdf).

Those surprised to find themselves victims of internet stalking, whether from violent ex-partners or total strangers with obsessive behaviour, may be advised by police and stalking charities to remove personal details from public websites that may allow the stalker to trace their whereabouts, for example by contacting community groups or organizations with which their material shows them to be linked. Removing personal data from a website may not be quick or easy to do. Webmasters of relevant websites may be difficult to contact and sometimes material may be left up on websites no longer attended to by any webmaster.

Future guidelines for people planning oral history projects might do well to include some good practice guidelines for protecting individuals from stalkers. The RCHP exemplified good practice, addressing concern expressed by one RCHP participant about being traced by a known stalker through the RCHP website, by substituting the textual version of the participant's name, easily traced by internet search engines, with a graphic image of the participants' name that could escape the beam of powerful internet search engines.

## Making material accessible to audiences who feel negatively about, prejudiced against or hostile towards the communities from which material is collected

The RCHP aim to challenge negative stereotypes about refugees by placing selected refugee life story material in the public realm was made explicit to all from the outset. Refugees consenting to give RCHP life story interviews understood personal material would very likely be encountered by people feeling negatively about, prejudiced against or hostile towards refugees.

One challenge for the RCHP team was to find ways of disseminating and sharing the material with people whose prejudices about refugees might make them initially reluctant to engage with the material.

RCHP material was displayed in a public space, in a public Museum Gallery open and accessible to all and with no prohibitive entry charge. Much thought went into the name that the exhibition should be given and the ways that it could be described in advertisements. The name chosen "Belonging", with connotations such as relationship to others and the world, "existential being" and "nostalgic longing", was in part a deliberate attempt to present a concept to which people from all communities could relate. The word "refugees" was given importance but placed in the strap-line "Voices of London's refugees", in the shadow of the name "Belonging".

A series of live music and dance performances were organized to take place in the exhibition area. These were well advertised and used to draw all sectors of the public into the exhibition area. The exhibition area itself was designed as a warm creative space, with colourful displays of artwork and artefacts, an area for children to create drawings and interactive displays. Oral history extracts were played aloud from speakers in different parts of the room as well as through different listening point headphones, so that people entering the space were immediately exposed to material.

The exhibition space could be entered by interviewees, people supportive of refugees and people negatively prejudiced towards refugees, simultaneously. It was a challenge for the project team to consider how best to "manage" the situations that may arise when people with prejudices about refugees encounter personal life story material about refugees. Whilst the team aimed to create a non-judgmental space for people of all points of view about refugees to engage with and reflect upon refugee life story material, to some extent there was an attempt to contain the feelings of people hostile towards refugees. Material was selected and presented in ways designed to elicit empathetic understanding. Care was taken to present life story material in ways that would promote respect for interviewees. Refugees are very often presented as villains or victims by the UK tabloid media. In the selection of material for public exhibition, the aim was not to elicit sympathy for the plight of refugees. Rather than dehumanizing refugees by casting them as passive victims, the team sought to use exhibition material to help deconstruct stereotypical views of "refugees" and present individuals as agents, and active citizens. The exhibition sought to present a multiplicity of voices and narratives, allowing different stories to emerge rather than trying to tell a singular story of "the refugee". Material was presented with lightness of curatorial voice; as far as possible refugees voices told their own stories with institutional voices and museum commentary kept to a minimum.

The success of the project team in achieving the aim of challenging negative stereotypes about refugees through the exhibition might best be judged by exhibition visitors and the interviewees themselves. The Museum encouraged visitors to leave comments about their experiences of the exhibition which included:

> Thank you for this clutch of ideas, stories, facts and momentos. It's a vast challenge to draw some examples from the multitude of experiences there are to draw from. I'm impressed that you haven't flinched from the political and the controversial. I hope that the exhibition encourages people to explore aspects – both social and political – of refugees coming to the UK.
> (Comment Posted on Exhibition Room Wall, Museum of London 2007)

Whilst comments left were overwhelmingly positive, some were derogatory or hostile towards refugees or other groups, for example "Gay ppl suk!" (*Visitors Comment Book, Museum of London,* 2007).

Those involved in monitoring public reaction to the exhibition took steps to neutralize the sting in some of the comments. For example, contrasting comments were displayed side by side on the Visitor's Comment Wall. Some abusive comments left were removed from public view. The RCHP team debated about the extent to which "comment cleansing" should be carried out. On the one hand it was argued that the best way to encourage people to abandon racist or prejudiced attitudes towards certain groups would be to afford a space where people felt free to speak their mind frankly, enabling prejudices and stereotypes to be unpacked and dismantled, rather than dangerously suppressed. On the other hand, it was argued that everything possible should be done to protect people from confronting hurtful comments and abuse. The potential for people to make abusive comments directed at the refugee participants was recognized and influenced the choice of extracts placed on public display.

### Sharing material with wider audiences: Controversies around context and frame

Careful decisions need to be taken about the kind of frame and context given to material shared with wider audiences. Simply presenting interview material without background information or context may leave "outside" audiences uncertain about how to access and make sense of material. Indeed it is often the context and frame given to the material, for example the wording of publicity posters advertising the material, or the catalogue headings assigned to material in an archive, or the titles given to an exhibition of sound recordings, that draws "outside" audiences to explore and engage with material in the first place. Where little framework is given, outsiders may drift away without engaging with material or, flailing around set material in an irrelevant context or understand it simply as an aesthetic experience.

In the case of the RCHP, material displayed in a public exhibition was given context by the exhibition space at the Museum of London. Material was hung upon different hooks to which people from diverse communities might relate. Rather than for example arranging material around concepts particular to certain communities, broad hooks within the conceptual vocabulary of people from all communities, such as "family life", were chosen.

A decision was made to contextualise sound-clips of refugee interviews through providing a time-line of migrant groups arrival in London printed across the length of an exhibition room wall. Much consultation was carried out about this time line which had to be designed to take into account constraints of wall space and different individual and community perspectives of historical events. The final information chosen for the Time line created controversy within visiting groups.

For example:

> Interesting exhibition identifying the issues and experiences of refugees BUT WHERE ARE THE PALESTINIANS! They are not even included in the Timeline          (*Visitors' Comments Book, Museum of London* 2007)

and

> very interesting, however as a Roma and lesbian where are the references, facts of lesbian and gay people settling in London fleeing persecution form countries that still disappear us…
> (*Visitors' Comments Book, Museum of London* 2007)

Had material simply been shared within a closed circle of oral history project participants such questions and may not have arisen. Opening up material to wider audiences creates a forum for disputes and encourages greater accountability on the part of the project participants. "Why this story and not that story?" is a question which may not be thought of, or not dared to be raised, or considered of much significance within a community where everyone knows everyone else.

In conclusion, oral life history material may be shared with wider audiences in a variety of ways with good intention. Those involved in oral history projects do well to bear in mind the possibility of negative consequences arising where individual life story material is placed in the public realm, or made available to people who may place it later in the public realm. Decisions about how material might be shared, in the best interests of the interviewee and interviewer and their friends, families and communities who may be affected, and of potential listeners from different communities in the present and in the future, need to be made with care. Benefits of sharing material by placing it in an open access public realm, such as a website, may be weighed against disadvantages. Oral history project planners should bear in the mind that whilst some people will be encouraged to participate in projects by the thought that life history material will be shared widely, others may be deterred or excluded from participation, unless the possibility of restricting general public access to material is offered at the outset.

Decisions about the sharing of material might best be made in consultation with individuals and communities concerned. Whilst oral history fieldworkers have responsibilities to the "tellers" and "sharers", there are also the interests of the "listeners" and "receivers" to consider. Besides talking through possible consequences of sharing material with a project team, oral history fieldworkers might consider seeking advice from an independent ethical advisory committee. Where no such committee exists, fieldworkers might collaborate with other groups to form an ethical advisory board independent to the project.

## References

### Website references

www.refugeestories.org (accessed 31.7.2007)
www.museumoflondon.org.uk/belonging (accessed 31.7.2007)
www.ohs.org.uk/ethics (accessed 31.7.2007)
www.webcredible.co.uk (accessed: 31.08.2005) Disability Discrimination Act
www.disability.gov.uk (accessed 31.08.2005) "Let's make it accessible"
www.stalkingsurvey.com (accessed 31.7.2007)
http://www.le.ac.uk/pc/aa/stalking/keyfindings.pdf (accessed 20.10.2007)

### Multimedia DVD References

Alfred, Z. 2005. *Childhood Landscapes.* London: Evelyn Oldfield Unit.
Buchuck, S. 2005. *Crossing Borders.* London: Evelyn Oldfield Unit.
Fayabi, P. 2005. *Life Journey: Afgan Community Oral History.* London: Evelyn oldfield Unit.

# Story – oral history – historiography

# The ethics of oral history

## Expectations, responsibilities, and dissociations

Brigitte Halbmayr

Institute of Conflict Research, Vienna, Austria

This article focuses on the mutual expectations of the oral historian and the interviewee – problems and opportunities that could arise from the rapport that is established between them. The (sometimes conflicting) expectations are elaborated in three stages: first, the interview setting itself; second, the level of interpretation and evaluation of the research results; and third, a possible ongoing rapport beyond the given research goal (as seen by the researcher). The author concludes that for each stage, balances must be found between the conflicting interests to meet the goals of the research project as well as to respect the dignity of the interviewee.

**Keywords:** oral history, ethics, goals of research, interviewee-interviewer relationship

For a long period of time, mainstream historiography refused to consider personal memories that were collected by oral historians as valid sources; on the contrary, personal memories and recollections were seen as adversaries of professional historians. Rapprochement of the former polar antagonists did not begin until after 1980, and oral history was eventually established as a special area of historiography. According to Aleida Assmann, this happened "in the wake of the Holocaust", and emerged from the quandary created by documents of the NS-era (see Assmann 2006: 47 passim). The latter – especially the documents created by the perpetrators – have never been able to render a true picture of the horrors, whereas eyewitnesses try to communicate, if at all possible, their very own experiences, both in terms of their inner selves and their surroundings. How else would we know about the hungry, starving Jewish ghetto children? How could we know about the desperate struggle for survival in the concentration camps? Or about the pain that is caused by the loss of one's entire family, a pain that never ceases for an entire lifetime? Such knowledge can never be communicated by statistics, by transport lists, or lists of names, but only by humans that remember and tell their stories. Personal memories of survivors are the ultimate source able to communicate the dimensions of Nazi horrors. Therefore, the survivors not only embody irreplaceable personal memories but also act as reminders for humanity (Assmann 2006: 48).

The knowledge produced by oral history has been, however, increasingly questioned. This began not only since the scientific community and the interested public were shaken by autobiographies, which, upon closer examination, proved to be either partially invented and/or forged. The case of Binjamin Wilkomirski, who invented a childhood for himself during the Holocaust – though he grew up in a Swiss village as a non-Jewish child[1] – gained notorious fame on the international stage (see Wilkomirski 1995). Whether this is a case of deliberate forgery or "false memory",[2] has yet to be sorted out. Another example is the two Spanish men who incorporated concentration camp imprisonments into their biographies. Enric M. declared himself a survivor of Flossenbürg, while Antonio P. M. claimed to be a former Mauthausen inmate. Actually, neither of them had ever been an inmate of a National Socialist concentration camp.[3] Interestingly, one of them, Marco, served as President of "Amical de Barcelona" for many years, being an important representative of former concentration camp prisoners.

These are but three examples of publicly known biographical forgeries, which increasingly lead to the question: What is true of these stories? Who is telling facts and who is telling fiction? And where is the dividing line?

This critical approach to oral history is also backed by recent research findings on memory (supported by brain research). Subsequent experiences and memories are superimposed on past experiences, which allows events of a distant past fade away and leads to their revaluation and reconfiguration. That means that each recollection puts old memories in new contexts, thus, actively reshaping them (see Tschuggnall 2003: 166 passim). Therefore, autobiographical stories are "much more closely linked to the real and immediate social situation of the interview than to things one would correlate with historic facts of lives lived" (Welzer 2003: 186; translation by the author).

---

1.   Wilkomirski is a pseudonim.

2.   False memories are memories that do not reflect real facts. With intense repetition of fictive events, over time the latter become indiscernible from "real" events and are believed to be real.

3.   Comp. Benito Bermejo and Sandra Checa: Comunicado, <http://www.exilioydeportacion.com/comunicado.htm> (Communication on 4 July 2006).

Such deliberations immediately lead us to the ethical problems of oral history. I would like to illustrate a brief theoretical introduction to these problems with the following examples.

I draw on experience based on two oral history projects concerning the Nazi concentration camps of Mauthausen and Ravensbrück: The international Mauthausen Survivors Documentation Project (MSDP) was a cooperative project of the Institute of Conflict Research, the Documentation Centre of Austrian Resistance, and the Ludwig Boltzmann-Institute for Historical Social Sciences with the participation of scientists from twenty (language) regions in Europe, USA, and Israel (2002–03). In this oral history project, biographical interviews with more than 800 survivors of Mauthausen were conducted. The Ravensbrück Project, which I worked on with my colleague Helga Amesberger at the Institute of Conflict Research in 1998–99, entailed narrative live story interviews with 42 Austrian survivors of the women's concentration camp of Ravensbrück.

In this article, I shall concentrate on the mutual expectations of the oral historian and the eyewitness, to show which problems and opportunities could arise from the rapport that is established between them. We find the (sometimes conflicting) expectations on three stages: first, the interview setting itself; second, the level of interpretation and evaluation of the research results; and third, a possible ongoing rapport beyond the given research goal as seen by the scientist.

It is my hypothesis that the oral historian is not only challenged in many ways by the personality and the expectations of the eyewitnesses during the specific interview setting, but also, and I underscore this, even more so after this "immediate dialog", thus possibly creating even more urgent ethical questions.

## The interview with concentration camp survivors

If a person who was persecuted by the NS regime is interviewed around the year 2000, a period of about 60 years has elapsed between the events and their rendering. During this period of time the events were frequently remembered, reshaped, and readjusted to life.[4] The way these recollections are rendered as autobiographical

---

4. This facilitates the transfer from short-term to long-term memory. Tschugnall argues that memory research demonstrated, in accordance with modern brain research, that recollections are not saved the way they are saved on a PC, and that recollections cannot be retrieved the same way at any time and at any place using a specific technology, as had been assumed for a long time. The original events have to be permanently repeated (in dialogues or silently). In other words, a permanent consolidation of memories is necessary to enable a precise rendering of memories. (Tschuggnall 2003: 166 passim)

reconstructions depends widely on the memory context, which is a context that is formed by many aspects. To a large extent, autobiographical stories are linked to the present and given present situations (see Welzer 2003). From the many factors that influence an interview setting, which have to be noted in this context and which have been discussed in other contributions (Leh 2000; von Plato 2000; von Plato 2002), for example: age, gender, health, education, linguistic competence of the interviewees (experienced versus first-time interviewee), I would like to deal with only one aspect – the mutual expectations of interviewer and interviewee – which I shall also discuss in the second and third section of this article. These expectations contribute significantly to the way they see each other and relate to each other. The interviewee is pursuing his/her own interests. Otherwise, s/he would not be ready to be interviewed, nor would s/he assume a special interest to the scientist, who has made the long trip to the interview. The interviewee tries in most cases to satisfy this interest by his/her stories.

Focusing on ethical aspects I want to stress that researchers have to be aware that by being interviewed, Holocaust or concentration camp survivors might experience a secondary traumatisation. On the other hand, however, there is no reason to be too worried that the interview situation might hurt the feelings of the interview partners because the latter wants to be asked, communicate memories, and pass down experiences. It is equally hurting not to respond to certain things that are communicated, if "offers" to talk about shameful and humiliating experiences are not accepted, met with disbelief, or discarded.

Secondary traumatisation can also be caused by pushy and badgering questions, which the interviewee would prefer not to answer. In such cases, the interviewer has to find a balance which places the well-being of the interviewee above the researcher's own "quest for knowledge", and also above his/her own fear of painful stories. This includes responding adequately to signs of overstrain or fatigue in the interviewee.

Another point I would like to stress is that narrative life story interviews require precise and intensive preparation from the person conducting them (in terms of knowledge of history, social skills, and determination of self-interests). A first analysis of interviews with Mauthausen survivors (conducted in the course of the Mauthausen Survivors Documentation Project (MSDP)) shows how important it is for the interviewer to know what to expect from the interview and to precisely know where his/her main interests are and to be able to (re)act flexibly in any situation. Possible expectations of the party that ordered the interview or of the project context also belong to the demands that should be met by the interviewers. The aim of the MSDP was to conduct biographical interviews and to extract not only individual experiences of the persecuted, but also to extract historical facts about the Mauthausen concentration camp and its branch camps.

These demands probably put some pressure on the interviewers. Some of them allowed very little space and time for stories that went beyond the persecutions. They did not ask additional questions, yet they did interrupt, pursue their own research questions, or simply follow the catalogue of questions, etc. In addition to ethical problems this creates, in the end it leads to partially unintelligible interviews of little substance. This could not be in the interest of either the interviewee or the interviewer. Therefore, such interviews require precise and intensive preparation on behalf of the interviewer, and an adequate measure of empathy and spontaneity during the interview.[5]

These results illustrate that it is not always easy to balance the interests of the interviewer and interviewee. Tensions can arise if opinions are voiced during the interview, which are not shared by the person asking the questions. How should one handle statements one does not agree with (for instance, racist or sexist remarks)? What is the best way to deal with contradictory or illogical statements? Or, for instance, if historical facts or dates are presented that are plainly wrong? The MSDP guidelines allowed such issues to be dealt with in the final phase of the interview (von Plato 2002: 18). However, the correction of historical facts is supposed to be done during the evaluation of the interview.

This leads us to the next stage.


## Research results: Interpretation and use

During the analysis and interpretation phase we see the tension between the interests of the interviewer and interviewee. As already shown in the interview section, the expectations of interview partners might be partially met or complemented: both want life experiences to be communicated, recorded, stored, and handed down; but they might also be contradictory in significant points. The interviewee expects encouragement, support, and understanding of his/her stories, while the interviewer tries to keep his/her critical distance to the interviewee's logic of hindsight interpretation. The interviewee expects an interpretation of his/her meaning and also of his/her interpretation, while the analyst might be more interested in ruptures and ambivalences in the story. For the interviewee, historic facts are just a general framework of his/her recollections, while the scientist might be mainly

---

5. MSDP started with an interview training that consisted of a theoretical introduction into methodical requirements as well as practical exercises; additionally, the interviewers were provided with a textbook about the Mauthausen KZ complex and a manual for conducting biographical interviews. Nevertheless, significant problems in implementing these recommendations could not be avoided.

looking for facts and figures, except if s/he is researching the process of remembering as such.

During his/her scientific work, the historian is required to differentiate these two levels of knowledge, which frequently occur in oral history: (1) Do I want to obtain knowledge about this person, his or her individuality, social background, and the way of remembering, or (2) Am I primarily interested in (main) historic events? As already indicated, both areas do not necessarily exclude each other, but they must be carefully considered.

Such deliberations lead to some ethical questions: It is of course inadmissible for me as a researcher not to contradict incorrect figures; for instance, the number of concentration camp victims which has definitely been proven wrong (like the often-quoted 92,000 murdered in Ravensbrück). (Deliberately) faked biographical stories must be rejected; for instance, the concentration camp imprisonments of the two Spanish men mentioned in the introduction. But even here it has to be considered how such things are to be corrected, especially if they are going to be published. And how do we handle extreme experiences of suffering during childhood, which are seen through the eyes and minds of children, but cannot measure up to the realities of grown-up people or to the scientific knowledge of a later period?[6] To what extent am I allowed to insist on precise historical facts if, by doing so, I destroy the basis of a person's own identity (as a victim)? If an eyewitness grants me the privilege to scientifically process and publish her memories, do I then have the right to disqualify her memories as wrong and (deliberately) misleading? Also, what about references to Jewish resistance fighters exclusively as Jews who did not see themselves as Jews – not even after 1945 – but who were (also) victimized in the Holocaust because of their being Jewish? Am I allowed to posthumously publish stories (in the interest of science) that run counter to social norms and expectations or evoke feelings of shame (such as experiences of rape), or must one respect the private and intimate life of a person beyond death? To avoid one-sided and flawed interpretations, caution is mandated for ethical reasons in such cases.

Then again, it certainly does not meet the expectations of eyewitnesses if audio or video records of their interviews are locked away from the public in (semi) private archives of researchers or in some small institutes. Both procedures are likely to hurt the dignity of narrator and to degrade eyewitnesses to mere research objects, which can be pulled out from the drawer whenever it is deemed appropriate.

---

6.  See Clare Parker's recollections on Lenzing, a branch camp of Mauthausen (Parker 2006).

## The art of dialogue beyond (social/historical) research interests

When using the interviews with Austrian survivors of the Ravensbrück concentration camp as the basis for a study, my colleague Helga Amesberger and I had the impression that the expectations of the women interviewed were very high (see Amesberger & Halbmayr 2001). On one hand, there was their hope of having their biographies published and having the picture presented "correctly"; for instance, highlighting solidarity and comradeship among the inmates, especially among the political prisoners, or omitting some taboos. On the other hand, we wished to pursue our goal to present a scientifically differentiated analysis and to improve the general knowledge of Austrian women in Ravensbrück. In addition, we wanted to maintain our ethical standards by not degrading these women to research objects, but by respecting their views on their lives as a form of "truth" as well.[7]

Because of our commitment to eyewitnesses – for several years we have been active in the Austrian Camp Association Ravensbrück – we are sometimes faced with a certain skepticism by our colleagues from the field of historical science, who see this involvement as a form of "taking sides for the victims", which might limit scientific objectivity.

Another experience was exaggerated expectations; for instance, expectations for help with applications for compensation and restitution was an area where we could not have any influence at all. Some colleagues of the Mauthausen project reported that some interviewees asked them to act as caring granddaughters or asked them for weekly visits. In such cases, too, interviewers are faced with expectations that often cannot be met. Both their own and others' standards and expectations create a tense atmosphere within which the researcher must act.

## Conclusion

In this article, I was only able to raise many questions which arise whenever ethical questions of oral history are discussed. It is impossible to present plain answers or clear-cut, general solutions, for the simple reason that there are none. For each situation, a new balance must be found.

The balance between the interests of the oral historian to learn about past situations which s/he cannot remember, and the interviewee's interest to protect his/her privacy and personal integrity.

---

7. This was the reason why we decided to add to our scientific analysis (Amesberger & Halbmayr 2001, volume 1) a volume with the women's life stories (Amesberger & Halbmayr 2001, volume 2).

The balance between perceiving the interviewees as information carriers of past experiences, and of perceiving them as acting subjects here and now, who in hindsight place, want to place, and have to place past events of their lives into a context determined by cause and effect.

The balance between a necessary scepticism toward facts and data of a life story, and the recognition, or at least tolerance of, a personal, biographical truth.

The balance between one's own demand for "siding with the victims" and the resulting need for keeping one's distance and the necessity of such distance.

Humans who are courageous enough to face memories of past sufferings over and over again are valuable for each society, since they help to build bridges between the past and present and hand down experiences that remind us of past events and fill us with hope for the future. I wish to conclude with a quote from Aleida Assmann: "Historical research needs memories for assessing significance and values. Memories need historical research for verification and correction" (Assmann 2006: 51; translation by the author).

The oral historian does his/her work within this framework of mutual dependency and mutual enrichment. Each research setting (and beyond) raises new questions of expectations, responsibilities, and the need for unbiased distance. This is exactly what keeps this area of historiography so demanding and alive.

## References

Amesberger, H. & Halbmayr, B. 2001. *Vom Leben und Überleben – Wege nach Ravensbrück. Das Frauenkonzentrationslager in der Erinnerung*, Vol. 1, *Dokumentation und Analyse*. Vol. 2 – *Lebensgeschichten*. Wien: Promedia.

Assmann, A. 2006. *Der lange Schatten der Vergangenheit. Erinnerungskultur und Geschichtspolitik*. München: C.H. Beck.

Leh, A. 2000. Forschungsethische Probleme der Zeitzeugenforschung. *BIOS – Zeitschrift für Biographieforschung und Oral History* 13(1): 64–76.

Parker, C. 2006. *Klaras Geschichte* [Mauthausen-Erinnerungen 1]. Wien: Bundesministerium für Inneres.

Tschuggnall, K. 2003. Favourite bits – Autobiographische Erinnerungen im Gespräch. In *Die Biographische Wahrheit ist nicht zu haben*, K.-J. Bruder (ed.), 163–182. Gießen: Psychosozialverlag.

von Plato, A. 2000. Zeitzeugen und die historische Zunft. Erinnerung, kommunikative Tradierung und kollektives Gedächtnis in der qualitativen Geschichtswissenschaft – ein Problemaufriss. *BIOS – Zeitschrift für Biographieforschung und Oral History* 13(1): 5–29.

von Plato, A. 2002. Some remarks on the interviews. In MSDP-Manual for Interviewers. Ms, Institute of Conflict Research & Documentation Archive of the Austrian Resistance & Ludwig Boltzmann-Institute of Social Scientific History (eds.), 16–21.Vienna.

Welzer, H. 2003. Was ist autobiographische Wahrheit? Anmerkungen aus Sicht der Erinnerungsforschung. In *Die Biographische Wahrheit ist nicht zu haben*, K.-J. Bruder (ed.), 183–
   202. Gießen: Psychosozialverlag.
Wilkomirski, B. 1995. *Bruchstücke. Aus einer Kindheit 1939–1948*. Frankfurt: Suhrcamp.

# Life story interviews and the "Truth of Memory"

## Some aspects of oral history from a historico-philosophical perspective

Karin Stögner
Institute of Conflict Research, Vienna, Austria

The interaction between an interviewee and an interviewer in a narrative life story interview is a relevant topic in oral history as well as in empirical social sciences in general. This relationship seems to be central especially with regard to the validity of memories produced in interviews as it affects in various ways the narrative and memory alike. The interview situation has immediate influence onto what is being remembered at all, which memories are being narrated and which are not.

Following such general considerations concerning the various problems of life story interviews this article sheds light upon some questions raised by philosophy of history, e.g. how the past becomes a "historic item". The major question addressed is how the present circumstances and conditions shape the way the past is narrated and how this has to be considered when dealing with life story interviews.

**Keywords:** philosophy of history, validity of memories, concentration camp survivors

## Introduction

This article is based on experiences with life story interviews gathered in the framework of the Mauthausen Survivors Documentation Project (MSDP), one of the largest oral history projects in Europe conducted with survivors of a single concentration camp.[1] In 2002 and 2003 about 860 life story interviews, most of

---

1. The scientific director of the MSDP was Gerhard Botz (Ludwig Boltzmann Institute of Social Scientific History, Vienna; Institute of Contemporary History, University of Vienna), the

which lasted several hours, were conducted in 23 different countries by on-site interviewers, mostly in Europe, but also in Israel and America. Nearly ten percent of the interviews were also videotaped.[2] The following considerations represent an attempt to situate the experiences made as an interviewer in the MSDP theoretically within the framework of some historico-philosophical considerations concerning the "truth of memory" and the process of authentication of "historic facts". As the perspective is based on direct experiences from interviews with Austrian concentration camp survivors, it is restricted to the Austrian situation and cannot easily be transposed to other countries that took part in the MSDP.

## "Historic event"

The significance of the interaction between interviewees and interviewers in the narrative life story interview is an important and widely discussed topic in oral history, but also in empirical social research. Especially with regards to the question of the validity and the "truth" of memories produced in life story interviews, this relationship is of central consideration, as it influences the method of narrating and hence memory itself. Therefore, the situational context of the interview directly affects what is remembered, which memories are narrated and which are not, which memories are regarded as important by the interviewee, how the narrative strands of memory are put together, and how they are assembled into an overall picture. All of this is highly influenced by the situation in which the interview takes place.

At this stage we are already concerned with a central issue of philosophy of history, namely how an event of the past becomes an "historic event" through the process of memory. According to the historico-philosophical theses of Walter Benjamin, a major representative of German philosophy of history who died in 1940 while trying to escape the Nazis, the past, and hence to a certain degree the construction of historic facts, have to be seen as a constant process which is

central project management was held by Brigitte Halbmayr and Helga Amesberger (Institute of Conflict Research, Vienna), the administrative coordination was taken over by Wolfgang Neugebauer and Christine Schindler (Documentation Archive of the Austrian Resistance, Vienna). As a researcher at the Institute of Conflict Research, I conducted interviews with Austrian survivors and was in charge of the database. This article is a thoroughly revised version of Stögner 2008. I would like to thank Helga Amesberger, Gerhard Botz, Brigitte Halbmayr, Johannes Höpoltseder, Kobi Kabalek, and Christine Schindler for their advice and critical annotations to this text.

2.   For a general overview of the MSDP see Botz/Halbmayr/Amesberger 2004; Amesberger/Botz/Halbmayr 2006. For the videotaped MSDP interviews see Klingenböck 2007.

eminently shaped by the political, societal, and economic constellations, not so much of the past, but of the current society where memory is actually situated. Thus, when asking for the "truth of memory", one always has to keep in mind that memory consists of constant actualisations of the past from the perspective of the present, which means we have to deal with images of the past being permanently reshaped and recollected. Benjamin repeatedly pointed to this very feature of the past and to the necessity of reflecting upon the part which the remembered/remembering actualisations have in the perception of the historic fact and of identifying the impact of the present onto memory (cf. Benjamin 2003, 2002a, 1991). As for a method to envision the past, he insisted on an approach representing "the past in our space, not us in the realm of the past" (Benjamin 1991: 273), meaning to represent the past in the context of the present, not the present in the context of the past. It is not so much about empathising with the past and looking at it "the way it really was" (Benjamin 2003: 391), as one leading German historian of the nineteenth century, Leopold von Ranke, defined the primary task of the historian. Benjamin, on the contrary, was aware that it is impossible to fulfil this task, yet trying it would mean to deny the relationship between the past and the present and to take the image of the past – the result of this relationship – uncritically for the past itself. Instead, Benjamin claimed a different, political and socio-critical way of dealing with the past, which could be described as some sort of receiving, rescuing actualisation of the past in the constellations of current society.

> The true image of the past flits by. The past can be seized only as an image that flashes up at the moment of its recognisability, and is never seen again. 'The truth will not run away from us': this statement by Gottfried Keller indicates exactly that point in historicism's image of history where the image is pierced by historical materialism. For it is an irretrievable image of the past which threatens to disappear in any present that does not recognize itself as intended in that image.
>
> (Benjamin 2003: 391)

Benjamin's demands concerning the exposure to history prove to be very important especially for the sphere of oral history. Here, the moment of the receiving present is fundamental, as memory takes place in the "here and now" of the interaction between interviewee and interviewer. Of course, Benjamin developed his materialistic approach not for oral history, but actually for dealing with the past in general; hence, for what may be called history of facts. Correspondingly, it has become standard in most branches of today's historical research to consider the double construction of the source and the object of history. This means that the historic fact is referred to as changing continually and as being (re-)constructed discursively, whereby the central role of the recipient(s) is always crucial (cf. Welzer et al. 2002: 35). However, the processes of perception and cognition which constitute memory cannot be transposed exclusively into the subjective sphere, but have to be viewed dialectically. Some sort of mediation takes place between the cognitive subject and the object to be recognised, as the historical object is never "mute" but imposes itself and thus comes into consideration according to its own specificities (cf. Benjamin 2003: 391). It is the mediation between the past and the present (the critical historian thereby being the mediator) which makes an historic object recognisable, perceptible, and thus able to be experienced. That an event or an experience of the past should be capable of being actualised at all and passed on to the present where they find some connecting point, implies that this event or experience represents a past problem, which has not yet been solved in current society and, therefore, recurs, with somehow changed features, in the current societal constellations (cf. Benjamin 2002a). This represents Walter Benjamin's socio-critical view which holds the present to a considerable degree responsible for the transmission of the past. Thus, whether an *historical* object, event, or experience will be remembered, thus becoming an *historic* object, or whether it will be forgotten depends not only on the cognitive subject, but in a decisive way on the time elapsed between the remembered past and the present, and on the way the past communicates with the present and the present is capable of understanding and experiencing.[3] These constellations are most likely to influence the development of cognitive interests in historians and social scientists, and thus have a lasting effect on the way the past is examined and interpreted. This is valid for the analysis of memory in general, taking place on the collective as well as on the individual level.

It can be assumed that in a life story interview the memories of the historical witness are aimed not so much at the remembered past, but much more at the receiving present. This means that memories are not simply a communication of the past, but to a high degree the expression of the past in the present. Hence,

---

3.   Forgetting itself has of course its own dialectic, so that productive forgetting has to be regarded as a precondition of memory, as is expressed in Walter Benjamin's 'Berlin Childhood around 1900': "We can never entirely recover what has been forgotten. The shock of repossession would be so devastating that we would immediately cease to understand our longing." (Benjamin 2002b: 395; cf. Stögner 2006). If there were not some specific kind of forgetting interposed between memory and the remembered experience or event as an intermediating instance, the individual would be exposed to the past experience in a very direct way, without reflecting distance, still caught in the past and not received in the constellations of the here and now. Indeed, the process of transforming the past experience into a narrated memory acquires a certain degree of reflected distance on the part of the interviewee to her/his own experiences in the past. In case this distance is not or is only insufficiently given, the interviewee is likely to still be in a kind of traumatic state. In these cases conducting an interview can be very difficult if not impossible.

life stories are always filtered by all which has happened between the time of actual experience and the time of narrating. Events and experiences that have taken *Palimpsest* place between the past event and the moment of remembrance function as distinctive layers (see von Plato 2002: 20). When interpreting an interview, the historian has to recognise which and how many of these layers have to be permeated in order to get access to the past event in question, as these layers themselves are an important part of memory and, thus, also constitute an aspect of the remembered event in question. Again, this holds true not only for dealing with life story interviews but to a certain degree also for the analysis and interpretation of historical documents and so-called historic facts of any kind. What we get to know is an idea of the past deposited in the present according to the historical, social, and political constellations of current society, of which historians always have to be critical when interpreting the past. As dealing with the past is always situated in the present, oral history and the narrative life story interview, if consciously handled, provide a possibility to situate memory adequately and to grasp an "irretrievable image of the past" (Benjamin 2003: 391). To reflect on this interaction and amalgamation of the past and the present, and to perceive both in their dialectical relationship – instead of instrumentalising the past against the present or vice versa – is a central task when it comes to analysing the memories of historical witnesses (cf. Rosenthal 1995: 17; 1998; Gahleitner, Pohn-Weidinger 2005).

## Interviewing camp survivors

With regard to life story interviews with concentration camp survivors, this dialectical relationship of the past and present – apparent in the politics of remembrance in Austria for example – is of particular importance, because the Shoah and National Socialism are always directly or indirectly elements of a family's story on the part of both victims and perpetrators and their respective descendants. Due to decades of denial, renunciation, and repression of the National Socialist past and the feeling of responsibility for this from the part of the Austrian majority, the way of passing on history becomes central. Thereby, (transgenerational) transmission of memory is important, as it implies the adoption of the narrated stories by the listening part of the interview community. Harald Welzer et al. consequently characterise the interaction between interviewee and interviewer in life story interview contexts as a "temporary community of memory" (2002: 35), a term which seems to be helpful when considering the impact of the interviewer's presence and the whole interview situation onto memory and the narrated life story. An interviewer takes over a mediating function between society and past experiences, which may have been held back for a long time and are recollected during the interview. Thus, a "temporary community of memory" is established and some form of mutual affiliation and togetherness develops in the course of envisioning the past. This implies that in a life story interview the interviewee and interviewer construct memory together in a mutual process.

Somehow memory can be seen as a sort of constant translation, namely of the past into the present. Simply by expressing experiences verbally and linguistically, they are brought into the present due to contemporary use of language which sometimes differs considerably from its use in the past. The past comes into current life in a transformed and changed shape. We have but translations of the past, the "language of the past" being in a continual process, which already begins with the initial "coding of the experience" in the past (cf. Goertz 2001; Schacter 1996). Nevertheless, concerning language use we are equally confronted with words and terms that seem to have outlasted all social and historical change and extend like columns from the past directly into the present, thus being immediate witnesses of the contexts in which they were initially coined. This is the case with, for example, "camp language", a specific jargon produced in concentration camp contexts, which Wolfgang Sofsky describes as follows:

> Camp language was direct, terse, and vulgar. There were almost no words to designate feelings, nor were there expressions for statements of satisfaction or retraction. It was a discourse of naming and address, threat and warning, command and demand. Other speech acts – such as descriptions, explanations, the giving of reasons or permission, and promises – were rendered marginal simply as a by-product of prevailing conditions. Camp jargon was a gesticulatory, abbreviated code for fleeting contacts, not for encounters and conversations. Its tone was often as brusque as its expressions were coarse. In the struggle for space and food, one inmate shouted at another, hurling words of rebuke or mockery. A friendly word was a rarity, and for that reason it often received special mention in prisoners' testimony. [...] It was an emergency language for an extreme situation. (Sofsky 1997:57)

As such, words and terms, when used in an interview, seem to give a direct and unmediated idea of the concentration camp situation. An adequate and thorough interpretation is nonetheless very difficult, as it is not easy to decide how the use of "camp language" in an interview is influenced by situations outside of camp.

When we interview a historical witness, we cause him or her to construct a life story which has to correspond to at least a minimum of cognitive requirements. Mostly this life story has a beginning and an end; and normally some linear development is expected, corresponding to the tradition of narrating. But unarticulated memory may actually work differently – more intermittingly than linear and by images more than words. In an interview these images are transformed into a more or less cohesive picture of the past, which implies that the interviewee has to correspond to at least a minimum of specific skills concerning the construction of an intelligible narration. However, we do have the possibility to leave space to the interviewees to develop their memory and to construct their own stories the way they see it. In the MSDP interviews, we asked in an open way and communicated to the interviewees that we were interested in their whole life stories, in which the specific concentration camp experiences should be situated. Every single detail – which the interviewee her/himself would otherwise have possibly taken for irrelevant – was important to us. If the purpose of a life story interview is also to collect specific information on life in concentration camps, there could emerge a further problem, namely that interviewees somehow expect memory and knowledge on the part of the interviewers. Although the interviewer is certainly familiar with the history of the concentration camp system, he/she has to convince the interviewee to tell every detail which might seem irrelevant or well known. If the interview is also to be intelligible to future generations who might work with the memories of the witness, the interviewee has to decode the well-known, the unexpressed, as well as the implied contents of the life story.

In order to initiate the narration, our very first question was, for example, "Could you please tell me your life story", followed by an explanation that the interviewee could begin wherever he or she wanted to. In order to encourage the interviewee to go into detail, we asked in a way which caused interviewees to envision certain events and incidents, to describe relatives and friends, but also perpetrators and daily routines in the concentration camp. This would also allow for some form of intermittent narration, which would be not so linear, and thus would correspond more to the way the human mind works. The aim of our open approach was to bring the interviewees to unfurl their life stories as far as possible on their own and to emphasise the issues which actually were important to them. In the beginning these narrative strands corresponded widely to structured biographical narratives and were influenced by the anticipations and expectations the interviewees had with regard to the interviewers and the respective focus of the academic interest of the project. So, even if the interviewer acts in a verbally and physically reserved, though well-considered way and would not actively structure or guide the narrative nor interrupt it, an interview is always an active interaction and hence the interview situation is never neutral. The narrative is always addressed to the listening part of the interview community as well as to the wider public. Therefore, we will never achieve a non-constructed, "authentic" grasp of the past in life story interviews, as in the course of narration memory is constructed in a mutual process between interviewee and interviewer. But here the question of the purpose for which the memory was constructed is decisive. In opposition to pure question/reply schemes of other interview methods, the life story interview leaves the agency of constructing the story mostly to the interviewee and thus allows him/her space to keep the arrangement of the narration, at least to a certain degree, aloof from hegemonic discourses, which otherwise constitute depersonalised master narratives.

Coming back to the question of the truth or validity of memory, our interviewing method also allowed for critical questions at the end of the narration. So, if an interviewee talked about things or events which the interviewer could not believe, or which did not correspond to the known historical facts, the interviewer could explore such discrepancies and try to work them up through discussion. In order not to interrupt or influence the narrative, critical questions should be asked only at the end of the interview. However, the interviewers of the MSDP scarcely made use of this possible critical point. This, of course, has quite serious effects on the "authentication" of narrated life stories, which has to be understood as a process between producers and recipients of the life story, who mutually accept the information given in the interview as "true" and "correct" (cf. Botz/Dewald/Prenninger 2004: 100). Among the authenticating recipients there are not only the interviewers directly involved, but also an imagined expert audience and also the public. The structure of this variously levelled public also has its impact on the interview in different ways: besides the effects on what is remembered, there is also the influence stemming from the specific way society deals with the past and, hence, from collective (non-)memory. So, the missing critical intrusion by the interviewers could also be seen as a consequence of the decade-long official and unofficial silence concerning the National Socialist past as well as its open denial from the part of institutionalised Austrian collective (non-)memory. This obviously impeded an autonomous and critical handling of the life stories and memories of the concentration camp survivors as a whole, including those scholars or scientists who showed a real and vivid interest in working critically through the past (cf. Adorno 2005). Sometimes the recipients' attitude is loaded by diffuse or concrete feelings of guilt, in front of which a critical discussion of the survivors' narrated life stories somehow seems "improper". Thus, it would be interesting to consider whether even those who deal with the National Socialist past on an academic level construct borders of speaking through the installation of master narratives, which afterwards are only reluctantly discussed critically. Maybe it was some sort of collective paralysis which also left its mark in the MSDP interviews, precisely from the reluctance on the part of the interviewers to ask critical questions and to discuss the survivors' memories. These considerations may be valid only for the German and Austrian context. However, there could also be a general, cross-national culturally prevailing mood which is addressed and emphasised by the stories of victims, as critical questions concerning the "truth" and validity of memory are also missing in interviews conducted in France, Italy, Israel, or the USA.[4]

As the effect of the interaction between interviewee and interviewer on the way the interviewee remembers cannot be fully prevented, it has to be consciously and actively reflected in the interpretative work of the historian. This is also true for dealing with other sources of history, which to a certain extent are also produced and reproduced through interpretation. As for dealing with documents, for example, it has to be assumed that the past events the documents refer to have already been shaped according to formal and structural rules of language and scripture and, even more importantly, according to the situation in the past. The document itself is an interpretation of an event, which has to be kept in mind when dealing with sources considered "authentic", reliable, true, and complete, as was the case, for example, in the official documents stemming from the Nazi perpetrators themselves. Thus, the interpretative work of the (oral) historian is always accompanied by the question of reliability.

Correspondingly, the question of how to deal with so-called "false memory" is central, in addition to the problem of who determines what is right or false memory. Quite often we are confronted with contradictions within the life stories themselves or between the memories and the so-called history of facts. Take, for instance, the following example: during an interview a survivor denies that his relatives were also persecuted or even murdered; yet, information contradicting this was known beforehand either from other interviews conducted when the survivor was younger, or by some other sources, such as transport lists of concentration camps. When this very survivor refuses to go further into the matter, the question of how to deal with such diverging memories becomes crucial. On the one hand, there is the question of protecting the interviewee against, for example, denigration from political or racist opponents who could deny the credibility and reliability of the survivor's personality, or the question of restitution and compensation payments which might be influenced by "false memory". But on the other hand "false memories" point to the contextualisation of the past in the present, for instance to the position of the present within the narration. The omittance or denial of bad experiences may also give a clue to this present situation. However, when the process of memory itself shall be analysed, the historic fact may become less relevant. We could also be confronted with a narrative intending to cover

---

4. Besides this impact of the collective way of dealing with and handling concentration camp survivors' life stories, it is also important to know that the MSDP interviews normally lasted several hours and that afterwards a questionnaire had to be filled in; for instance, that the interviewee and interviewer alike were sometimes too exhausted to critically discuss the story told in the interview.

bad experiences or specific events the interviewee cannot or does not want to address openly, or which he/she has forgotten. We may also be confronted with something the survivor did not live through personally, but which he/she had witnessed or heard about, or maybe even a film sequence which the survivor had saved as his/her "own" memory in deeper layers of consciousness (cf. Roseman 1998). In the MSDP interviews we were quite often confronted with narrations which seemed to be extremely influenced by well-established master narratives concerning everyday life in the concentration camps as well as by public discourse (cf. also Ecker 2008). We always have to be critical of such things when interpreting life story interviews and try to find out what "false memories" stand for, what they hide, etc. In the end they can tell us a lot about the relationship between the past and the present on the individual as well as on the societal level. This does not mean that we should give way to a mere subjectivity in the interpretation of history, but that oral history provides us the possibility to reflect on so-called "historic facts", which are also produced and interpreted in the dialectical framework of subjectivity and objectivity, but which are generally considered as objective and "authentic".

According to Benjamin, the task of the historian is to consciously reflect on the myth of "objectivity" and to detect the subjective part in the perception of the past. By being aware of these problems concerning the process of remembering and interpreting the past, oral history is in opposition to the installation of an undialectical and fixed image of the past, and thus corresponds to a major requirement in Benjamin's philosophy of history.

## References

Adorno, T. W. 2005. The meaning of working through the past. In *Critical Models: Interventions and Catchwords*, translated by H. W. Pickford. New York NY: Columbia University Press.

Amesberger, H., Botz, G. & Halbmayr, B. 2006. Le camp de concentration de Mauthausen dans le souvenir de 800 survivant(e)s. *Etudes sur le témoignage audiovisuel des victimes des crimes et génocides nazis (Studies on the audio-visual testimony of victims of the Nazi crimes and genocides)*, juin 2006, 57–74.

Benjamin, W. 1991. *Das Passagen-Werk* [Gesammelte Schriften V]. Frankfurt: Suhrkamp.

Benjamin, W. 2002a. Eduard Fuchs, collector and historian. In *Selected Writings*, Vol. 3, 1935–1938, translated by E. Jephcott & H. Eiland, 260–302. Cambridge MA: Belknap Press.

Benjamin, W. 2002b. Berlin childhood around 1900. In *Selected Writings*, Vol. 3, 1935–1938, translated by E. Jephcott & H. Eiland, 344–413. Cambridge MA: Belknap Press.

Benjamin, W. 2003. On the concept of history. In *Selected Writings*, Vol. 4, 1938–1940, translated by E. Jephcott & H. Eiland, 389–400. Cambridge MA: Belknap Press.

Botz, G., Dewald, B. & Prenninger, A. 2004. Mauthausen erzählen – Narrating Mauthausen. In *Das Gedächtnis von Mauthausen*, Bundesministerium für Inneres, Archiv der KZ-Gedenkstätte Mauthausen (ed.), 76–103. Vienna: Bundesministerium für Inneres.

Botz, G., Halbmayr, B. & Amesberger, H. 2004. Zeitzeugen- und Zeitzeuginnenprojekt Mauthausen (Mauthausen Survivors Documentation Project – MSDP). Genese und erste Ergebnisse. In *Jahrbuch 2004. Mauthausen*, Dokumentationsarchiv des österreichischen Widerstandes (ed.), 30–67. Vienna: LIT Verlag.

Ecker, M. 2008. "Ich habe erst viel später erfahren, dass das Mengele war" – Über den Einfluss öffentlicher Diskurse auf die Erzählungen von Holocaust-Überlebenden. In *Die "Wahrheit" der Erinnerung. Jüdische Lebensgeschichten*, E. Lappin & A. Lichtblau (eds), 35–45. Innsbruck: StudienVerlag.

Gahleitner, D. & Pohn-Weidinger, M. 2005. Biographieforschung: Erzählte Lebensgeschichten als Zugang zu Vergangenem. Theoretische Annahmen und methodisches Vorgehen. In *Jahrbuch 2005. Frauen in Widerstand und Verfolgung*, Dokumentationsarchiv des österreichischen Widerstandes (ed.), 175–195. Vienna: LIT Verlag.

Goertz, H.-J. 2001. *Unsichere Geschichte. Zur Theorie historischer Referentialität*. Stuttgart: Reclam.

Klingenböck, G. 2007. Between memory and audiovisual representation: Changes of paradigm, questioning the approach to the "eyewitness" in the "digital age". *Etudes sur le témoignage audiovisuel des victimes des crimes et génocides nazis (Studies on the audio-visual testimony of victims of the Nazi crimes and genocides)*, juin 2007, 71–84.

Roseman, M. 1998. Erinnerung und Überleben. Wahrheit und Widerspruch im Zeugnis einer Holocaust-Überlebenden. *BIOS. Zeitschrift für Biographieforschung, Oral History und Lebensverlaufsanalysen* 11(2): 263–279.

Rosenthal, G. (ed.). 1998. *The Holocaust in three generations. Families of victims and perpetrators of the Nazi regime*. London: Cassell.

Rosenthal, G. 1995. *Erzählte und erlebte Lebensgeschichte. Gestalt und Struktur biographischer Selbstbeschreibung*. Frankfurt: Campus.

Schacter, D. 1996. *Searching for Memory. The Brain, the Mind, and the Past*. New York NY: Basic Books.

Sofsky, W. 1997. *The Order of Terror. The Concentration Camp*. Princeton NJ: Princeton University Press.

Stögner, K. 2006. Erinnern und Vergessen. Zum Begriff des Eingedenkens bei Walter Benjamin. In *Jahrbuch 2006. Erinnerungskultur*, Dokumentationsarchiv des österreichischen Widerstandes (ed.), 37–47. Vienna: LIT Verlag.

Stögner, K. 2008. Lebensgeschichtliche Interviews und die "Wahrheit der Erinnerung" – Einige Überlegungen zum Mauthausen Survivors Documentation Project (MSDP). In *Die "Wahrheit" der Erinnerung. Jüdische Lebensgeschichten*, E. Lappin & A. Lichtblau (eds), 169–179. Innsbruck: StudienVerlag.

von Plato, A. 2002. Some remarks on the interview. In *Manual for Interviewers*, Institute of Conflict Research, Documentation Archive of the Austrian Resistance (eds.), 16–21. Vienna: IKF & DÖW.

Welzer, H., Moller, S. & Tschugnall, K. 2002. *"Opa war kein Nazi". Nationalsozialismus und Holocaust im Familiengedächtnis*. Frankfurt: Fischer.

# Index

In the series *Studies in Narrative* the following titles have been published thus far or are scheduled for publication: